IMAGES
of America

COLUMBIA, MARIETTA,
AND WRIGHTSVILLE

On the cover: Columbia Malleable Casting Corporation workers pause at the plant at Second and Linden Streets in Columbia in back of the molds they will use to produce iron castings. They and the operation are representative of all three river towns, Columbia, Marietta, and Wrightsville, at the beginning of the 20th century. (Courtesy Columbia Historic Preservation Society.)

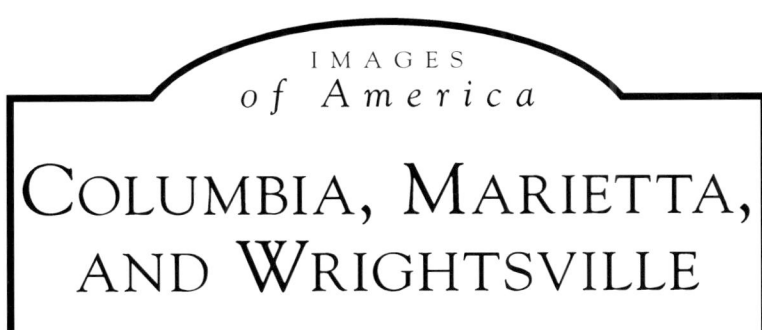

IMAGES
of America

COLUMBIA, MARIETTA, AND WRIGHTSVILLE

Frederic H. Abendschein

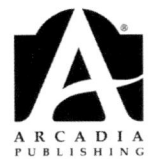

Copyright © 2009 by Frederic H. Abendschein
ISBN 978-0-7385-6473-9

Published by Arcadia Publishing
Charleston, South Carolina

Printed in the United States of America

Library of Congress Control Number: 2008939954

For all general information contact Arcadia Publishing at:
Telephone 843-853-2070
Fax 843-853-0044
E-mail sales@arcadiapublishing.com
For customer service and orders:
Toll-Free 1-888-313-2665

Visit us on the Internet at www.arcadiapublishing.com

*To my wife, Mary Virginia Abendschein,
for all her encouragement, understanding, and support.*

CONTENTS

Acknowledgments 6

Introduction 7

1. Columbia 11

2. Marietta 97

3. Wrightsville 111

Bibliography 127

Acknowledgments

There are many people I have to thank for their help, but for any errors that might have crept in, I'm responsible. I'd like to thank the following individuals and organizations.

First and foremost, Erin L. Vosgien, junior publisher of Arcadia Publishing, patiently listened to all of my questions, answered them, did the initial editing, and guided me through the process.

Claire Storm, Rivertownes PA USA president, put me in contact with Arcadia and encouraged me to do this project. Bob and Florence Miller, Columbia Historic Preservation Society, spent many hours at the society's museum while I went through finding and scanning many of the photographs. Melissa Glenn, Susquehanna Valley Chamber of Commerce, supplied with the great aerial view of the three towns.

Mary Barninger, Susquehanna Fire Company, one evening turned out many company members to go though the company's photograph collection and their own and loan photographs to me. John Hinkle Jr., third generation in the family's pharmacy and restaurant business, lent many photographs from his collection. Mary Wickenheiser and Cleon G. Berntheizel went through their collections for photographs and information for captions. Kevin Shue and Marianne Heckles, Lancaster County Historical Society (LCHS), steered me through LCHS's electronic catalog and provided scans.

The Board of Historic Wrightsville, Inc., members listened to my description of this book and gave me permission to access their photograph collection. Bonita Emenheiser, Historic Wrightsville, Inc., museum director, pulled photographs and told me about them while I scanned.

The late John Denney Jr. was a friend, historian, author, and great collector of railroad and trolley photographs from the three towns. Many photographs from his former collection appear in this book. The late Thomas Hoch documented buildings throughout Columbia from the late 1940s through the 1960s. He often climbed up on roofs and in steeples to get unusual vantage points. He took many of the Columbia photographs from this time period.

Lastly, I thank all of the citizens of Columbia, Marietta, and Wrightsville, who make these three river towns, at the center of the Lancaster-York Heritage Area, a great place to live and work.

INTRODUCTION

Columbia, Marietta, and Wrightsville are three communities on the lower part of the 444-mile long Susquehanna River. This river, the longest on the eastern seaboard, links the three towns and was the reason for their founding and initial growth.

The towns are about 25 miles downstream and southeast of Pennsylvania's capital, Harrisburg, and about 45 miles upstream of the Susquehanna River's mouth at the Chesapeake Bay at Havre de Grace, Maryland. This places them about 75 miles west of Philadelphia and north of Baltimore.

Columbia and Marietta are on the river's east shore while Wrightsville is on the west shore across from Columbia.

A tongue-in-cheek legend says that Susquehanna is a Native American phrase meaning "mile-wide, foot-deep." This shallowness makes it the longest non-navigable river in the country.

However, in late winter or spring, melting snows can raise the river's level to flood stage and beyond. Ice jamming at Turkey Hill, a few miles downstream where the river suddenly narrows, down to only a half-mile wide can create or make flooding worse at Columbia and Wrightsville.

Just before European settlement in what became Columbia, Native Americans in the area included the Shawanese and the Susquehannocks.

William Penn gave a patent of 3,000 acres in 1701 on the area to George Beale. Actual settlement did not start until the 1720s when the Blunston, Wright, and Barber families arrived.

Quaker preacher John Wright set up a ferry to run across the river in 1730. His family name and operation became what settler's first called the area, Wright's Ferry. John's son James and daughter Susannah were settlers, with James building a 10-room home for his sister. The home still stands and is the oldest in town. James's son Samuel laid out the town in 1788, surveying the land, laying out streets, and chanced off the first 160 lots.

Renamed Columbia in hopes of becoming the new nation's capital, the town came close to winning the honor, but southern states wanted it located farther south. Soon joining settlers of English heritage were ones from the German speaking states and freed or escaped African American slaves.

The first bridge from Columbia over to Wrightsville went up in 1814 over the Susquehanna River between the present two bridges. Destroyed by ice in 1832, little remains of this covered bridge.

In 1833, what became part of the State Works of Pennsylvania opened in Columbia. The Eastern Division of the Pennsylvania Canal ran to the northwest toward Harrisburg. The following year, another link in the State Works reached Columbia from Lancaster. The

Philadelphia and Columbia Railroad (P&C) ran between its namesakes and reached Columbia via an inclined railway.

In the mid-1800s, railroad lines began radiating out from Columbia. A line ran over the second bridge toward Wrightsville and York. Another line extended north toward Marietta and Harrisburg. Still another railroad ran downstream on the eastern bank of the Susquehanna. By 1877 the Pennsylvania Railroad (PRR) had control of all these and the P&C too.

In the midst of the Civil War, the Reading and Columbia Rail Road, ultimately absorbed by the Reading Railroad, linked the two municipalities together.

After the Civil War when retreating Union forces burnt the second bridge, a third bridge took its place and lasted until 1896, when a hurricane destroyed it. The PRR built a steel bridge as a replacement in 1897.

At the end of the 19th century, the trolley arrived in town from Lancaster. Ultimately operating as the Conestoga Traction Company, the trolley extended its line to Marietta.

Major industries manufacturing such diverse items as silk, lace, wagons, industrial laundry equipment, stove, cast-iron pipe fittings, portable air compressor, clothes, and commercial cast iron all took root in Columbia and grew. At the same time, small businesses such as bakers, a brewery, hotels, livery stables, butchers, shoe and clothing stores, drugstores, restaurants, and corner grocery stores also developed.

Residents invited family and others who moved away back to celebrate their prosperity in 1905 and 1913 for Old Home Weeks and in 1888 for the town's centennial and again in 1938 for its sesquicentennial. These reunions were particularly rich sources of historical photographs.

In 1906, the PRR opened its Atglen and Susquehanna Branch low graded freight bypass sending many more through freight trains via Columbia. In 1930, the fourth bridge opened for vehicular traffic over the Susquehanna River on the Lincoln Highway, eliminating a bottleneck. Eight years later, the PRR electrified its Lancaster County lines through Columbia.

Columbians have always fought in the country's wars. African Americans traveled north to join the famous 54th Massachusetts that fought in the Civil War. Citizens enlisted during the Spanish-American War, World War I, World War II, Korean War, and Vietnam War, and started and joined military fraternal organizations when they returned home. Columbia was home to eight generals and admirals, an unusually high percentage.

Columbia has continued to change with the time diversifying its economy into tourism with such attractions as the world-renowned National Association of Watch and Clock Collectors' Museum. The town is home to Anvil International, makers of cast-iron pipe fittings and Colonial Metals, caster of brass and bronze ingots.

In 1719, Scotsman George Stewart began settlement on several hundred acres at what became the east end of Marietta. In 1748, David Cook bought the land and it passed down through his family. A grandson also named David Cook began to lay out a town on part of the property in 1803, called it New Haven, and distributed the first 100 lots by lottery.

Jacob Grosh acquired some of the first Cook's land, and in 1814, he started a town he called Moravian Town, nicknamed Bungletown, to the east of New Haven.

Switching to the west of New Haven and going back in time to 1719, James Wilkins acquired 300 acres. Donegal Church pastor John Anderson bought the land in 1727. His son James started a ferry over to the York County side. In 1804, James Anderson, descended from John and his son James, laid out the town of Waterford. Anderson too gave away lots based on a lottery that cost $60 per ticket.

To the north of Waterford, Benjamin Long had bought part the original 300 acres and laid out a continuation of Waterford. In 1812, the founders of New Haven and Waterford, Anderson and Cook respectively agreed to combine the town and seek a charter from Pennsylvania.

There are three stories on how the name Marietta came to be, all involving wives or daughters named Mary and Henrietta of Anderson and/or Cook. The resulting town ran along the east shore about a mile and a half, but because of the bends in the river the shore was geographically north.

The first major industry in town was a waypoint on shipping lumber, bundled into rafts, downriver. In 1814, there were nine lumber merchants. The canal and railroad arrived resulting in even more traffic moving through town. To the east of town from the mid-19th century into the early 20th century, anthracite iron furnaces operated. At one time there were six running concurrently. Today Marietta's large industries are GlaxoSmithKline, which continues in work of predecessors manufacturing vaccines, and Armstrong World Industry's ceiling plant.

That leaves the formation of Wrightsville. Ferry operator John Wright's son, John Wright Jr., directed the west shore operation for his father at what is now the foot of Hellam Street while his father sent the ferry across the river from the foot of what is now Walnut Street on the east shore.

In 1811, the Wright family sold the west shore land to Jacob Kline who laid out the 101-lot town of Wrightsville. In 1812, establishment of the adjoining town of Westphalia occurred, as did Wrightsville Extended in 1813. In 1834, all were incorporated into Wrightsville Borough.

Gen. John Gordon's brigade of Early's Division of Gen. Robert E. Lee's invading Confederate army approached Wrightsville on Sunday, June 28, 1863. After a brief encounter, hastily assembled defending Union forces retreated across the bridge toward Columbia. The defenders attempted to destroy the bridge's center section, but instead fire destroyed the whole bridge. The Confederates turned back only to fight the Union army again a few days later at Gettysburg.

The Susquehanna and Tidewater Canal opened in 1840 and ran 45 miles downstream to the Chesapeake Bay. Traffic, consisting of grain, iron, lumber, and coal barges, peaked in 1870.

Canal boats, pulled by mules on a special double-deck towpath section of the bridge, crossed over from the Pennsylvania Canal at Columbia to the Susquehanna and Tidewater Canal's start at Wrightsville.

Over the years, Wrightsville has been home to such diverse businesses as cigar manufacturing, quarries, limekilns, lumber mills, a silk mill, a flour and feed mill, and hardware manufacturing. Today the largest industry is Riverside Foundry of Donsco, Inc., which makes gray iron castings.

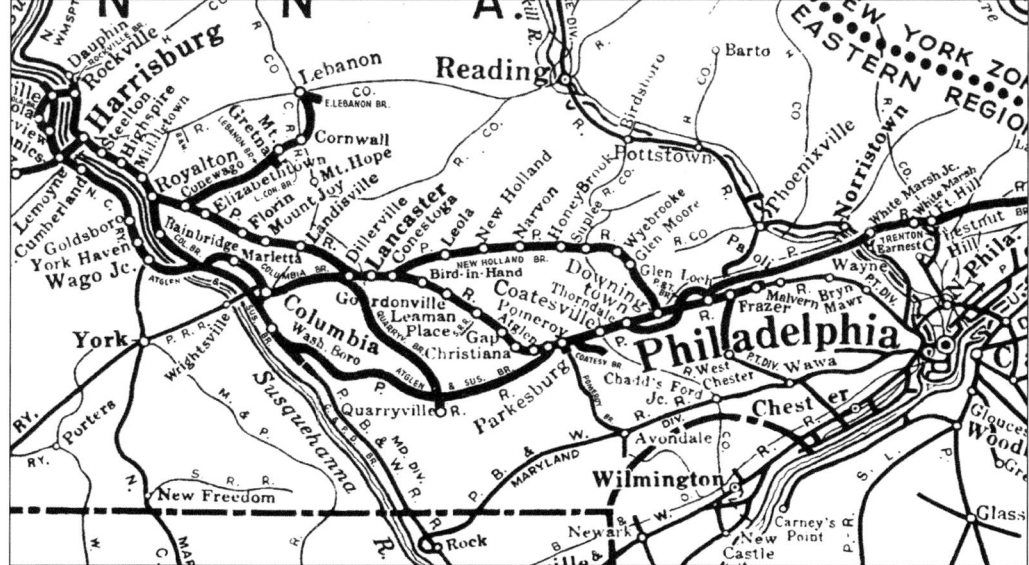

This 1941 Pennsylvania Railroad (PRR) map illustrates where Columbia, Marietta, and Wrightsville are with respect to the lower Susquehanna River, Harrisburg, York, Lancaster, Philadelphia, and other southeastern Pennsylvania communities. Columbia was an important location on the PRR with the Columbia, Atglen and Susquehanna; Frederick; and Columbia and Port Deposit Branches all focused on it. (Author's collection.)

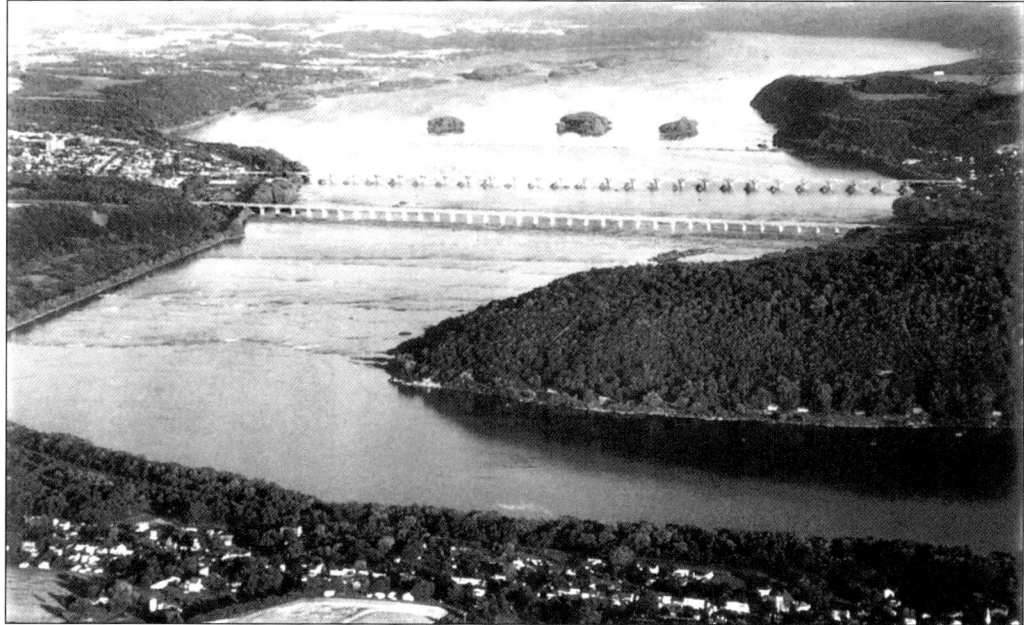

Looking down the Susquehanna River, this aerial view shows how the Susquehanna River dominates the Columbia, Wrightsville, and Marietta area. Marietta stretches along the foreground, Columbia is to the upper left, and Wrightsville is to the upper right. Joining the latter two are the 1972 and 1930 bridges. Roundtop juts out along on the York County side, forcing the river to make a 90-degree bend. (Courtesy Susquehanna Valley Chamber of Commerce.)

One

COLUMBIA

Geography determined Columbia's physical growth pattern. Starting at a natural Susquehanna River crossing, the town spread out along the river's east shore north to Chickies Hill and south to the river hills. When growth encountered those physical constraints, it accelerated eastward where the land was much gentler and more conducive to construction. The result was a town roughly of equal dimensions along the river and eastward away from it.

East–west Locust Street divides the town into north and south. Running parallel to Locust are other tree-named streets. Going north from Locust, there are Walnut, Chestnut, Poplar, Maple, Linden, and Cedar Streets. To the south of Locust the main streets are Cherry, Union, and Manor Streets.

North–south streets are numbered streets, roughly parallel to the river and starting there with Front Street and proceeding east with Second, Third, and so on. Any numbered street with the adjective *north* in front of it runs in that direction from Locust Street.

There are other streets throughout the town. For example there is a cluster of short streets named after the town founders: Mifflin, Houston, Blunston, and Wright with a longer one, Barber Street, off by itself. Scattered about are ones with names such as Central Avenue, Franklin Street, and Penn Street.

Long alleys run east from near the river and are called avenues. Their names are letters of the alphabet starting with A Avenue at the north end of town. There are other, shorter ones, such as Stump, Tank (named for a railroad water tower nearby), Elbow (it has a bend in the middle), and Concord Avenues.

The downtown is along Locust Street from Front Street to Fifth Street and along the numbered streets one block north and south of Locust Street.

PA 462, the Lincoln Highway and the old US 30, crosses the 1930 concrete arch bridge from Wrightsville and it then becomes Chestnut Street. At Fifth Street, the Lincoln Highway abruptly turns right and follows Fifth Street for two blocks to Locust Street. There it becomes Lancaster Avenue, which heads off at an angle toward its namesake city. Businesses are spread out along this Lincoln Highway corridor.

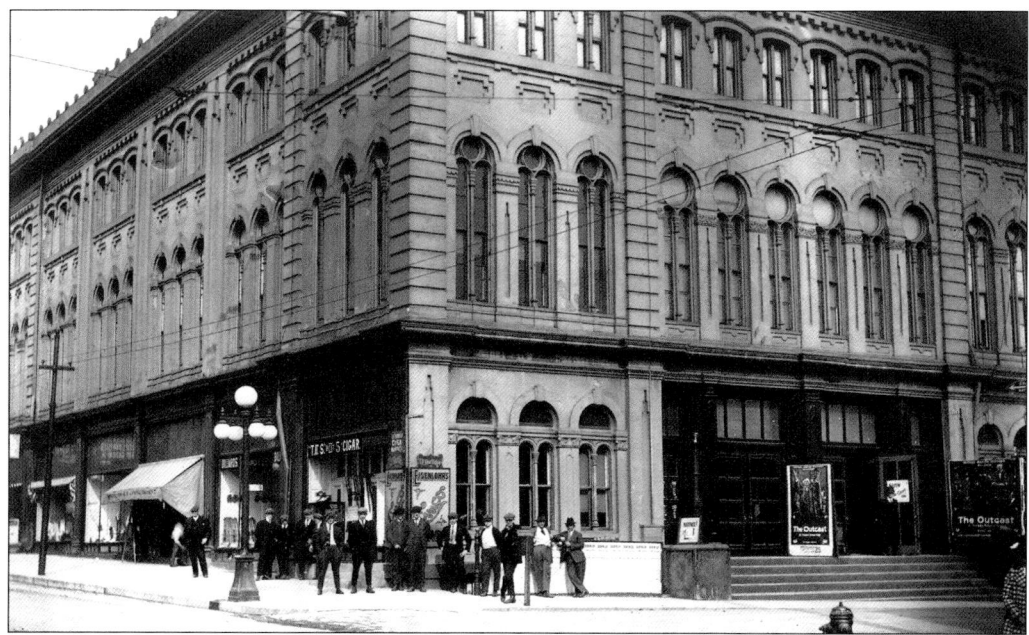

Columbia's opera house, built in 1875 at on the southeast corner of South Third and Locust Streets to replace the original 1828 town hall, was the home to borough offices, small shops and businesses, and an auditorium for opera, vaudeville, and movies. The advertisement on the steps is for *The Outcast*, a silent film released in 1915. (Courtesy Columbia Historic Preservation Society.)

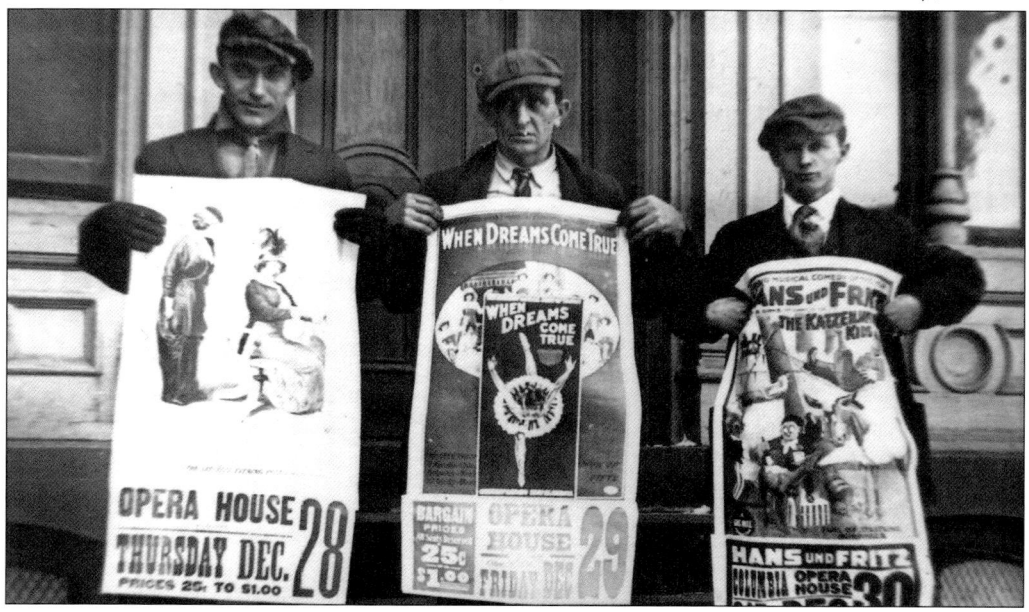

Three men line up with posters showing what was playing between Thursday, December 28, and Saturday, December 30. The poster on the left is for an unknown event. In the center is *When Dreams Come True*, whose company of 50 played for months at a time in Chicago, New York, and Boston. The right one is for the "Hans und Fritz, the Katzenjamer Kids." (Courtesy Columbia Historic Preservation Society.)

On February 19, 1947, fire broke out in the opera house, destroying the building. According to the newspaper, "Tears welled in the eyes of many among the awe-struck spectators as they saw the stately tower with its traditional clock—flames and smoke belching from all four faces–writhing and twisting and finally crumpling in blazing chunks with a sickening roar to the street more than 100 feet below." (Courtesy Columbia Historic Preservation Society.)

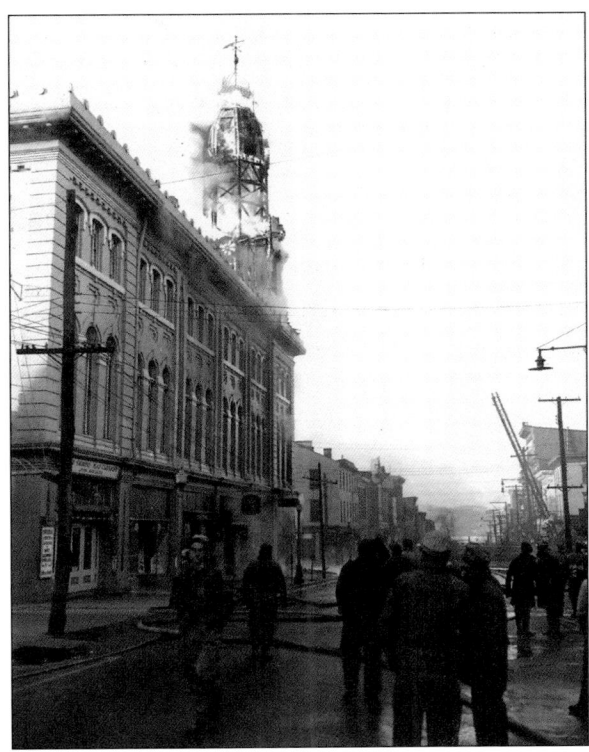

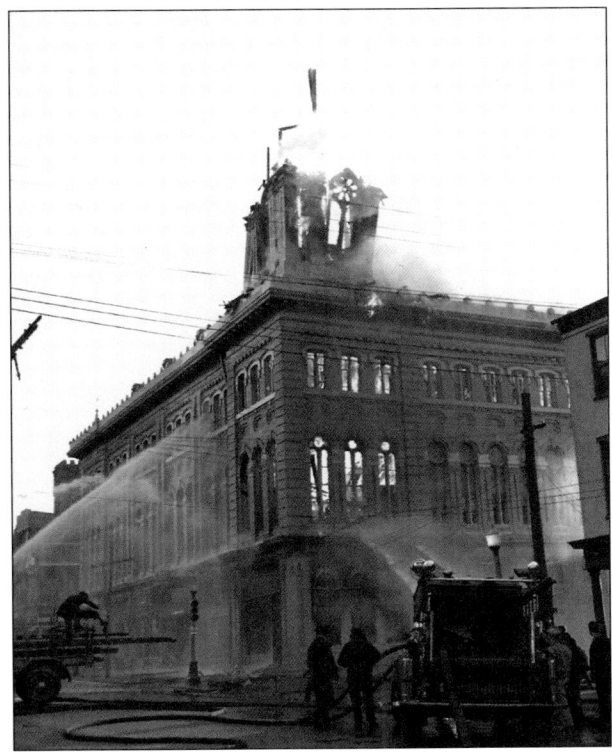

The day the opera house burned became known as "Black Wednesday" in Columbia. All local residents alive on that fateful day can remember where they were when the hours-long and "ruthless destroyer" fire struck "to devastate and reduce to ruin the very heart and pulse-beat of this community." (Courtesy Columbia Historic Preservation Society.)

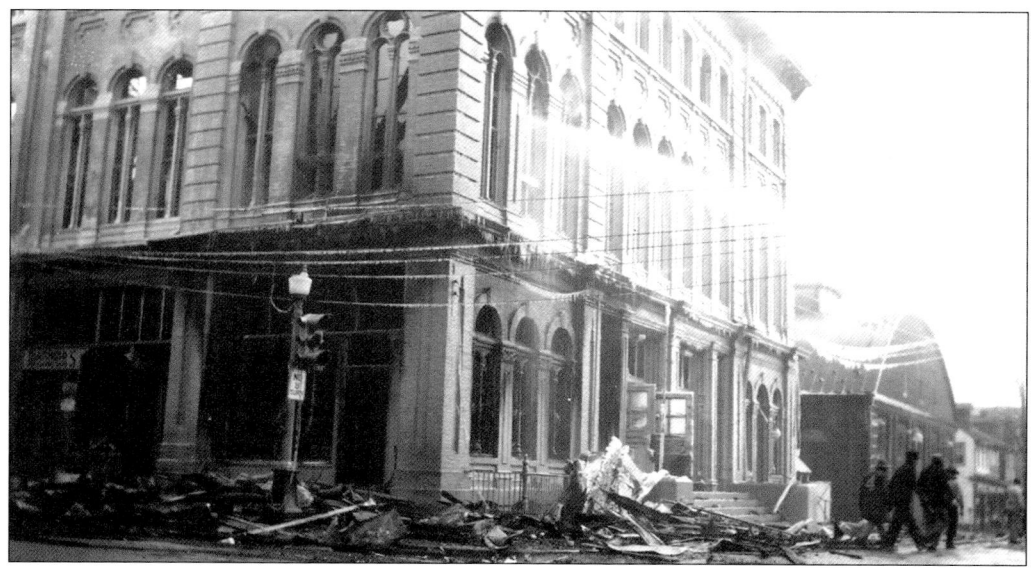

Later that day, after the fire companies extinguished the blaze, only the building's ice-encased shell remained. Fortunately the flames did not spread to engulf the Columbia Market House to the right on South Third Street. Ultimately, the borough council decided to save what it could and rebuild it as a one-story municipal building, which is still in use. (Courtesy Columbia Historic Preservation Society.)

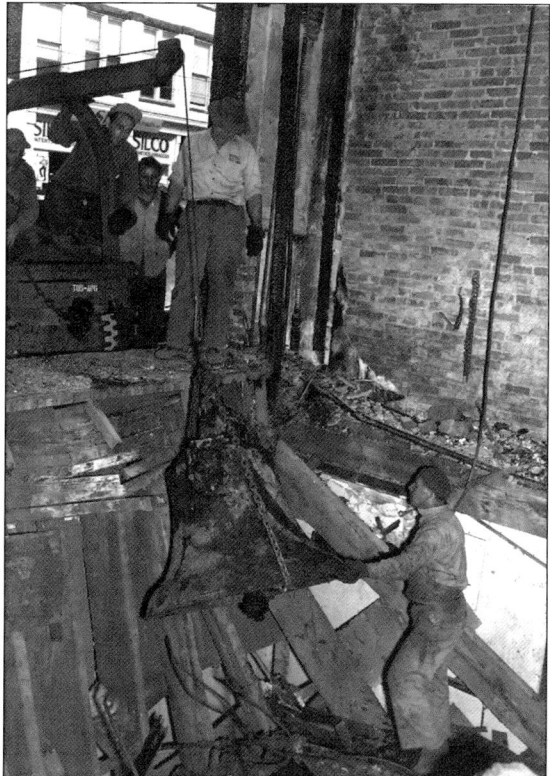

The fire, in burning the tower, not only destroyed the town clock, but it also caused the tower bell to break loose and come crashing down to the basement below. During the building's reconstruction, workers used a tow truck to hoist the destroyed bell up to street level for subsequent recovery. (Courtesy Columbia Historic Preservation Society.)

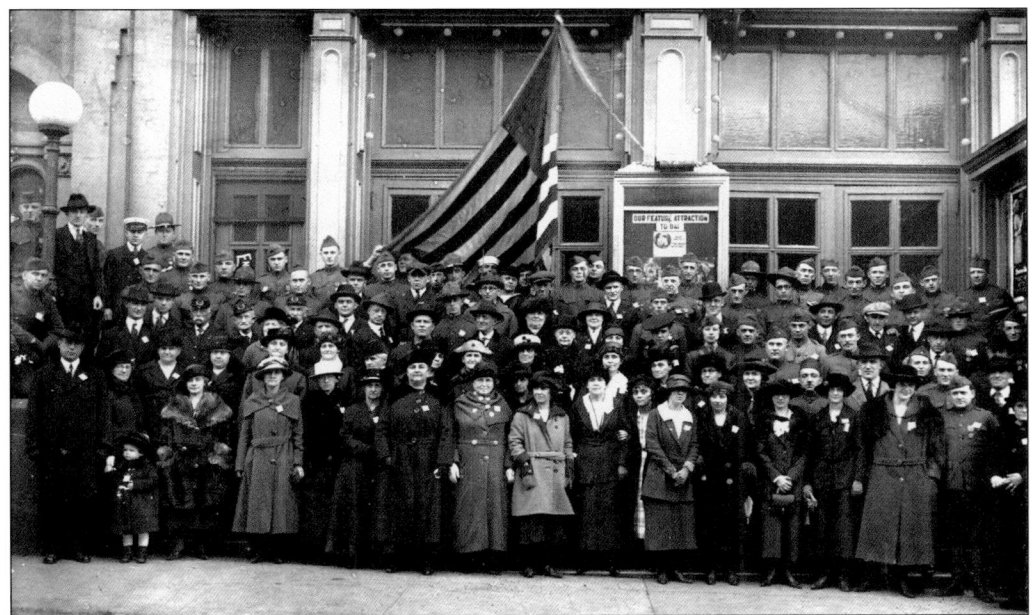

A large group poses beneath the flag on the opera house steps. There appear to be many veterans in the group. Judging from their uniforms, they appear to have served in the Civil War, the Spanish-American War, and World War I. Both the U.S. Army and the U.S. Navy seem to have representatives. (Courtesy Cleon G. Berntheizel.)

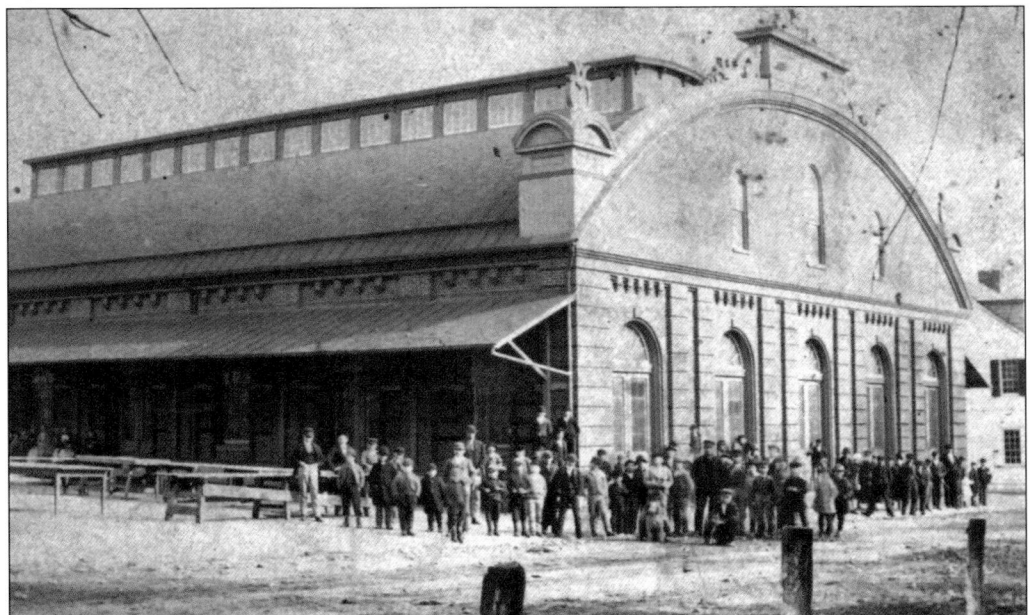

Completed in 1869 at a cost of about $20,000 (around $250,000 in today's dollars), Columbia Market House is on South Third Street. Seen soon after its opening, the building does not have its long-standing neighbor to the left, the opera house. The 118-foot-long by 40-foot-wide building at one time had 180 stalls inside with more outside under the cantilevered roof. (Courtesy Lancaster County Historical Society.)

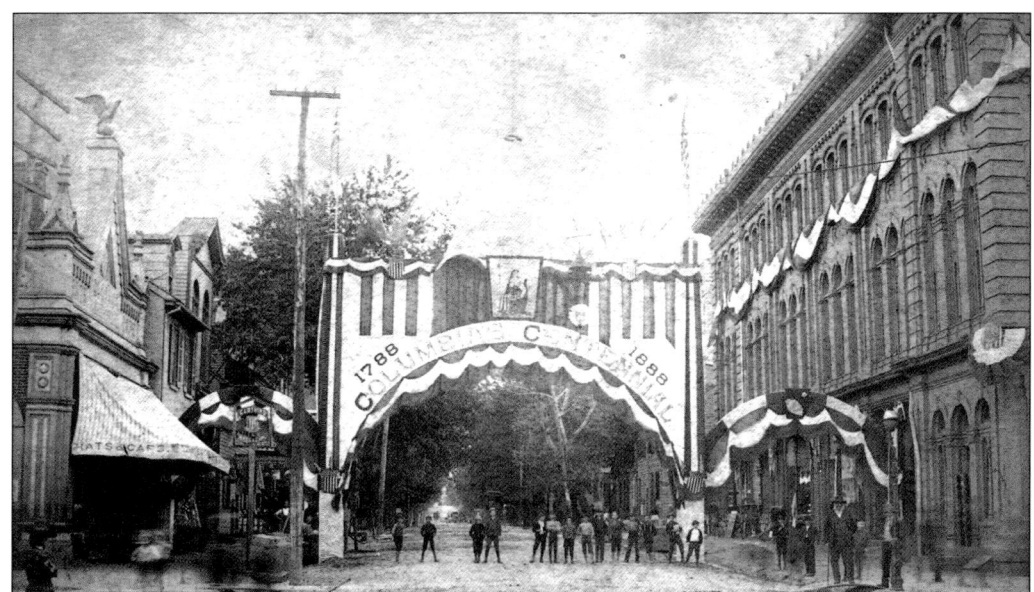

The first celebration widely captured photographically in Columbia was the town's 1888 centennial marking when the town was established as a borough. Decorations and arches appeared throughout the town. One of the largest was on Locust Street just east of Third Street. The opera house is on the right. (Courtesy Columbia Historic Preservation Society.)

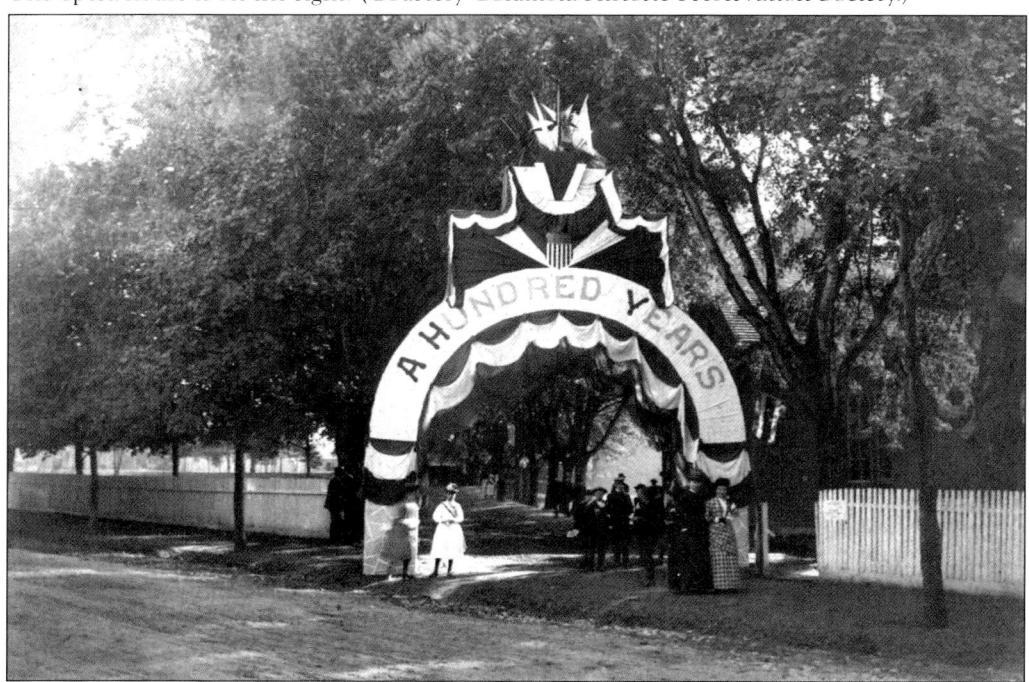

In 1888, the Fifth Street and Locust Street entrance to Locust Street Park did not look at all like it does over 100 years later. A huge bicentennial arch proclaiming "A Hundred Years" stood over the entrance. A picket fence ran along Locust Street. The park served as a focal point for the bicentennial parades and speeches. (Courtesy Columbia Historic Preservation Society.)

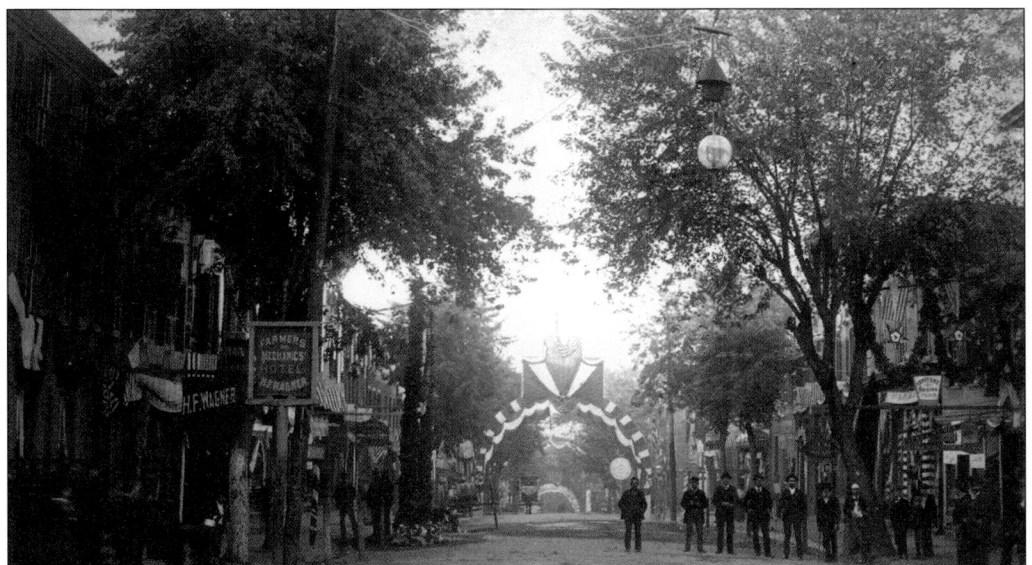

This view is looking west down Locust Street from Third Street in 1888. One arch is midway down the block and another is off in the distance. Henry F. Wagner's Farmers and Mechanics' Hotel is on the left on the southwest corner. On the north side are John Weimer's cigar and tobacco shop and the Keystone Social Club. (Courtesy Columbia Historic Preservation Society.)

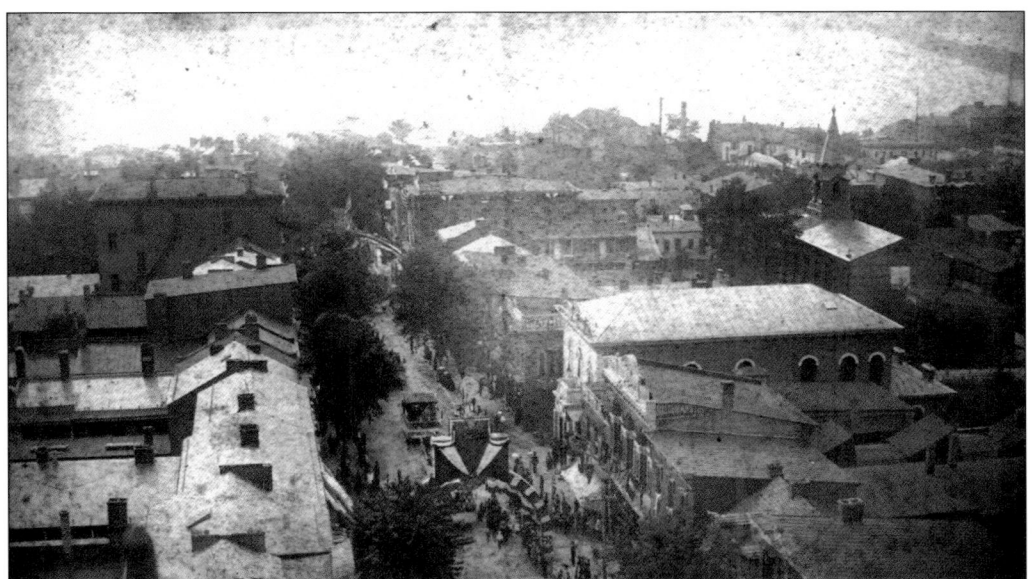

Climbing up in the opera house gave the photographer a good view west on Locust Street to the Susquehanna River in the distance. Spreading across Locust Street are two centennial arches: one is visible in the center while the other, at Second Street, is only half visible because of trees. The First English Lutheran Church on North Second Street is also visible. (Courtesy Columbia Historic Preservation Society.)

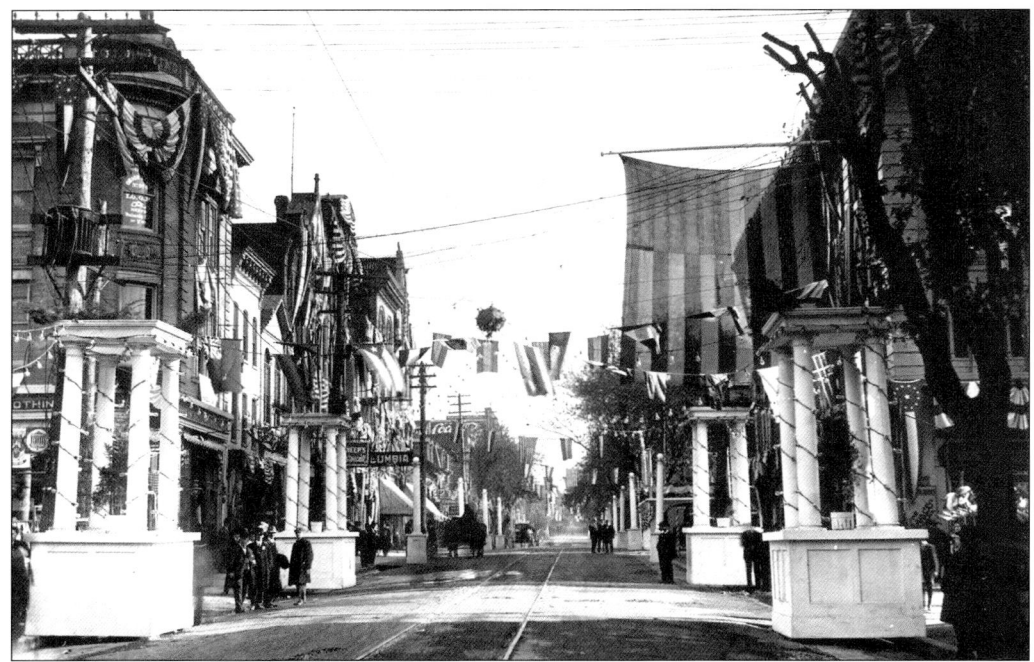

For the 1913 Old Home Week, a translucent United States flag is suspended from the opera house over Third and Locust Streets. On each of the four corners there is a temporary group of four columns coming out of common bases. Strings of lights spiral around each column and the trolley tracks run on Locust Street's center. (Courtesy Columbia Historic Preservation Society.)

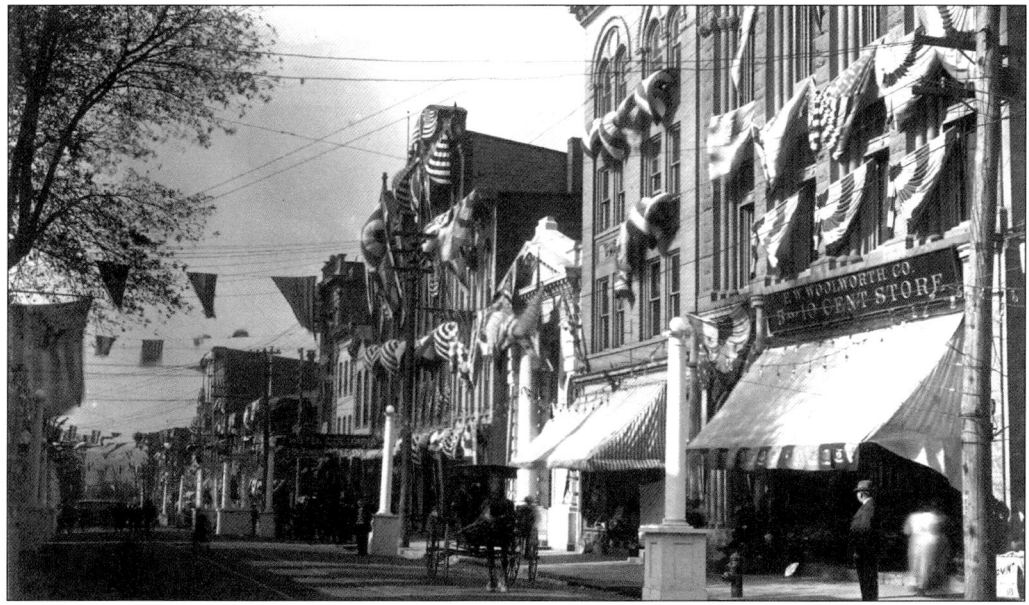

Arguably the most decorated part of town was Locust Street. Buildings were covered with patriotic colors and lining the street were temporary lighted columns with lights strung between them. Looking west down to Third Street, F. W. Woolworth Company 5 and 10 Cent Store is in the foreground in the Masonic building. (Courtesy Columbia Historic Preservation Society.)

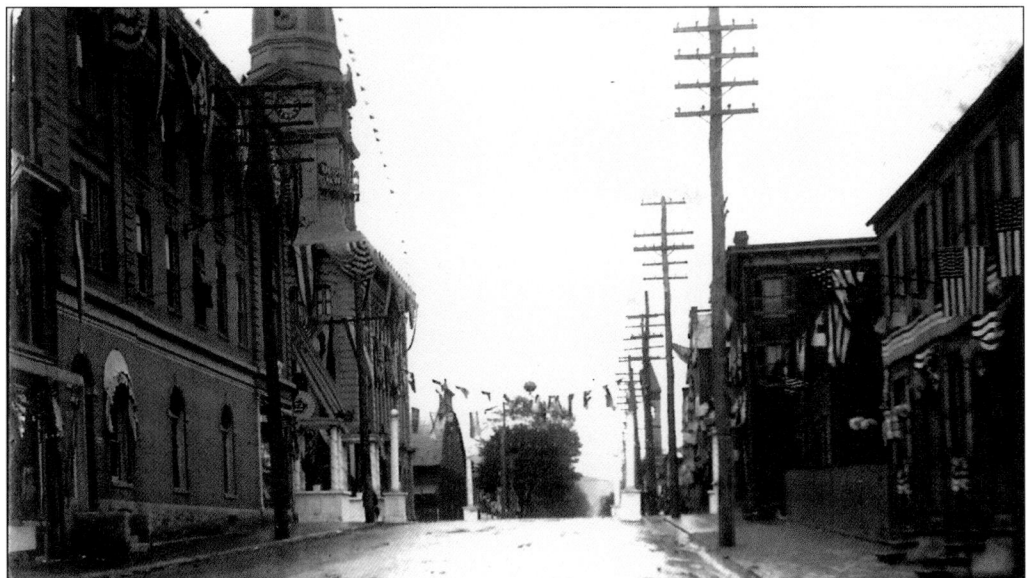

The photographer aimed his camera south along Third Street toward Locust Street during the 1913 Old Home Week. On the left from front to back are the Eagle Building, Locust Street intersection, the opera house, and the Columbia Market House. On the right are homes and, at the intersection, Schroeder and Hinkle Druggists. (Courtesy John Hinkle Jr.)

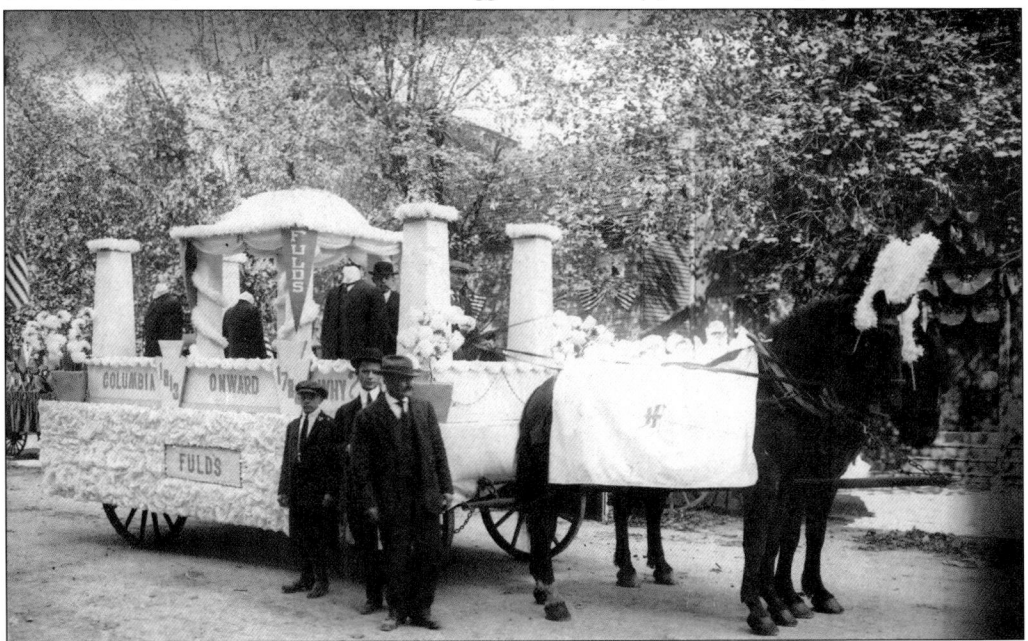

Fulds, a "Clothier & Men's Furnisher" store at 207 Locust Street, built a horse-drawn float for the 1913 Old Home Week parade. The float carried the idea of columns off the street and on to a mobile platform. On the float's side was the week's motto, "Columbia Onward 1788–1913, Why Not?" The mannequins display some of the men's clothes the store carried. (Courtesy Columbia Historic Preservation Society.)

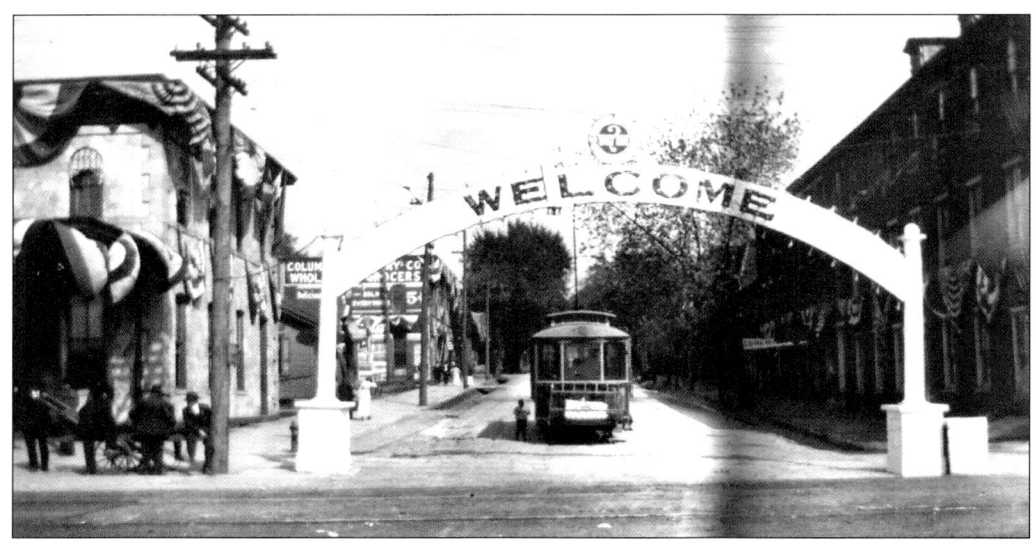

Columbia's Old Home Week in 1913 was held October 12–19. Visitors to town were welcomed to Columbia by numerous arches. This one is at Front and Walnut Streets. Over the lighted Welcome at the top of the arch was the theme log, two concentric circles saying Columbia Onward 1788–1913 in the blue outer one and Why Not? in the red inner one all in white letters. (Courtesy Columbia Historic Preservation Society.)

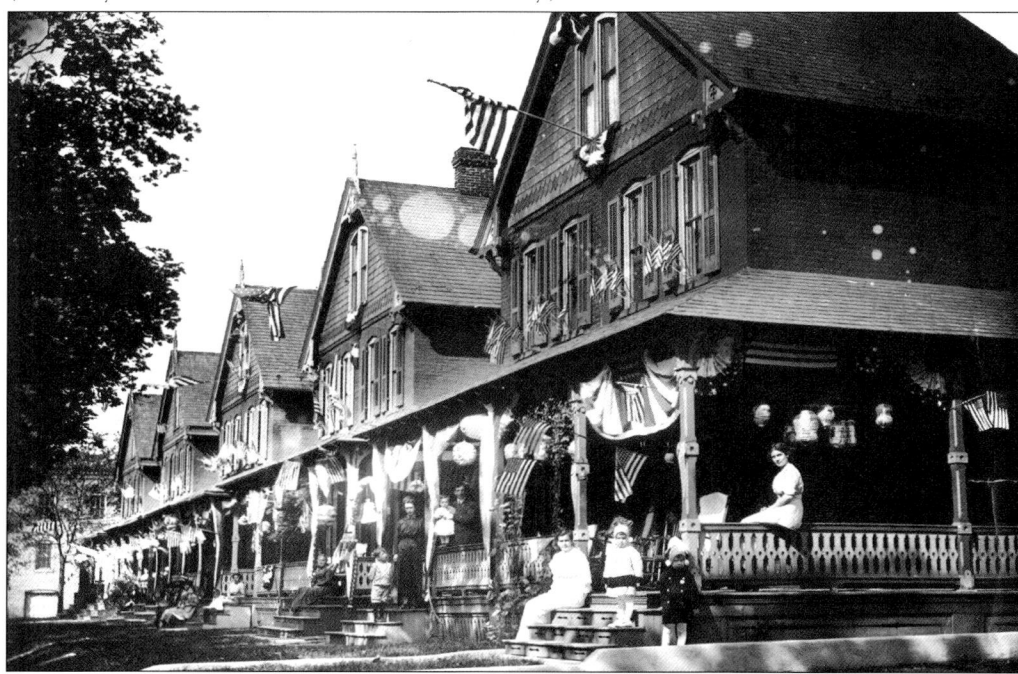

Based on a New England tradition that spread across the United States, old home weeks were popular at the start of Columbia. Citizens would invite family and friends to come back to the hometown for a few days. Residents along the east side of North Third Street between Poplar and Maple Streets decorated their homes for the event. (Courtesy Columbia Historic Preservation Society.)

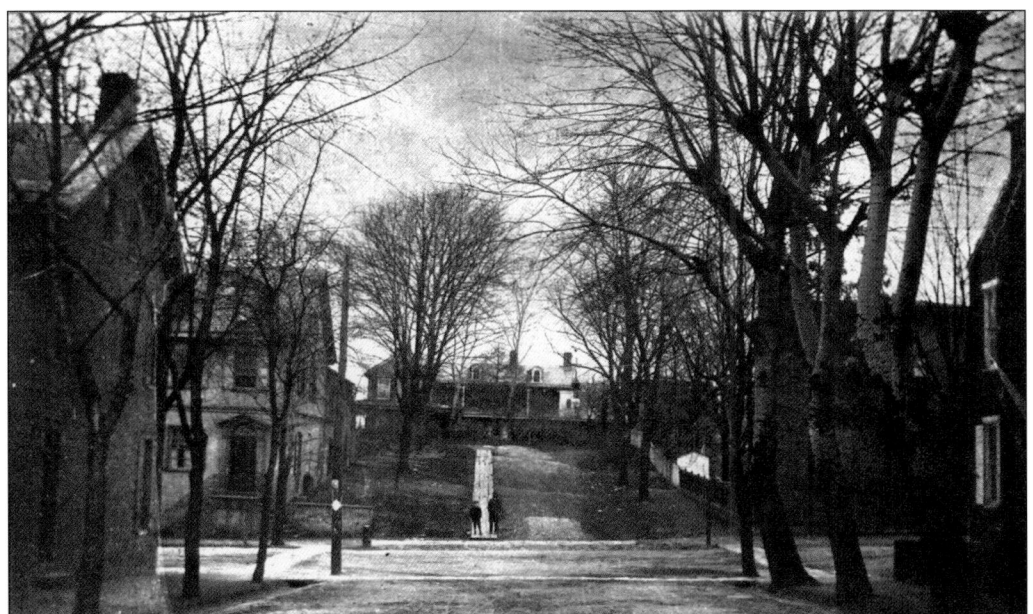

The camera is pointed north on North Second Street toward the cross street, Walnut Street. The house with the stairs in front on the right was the birthplace of the poet Lloyd Mifflin, known as "America's Sonneteer." Later his home became the PRR's Young Men's Christian Association. Straight ahead on the rise in the distance is Mount Bethel. (Courtesy Columbia Historic Preservation Society.)

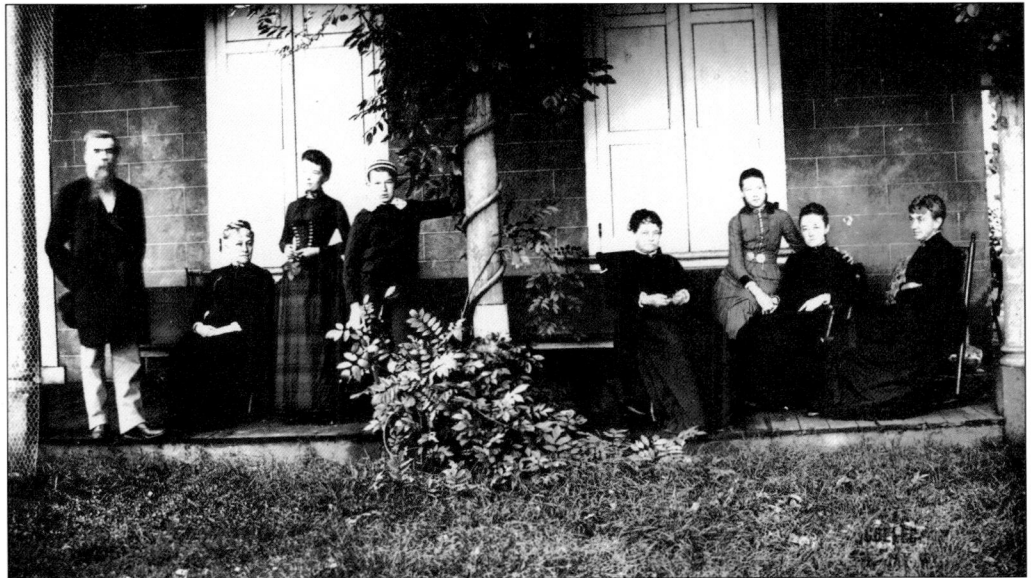

Samuel Blunston, an early surveyor known among genealogists for his Blunston Warrants, built a home on a rise overlooking the Susquehanna River. The home was known as Bellmont until the Bethel family, some of whom are on the porch, took it over and renamed it Mount Bethel. Demolition of the home happened during construction of the Columbia entrance to the 1930 bridge. (Courtesy Columbia Historic Preservation Society.)

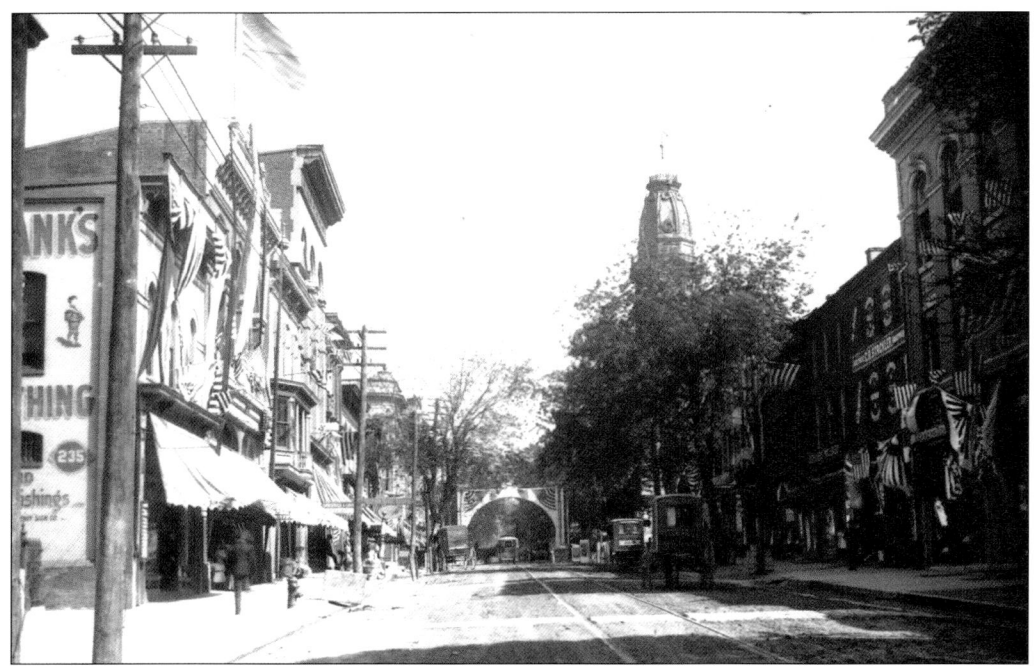

Columbia's first Old Home Week was held in 1905. Notice Locust Street's lack of automobiles, which would not be the case only eight years in the future when the town welcomed returning former residents and visitors for its second Old Home Week. Also notice the awnings on the north or sunny side of the street and their absence on the south side. (Courtesy Columbia Historic Preservation Society.)

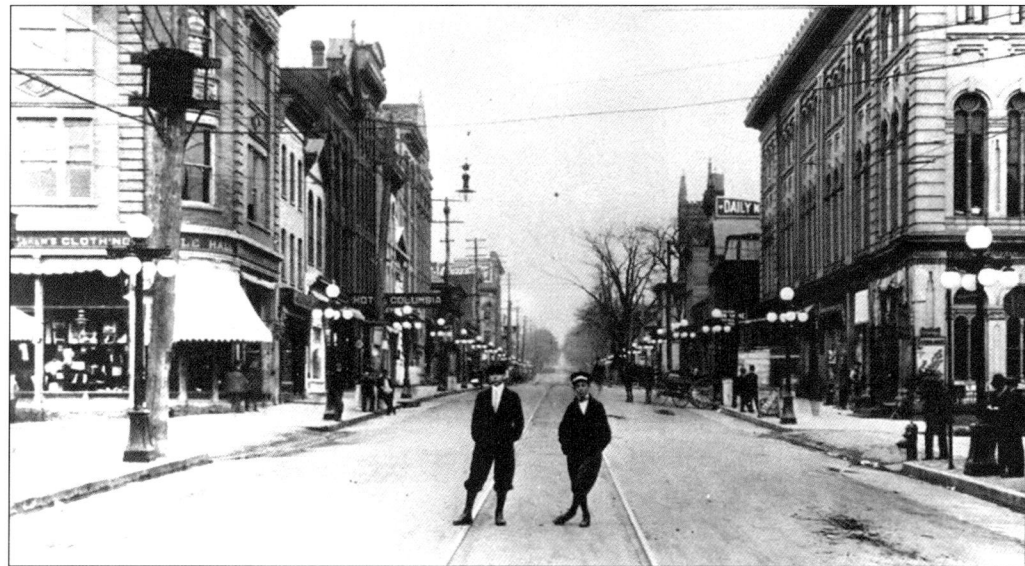

Traffic is light, allowing the young men to pose for the camera in the middle of the trolley track on Locust Street. Columbia's street lighting for Locust Street at the start of the 20th century consisted of five electric globes on posts supplemented by suspended electric lights at intersections. (Courtesy Columbia Historic Preservation Society.)

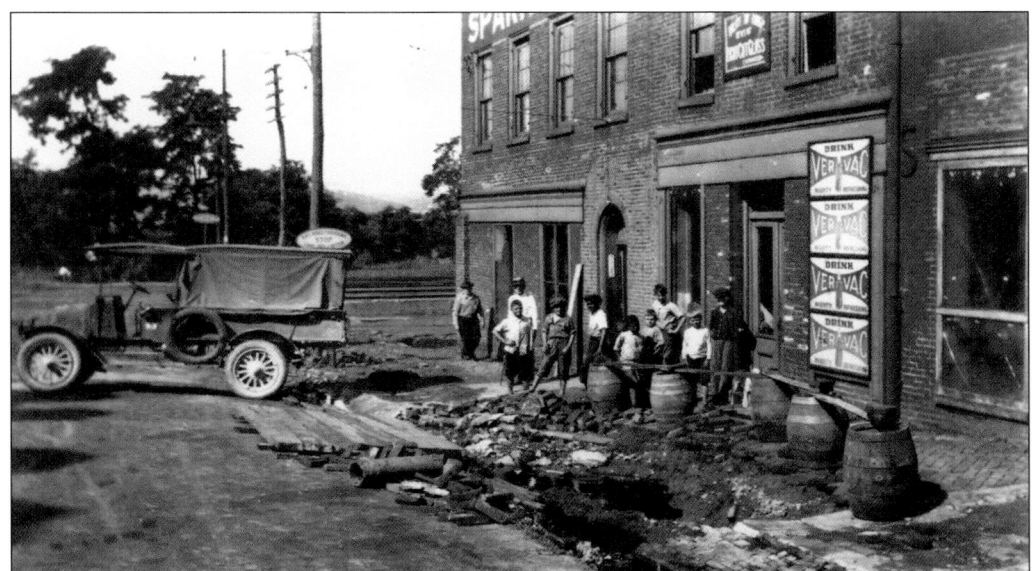

Some major repairs are underway to the brick sidewalk on the north side of Locust Street at its intersection with Front Street. On the left, Locust Street crossed the PRR tracks on its way to the Susquehanna River. The four signs on the building advised the reader to "Drink Ver-Vac," a soft drink, as it was "mighty refreshing." (Courtesy Columbia Historic Preservation Society.)

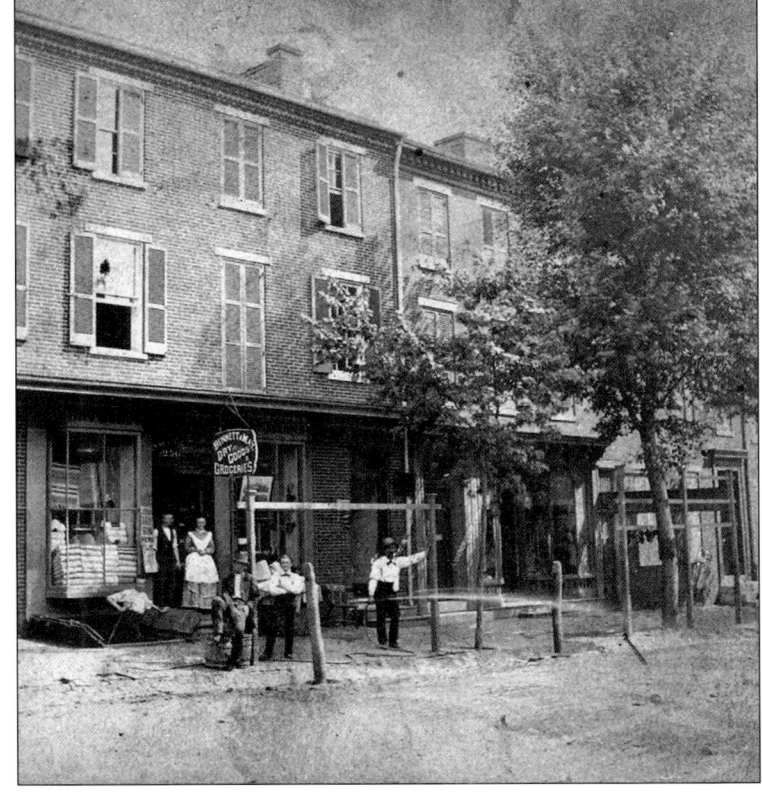

In 1892, F. A. Bennett had a dry goods, carpets, groceries, boots, and shoes store at 233 and 235 Locust Street, while a few doors east at 255 Locust Street, Lewis A. May had a fancy grocery store. They combined as Bennett and May, Dry Goods and Groceries in one location. (Courtesy Cleon G. Berntheizel.)

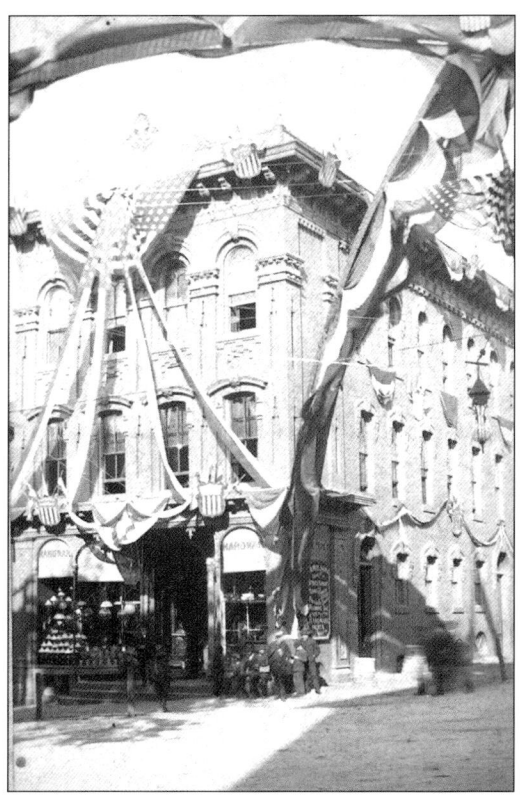

The cornerstone date is 1876 for Hiram Wilson's three-story hardware store. Wilson decorated it as shown for Columbia's centennial in 1888. One anchor for the four-corner soaring celebration arch was by his store on the northwest of Second and Locust Streets. The window on the left had a display of lights and a furnace sat on the steps. (Courtesy Columbia Historic Preservation Society.)

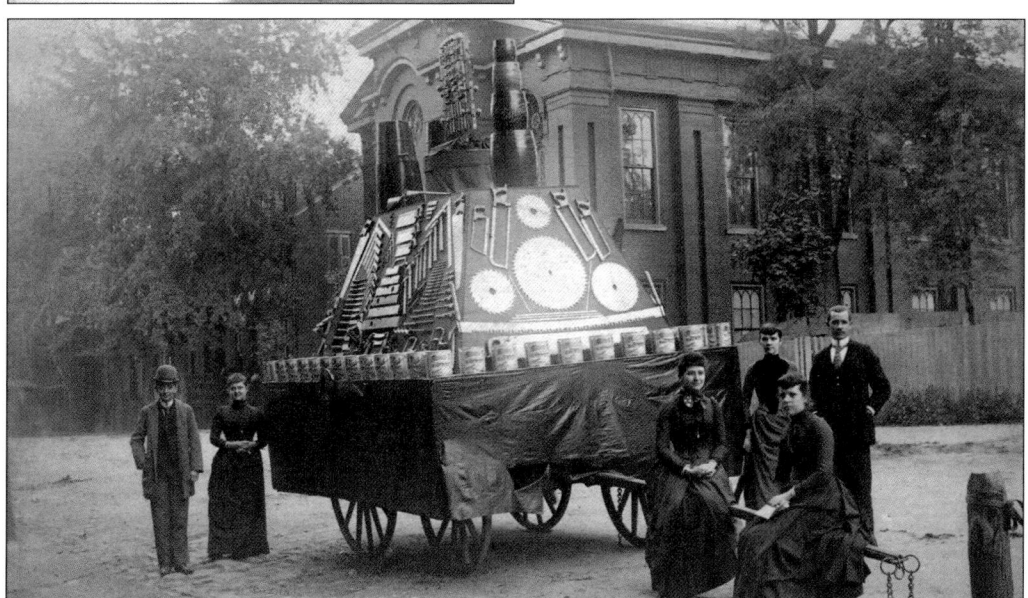

Sunlight glints off circular saw blades as the Wilson family members pose with their float for the centennial parade. The float displays tools such as saws, hammers, planes, levels, and drills, all surrounded by paint buckets. First English Lutheran Church is in the background, and Wilson's building is out of view to the left. (Courtesy Columbia Historic Preservation Society.)

By 1913, the Columbia branch of Follmer, Clogg, and Company was using the building to manufacture umbrellas and parasols. However, the building still has a sign painted on the side that said Wilson's. Note that a fourth floor now appears with a trace of the old roofline between it and the third floor. (Courtesy Columbia Historic Preservation Society.)

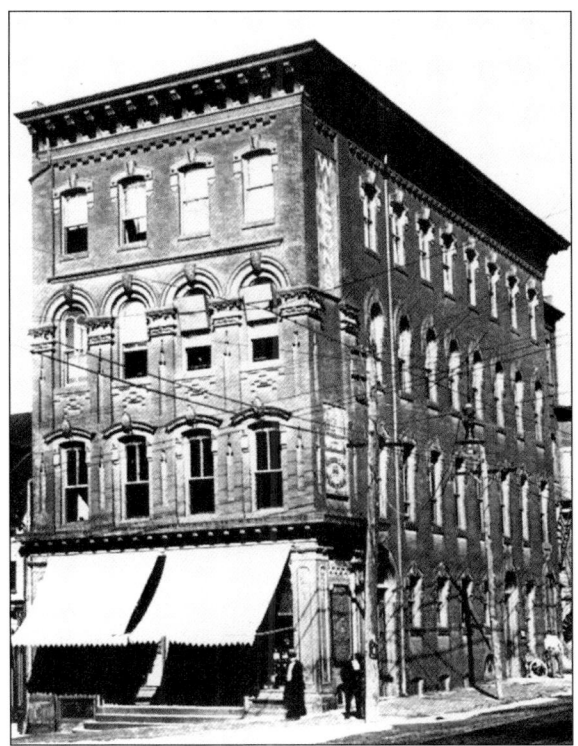

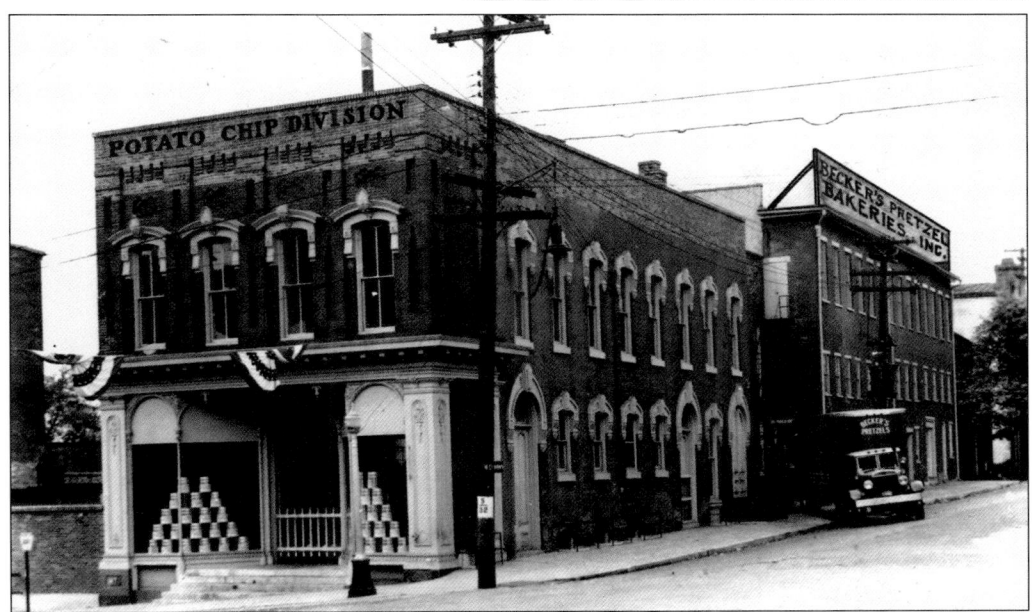

By 1919, the Columbia Baking and Manufacturing Company was at this location, and by 1940, it was Becker's Pretzel Bakeries, Inc. The latter located its potato chip division in the building. The top two stories are gone, as is the fancy roof trim. A truck is parked at the dock at an angle so as not to block Second Street. Cans of potato chips are neatly stacked in the windows. (Courtesy Columbia Historic Preservation Society.)

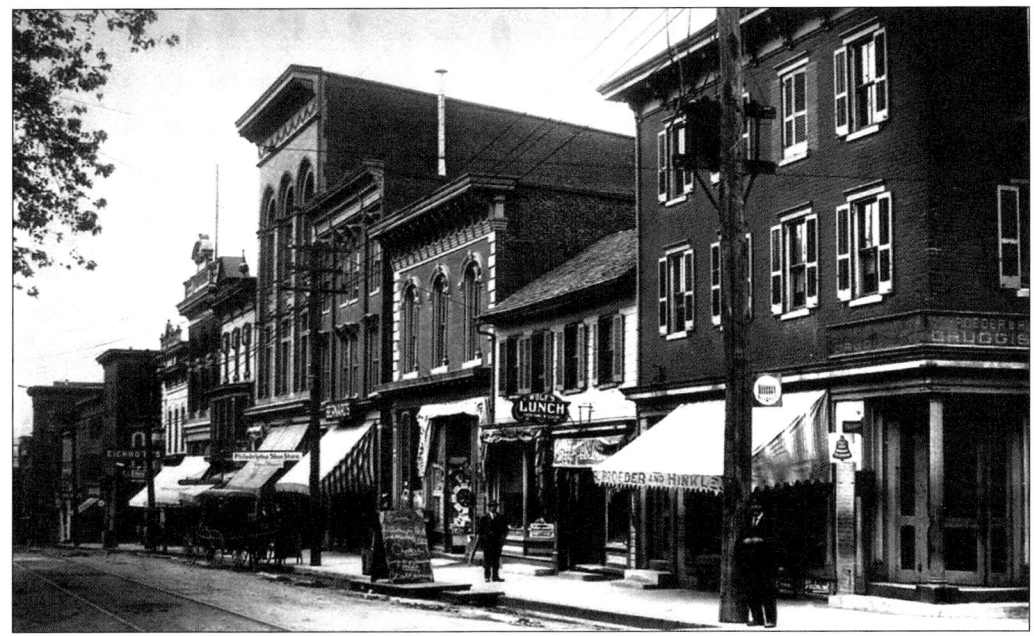

Looking west down Locust Street from Hinkle's, the next building held Wolfe's Lunch. In a 1902 advertisement he said, "Meals at all hours. Regular meals 30 cents. Ice Cream in Season." Farther down the street a horizontal sign projecting out over the sidewalk was for Eichorn's, a men's clothing store. (Courtesy John Hinkle Jr.)

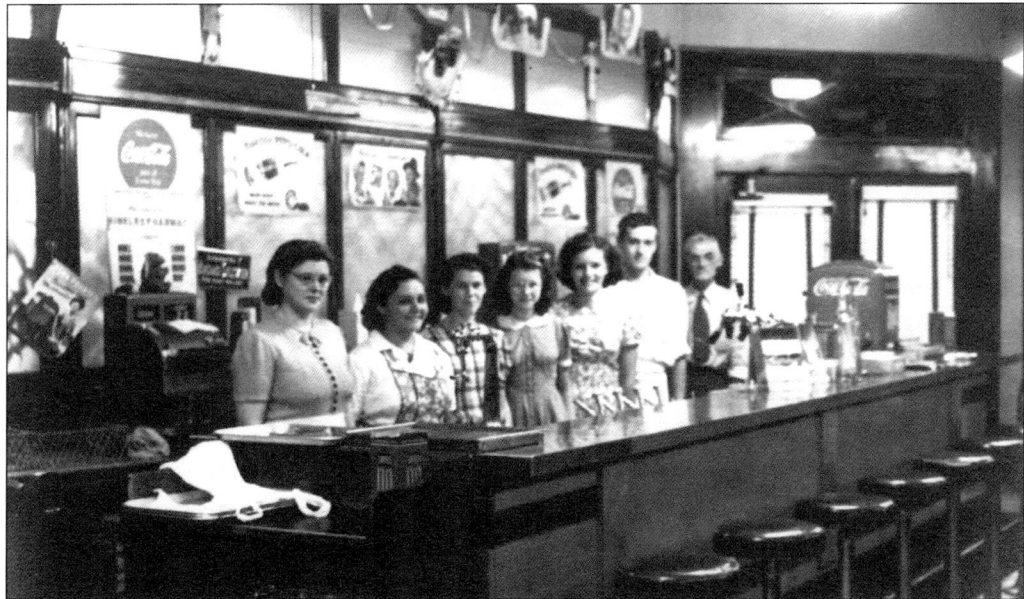

Inside Hinkle's, the staff all lines up behind the counter to have their photograph taken. Notice the mechanical cash register on the left. Two Coca-Cola advertisements are on the wall behind the counter, the typical bright red Coca-Cola machine is on the right and behind it are the angled double doors opening on to the North Third Street and Locust Street intersection. (Courtesy John Hinkle Jr.)

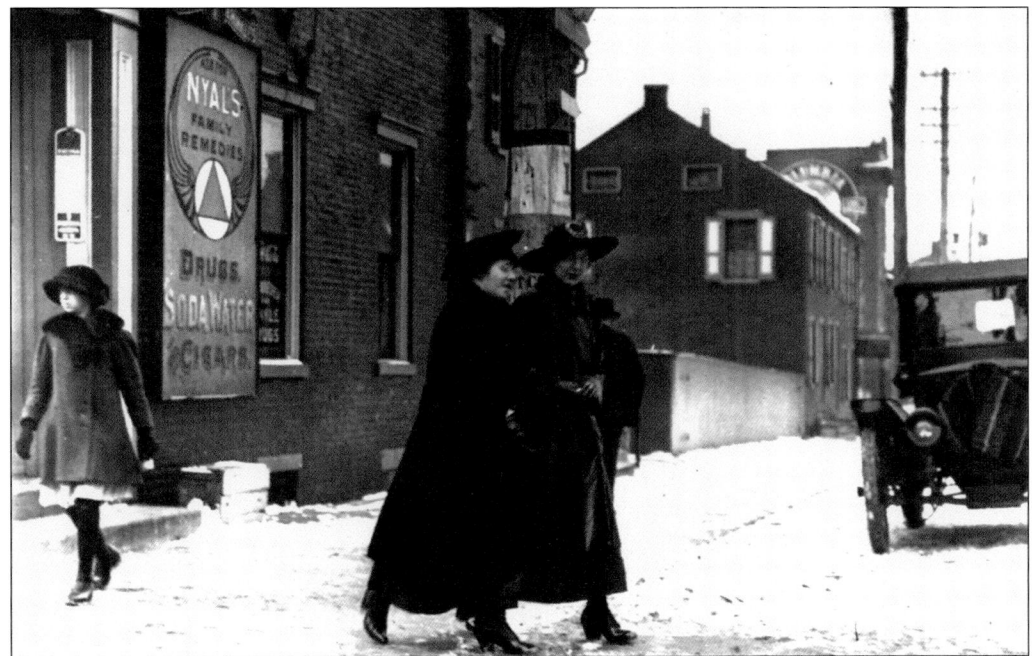

A light snowfall has covered the ground, but it is not enough to stop pedestrians from using North Third Street in front of Hinkle's. On the side of the building the large sign says "ask for Nyal's Family Remedies" and "drugs, soda water, and cigars." The owner of the car on the right has covered the radiator with a blanket with the hope of retaining some heat in the cooling water. (Courtesy John Hinkle Jr.)

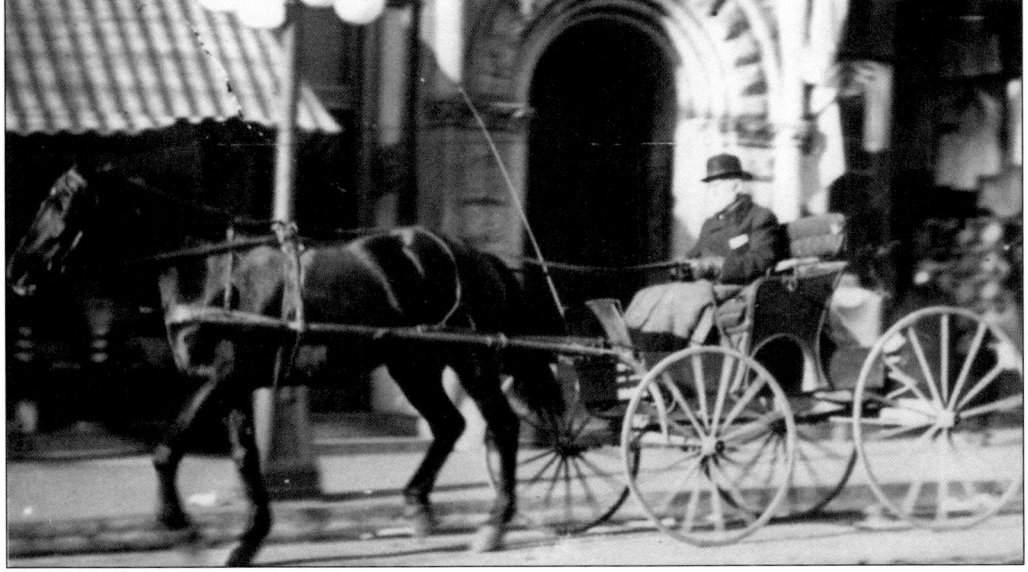

Dr. Houston Mifflin is in his carriage heading west on the 300 block of Locust Street by a five-globe streetlamp. Behind him is the Masonic building with its arched entrance. Mifflin was a member of one of the oldest Columbia families and, in addition to being a physician, was in real estate. (Courtesy Cleon G. Berntheizel.)

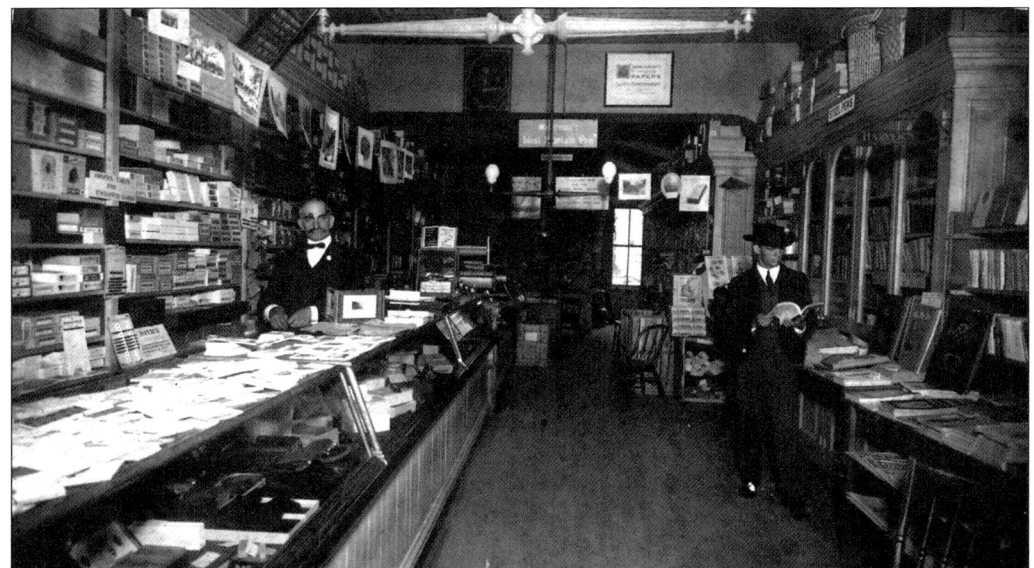

Clarissa Richards and Mary E. R. Eckman operated the Richards and Eckman store that was located at 215 Locust Street and that sold books, stationery, and wallpaper. The two women and their families lived next door at 213. In this 1905 view, the sign above the rear gaslight fixture reads Waterman's Ideal Fountain Pen. (Courtesy Columbia Historic Preservation Society.)

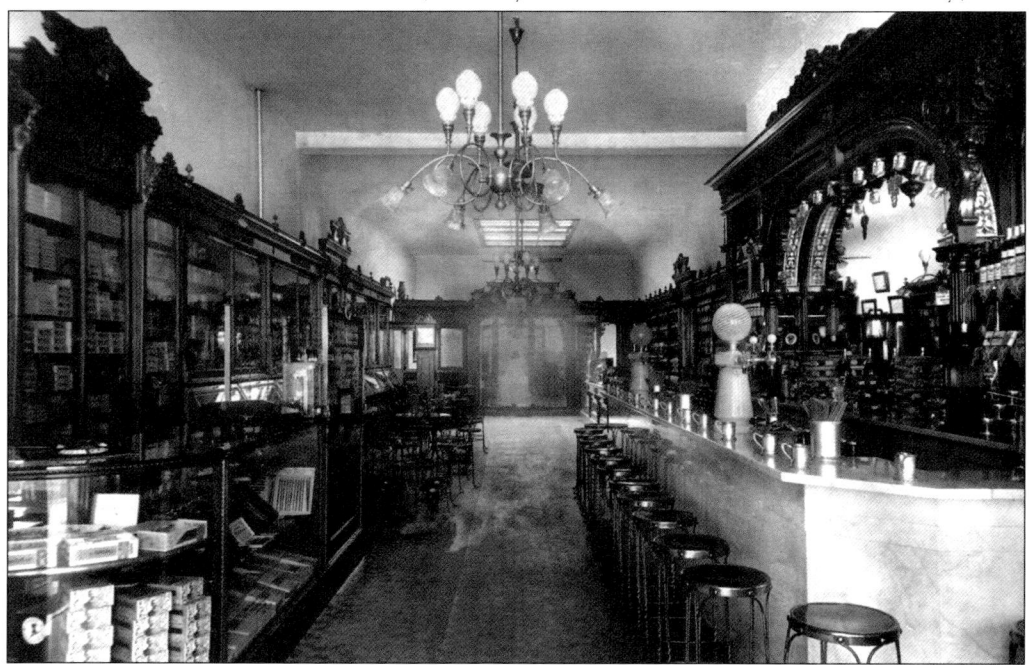

Harry W. Zeamer had a drugstore at 240 Locust Street. Inside, on the right, is the soda fountain featuring 14 seats beneath an ornately framed mirror. Patrons also could choose to seat themselves at the tables to the left. Cigar boxes line the other ornate wall cabinet to the left and the floor display cabinet, which has an ashtray for Leda Havana Cigars on its top. (Courtesy Columbia Historic Preservation Society.)

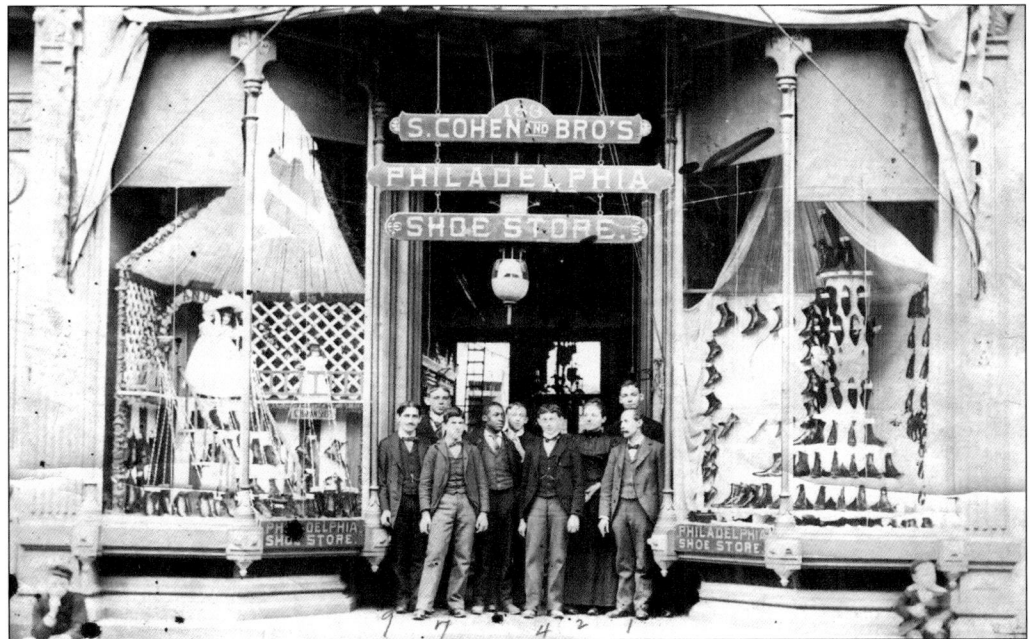

In 1892, Selig Cohen and brothers operated their Philadelphia Shoe Store at 163 Locust Street, pictured here. They carried a wide variety of shoes, many of which they displayed in their store's window. After the dawn of the 20th century, they moved about a block east to 247 Locust Street. (Courtesy Columbia Historic Preservation Society.)

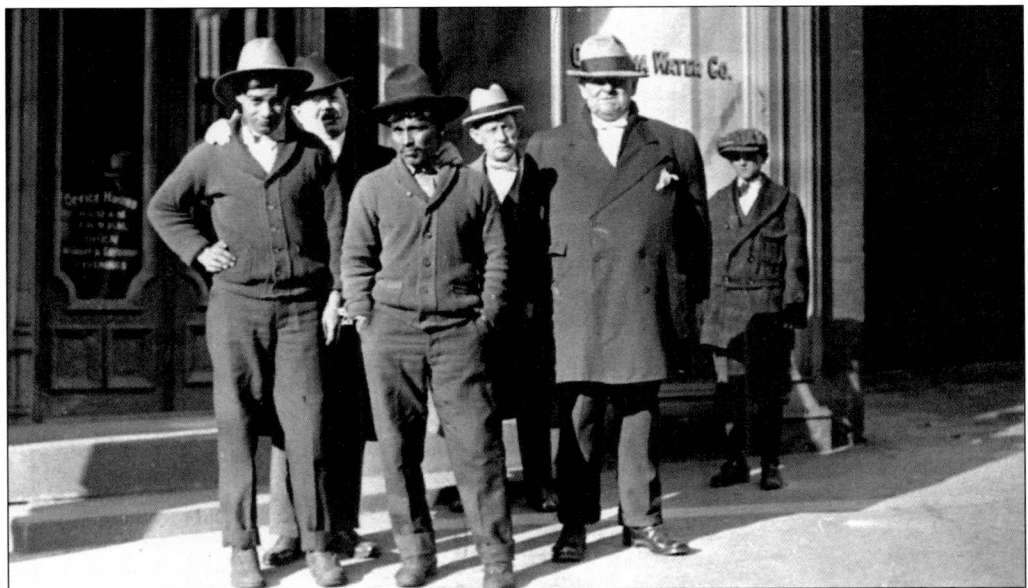

Many municipalities own their water system, but the Columbia Water Company is privately owned. Filtering and pumping starts at the foot of Locust Street by the Susquehanna River with pipes distributing water through the town and surrounding area. Here company officials and employees gather in front of the office at 225 Locust Street. (Courtesy Columbia Historic Preservation Society.)

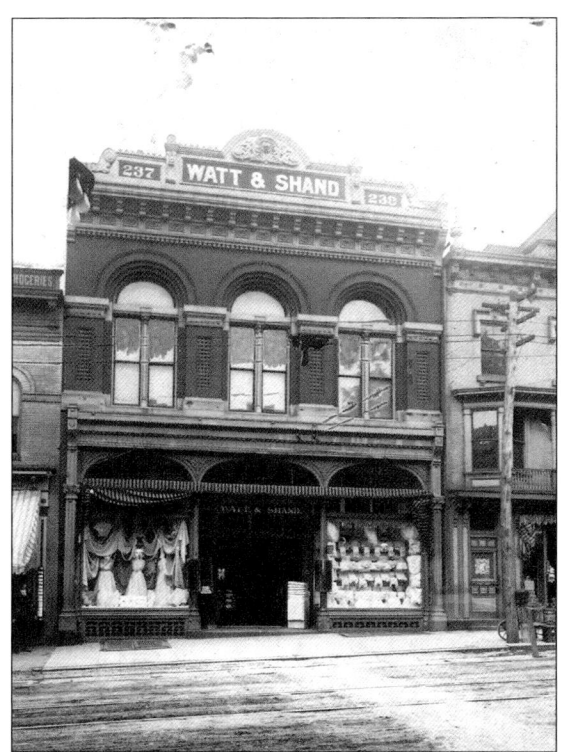

Watt and Shand was a Lancaster department store with a branch in Columbia. The store took over the building of another local department store, Heistand's, at 237–239 Locust Street after the Civil War. On this day, the store has displays of dresses in the left window and shirts in the right one. (Courtesy Columbia Historic Preservation Society.)

Fire broke out in Watt and Shand one day in 1906 and extensively damaged the building, but not to the point that the company had to tear it down. After firemen contained the blaze, they continued a stream of water on the second story to prevent reignition and to cool the structure down so that salvage operations could begin. (Author's collection.)

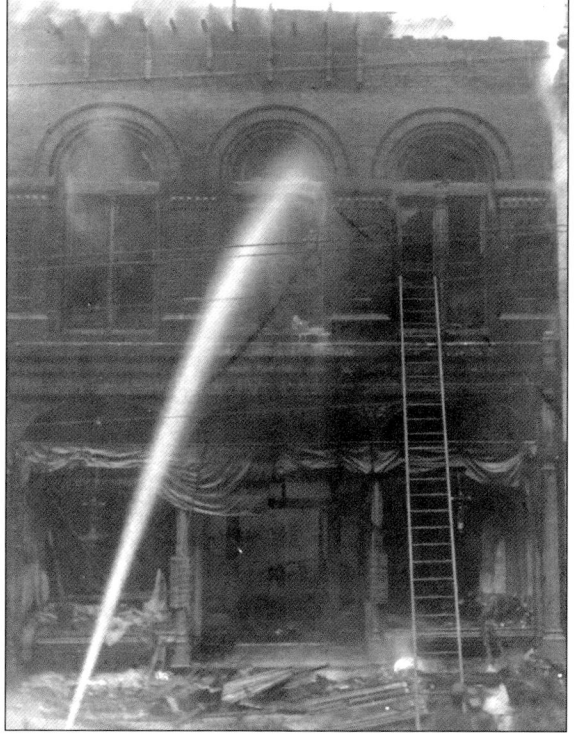

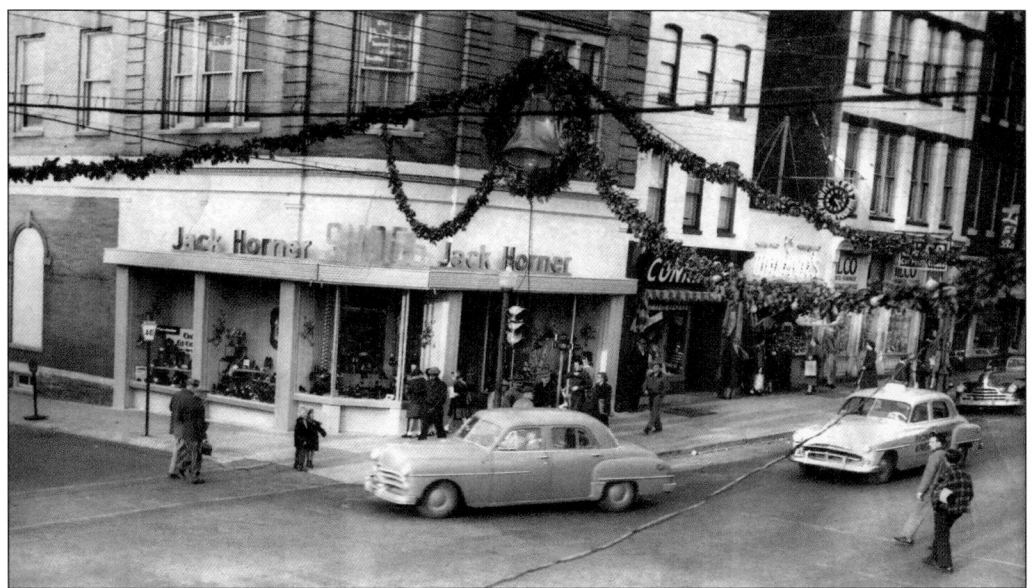

By the clock over Walker's Jewelers it is 3:25 p.m. on a day during the holiday season in the 1950s at Third and Locust Streets. On the northeast corner is Jack Horner's shoe store. Over the intersection is a holiday decoration of a lit bell and garlands draped to the four corners. (Courtesy Columbia Historic Preservation Society.)

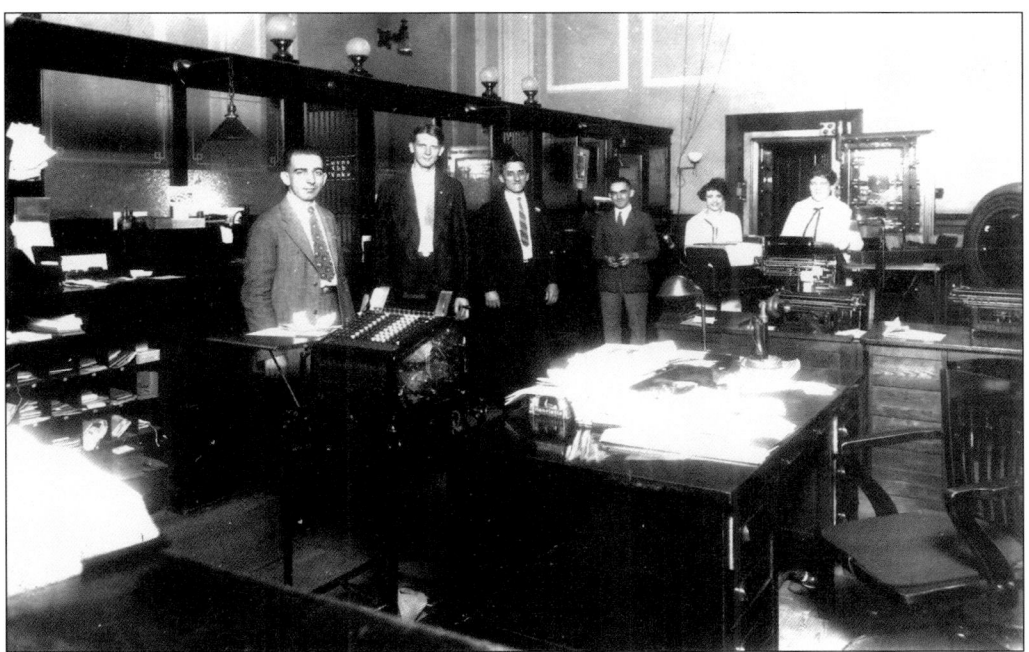

The building of what was the Central National Bank of Columbia at 323 Locust Street is small but imposing, outside with tall columns. Inside the bank exuded confidence typical of small-town banks across the country. There was a small staff behind barred teller stations with a safe often kept open during business hours. (Courtesy Columbia Historic Preservation Society.)

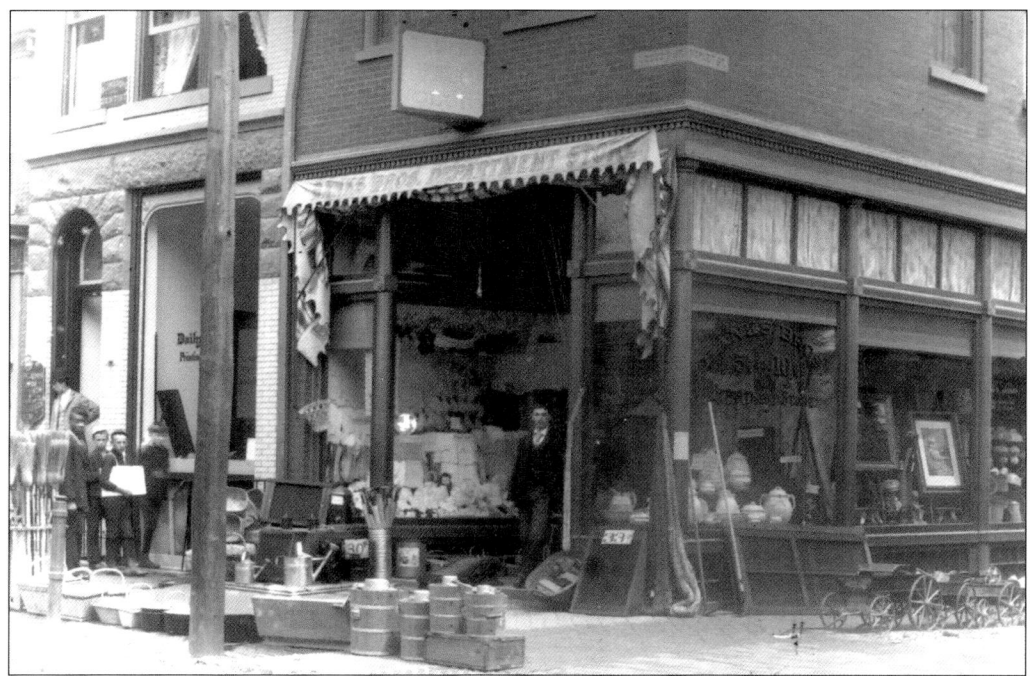

Banks Brothers Five and Ten Cent Department Store was at 324 Locust Street at the intersection with Market Street. The store display on the sidewalk features brooms, baskets, watering cans, washboards, churns, and carts. To the left is the Columbia Daily News building. The four boys outside may have delivered the *News* based on what one is holding. (Courtesy Cleon G. Berntheizel.)

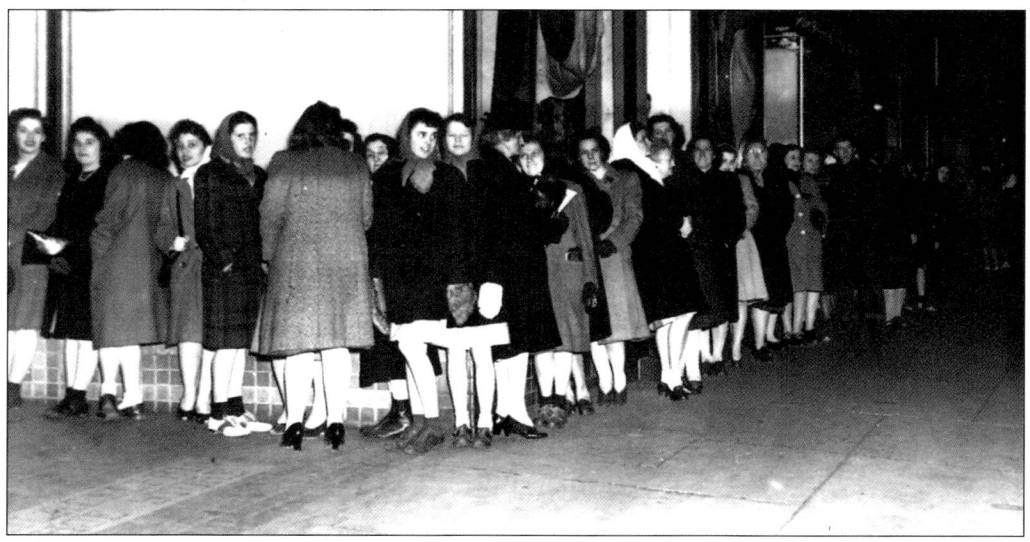

Judging by their dress, it appears these women are standing in a line during a cold winter's night during World War II for something that was severely rationed. However, it is 1946, and they are waiting at Heineman's store to buy nylon stockings. Invented in 1935, nylon did not get used in stockings until 1940, and then the government pulled it from the market during the war to substitute for silk in parachutes. (Courtesy Columbia Historic Preservation Society.)

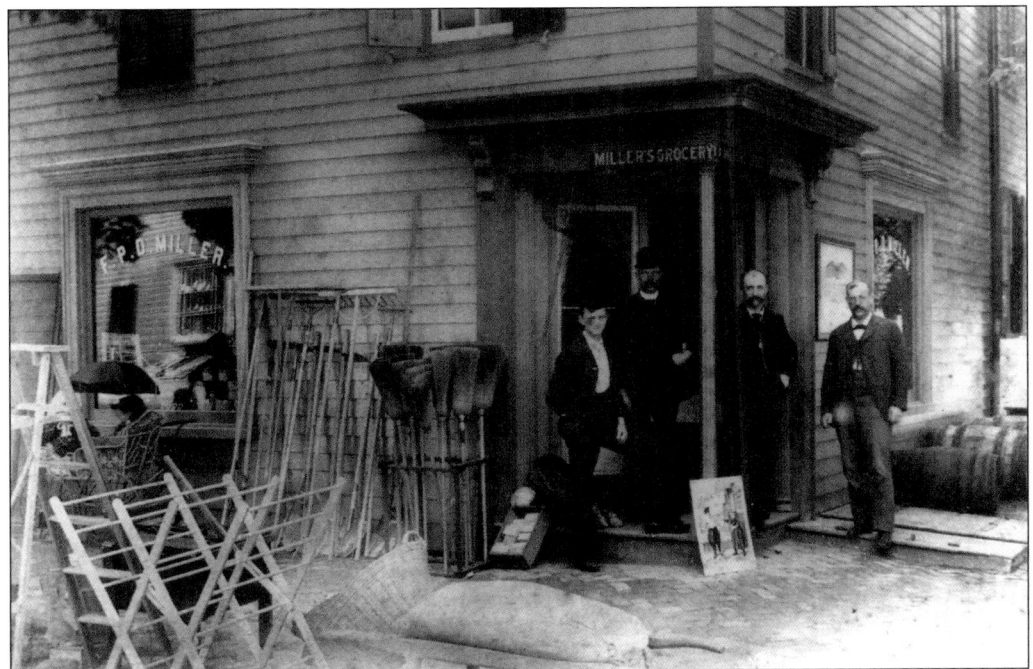

From at least 1892 to 1919, Frank P. D. Miller had a "Groceries, Provisions, and Notary Pubic" operation on the southeast corner of Fourth and Locust Streets. An assortment of rakes, hoes, brooms, baskets, and racks are on the Locust Street pavement in front of his store. He promised "Goods Delivered Free to all Parts of Town." (Courtesy Columbia Historic Preservation Society.)

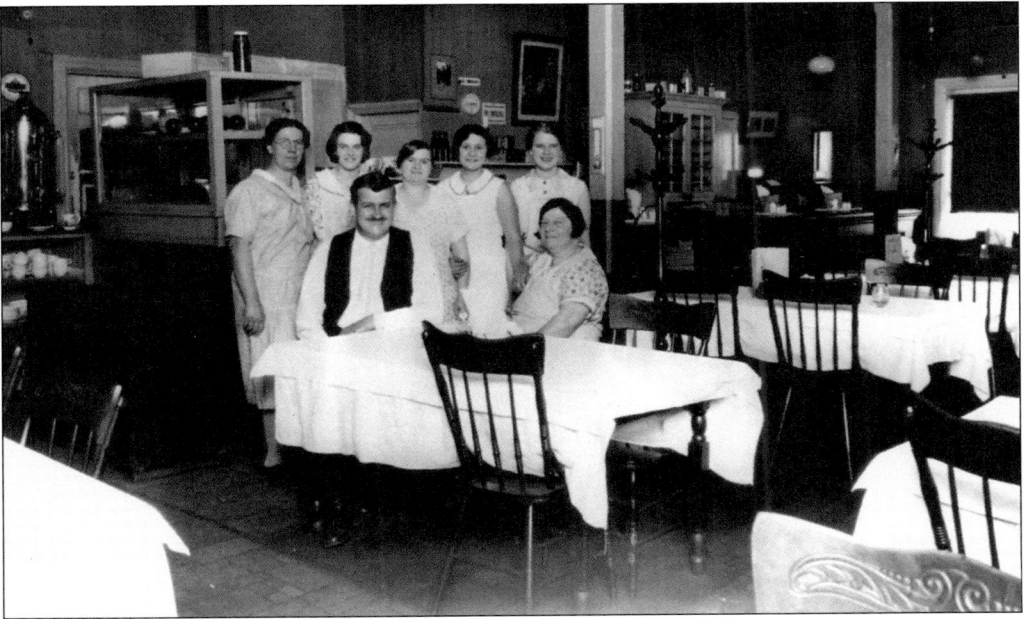

By 1926, Tuffield (Tuffy) Olena had the Columbia Cafe in place of the grocery and operated there until at least 1940. He sits at the table surrounded by employees. (Courtesy Columbia Historic Preservation Society.)

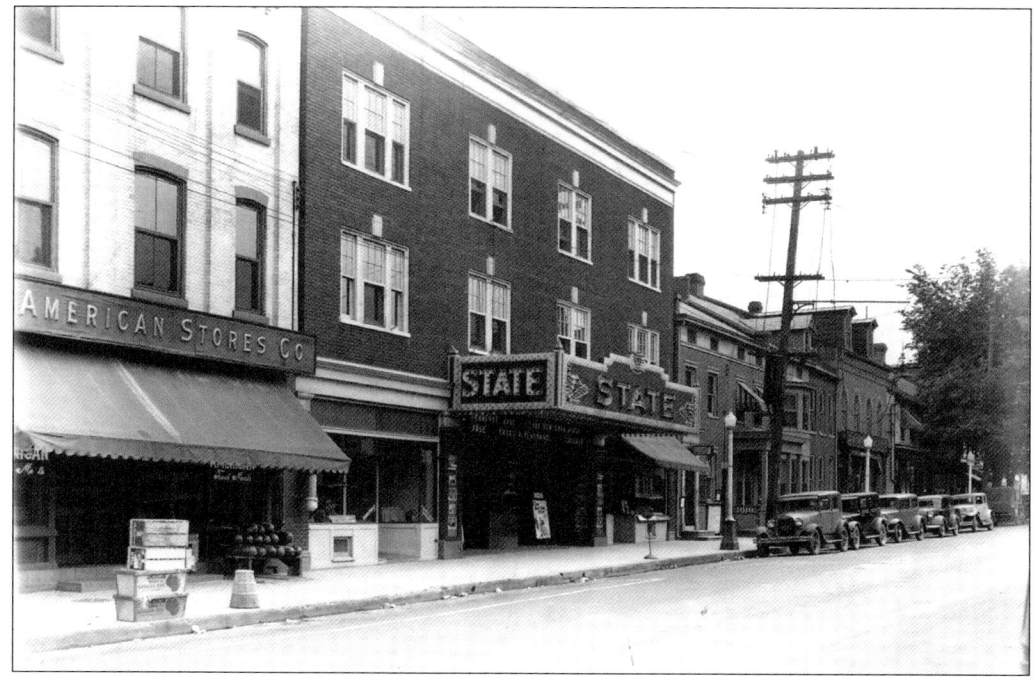

It is 1935, and Franchot Tone is starring in *One New York Night* at the State Theater at Locust Street. To entice moviegoers the State offered free "Emerald Glassware" on Tuesdays. The building had shops on both sides flanking the box office and apartments overhead. To the left down Locust is the Acme grocery store, while to the right is another chain store, the Atlantic and Pacific. (Courtesy Columbia Historic Preservation Society.)

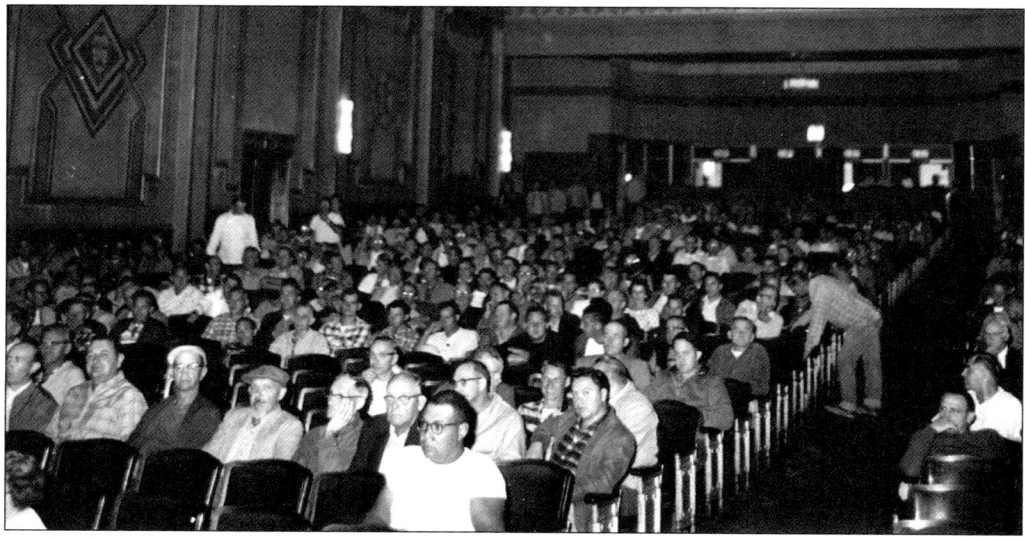

Inside, the State Theater sloped from the Locust Street entrance to the screen. The walls and light fixtures were art deco style. When the lights were low, the atmosphere was most appropriate for film noir movies of the 1930s to 1950s. Midcentury boys and girls would flock there to load up with candy for Saturday afternoon matinees of cartoons, newsreels, and B cowboy movies. (Courtesy Columbia Historic Preservation Society.)

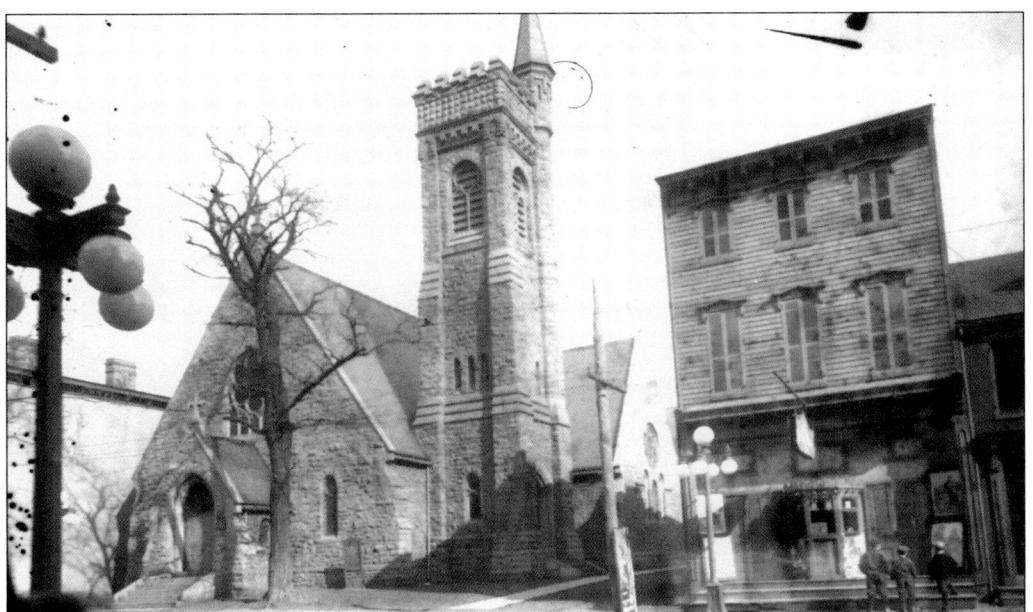

The three boys, outside the Happy Hour Theatre at 336 Locust Street, examine the posters to find out what movies are playing. To their right and high above the boy in the black jacket is a poster featuring Roscoe C. "Fatty" Arbuckle, famous silent-era movie comic star. Left of the theater is St. Paul's Episcopal Church. By 1926, the Liberty Billiard Parlor and Cigar Store had replaced the theater. (Courtesy Columbia Historic Preservation Society.)

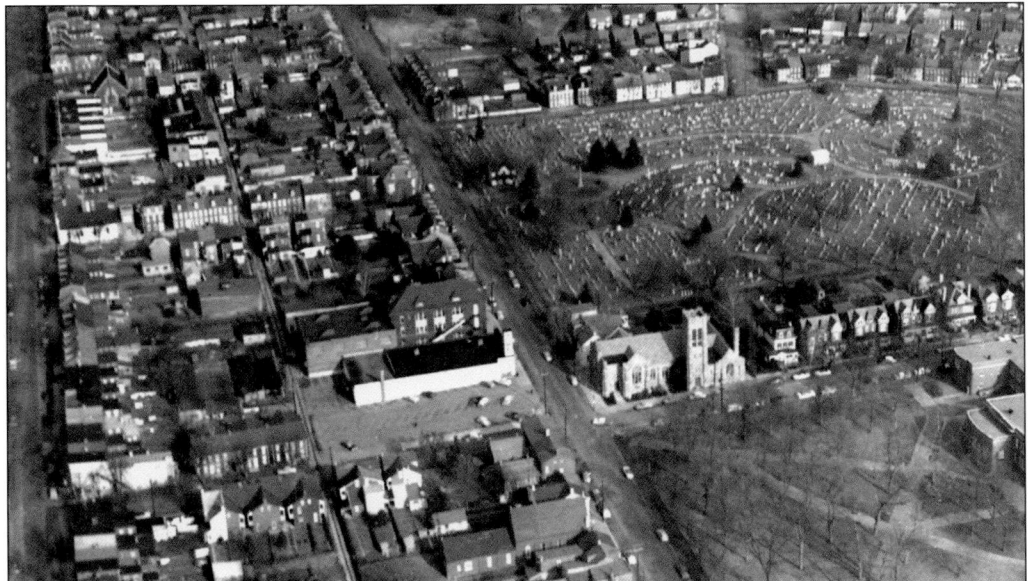

Dominating this 1950s aerial photograph is St. John's Lutheran Church at South Sixth and Locust Streets. Locust runs vertically and the street parallel running to the left is Walnut Street. Above the church is Mount Bethel Cemetery, one of the main ones in town. Below the church to the west is Locust Street Park. Across Locust Street is the Acme supermarket and the larger building above it is Columbia No. 1's station. (Courtesy Columbia Historic Preservation Society.)

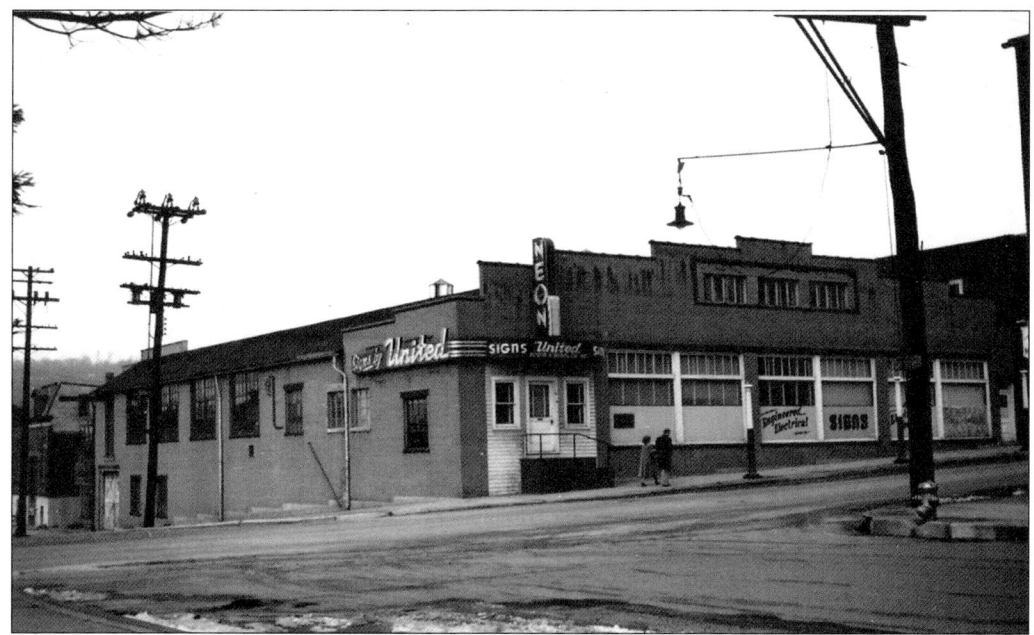

United Sound and Signal Company, Inc., located in 1949 on the northeast corner of North Second and Chestnut Streets, produced engineered electrical signs, specifically of the neon variety. Naturally the company used what it produced to advertise with a sign that wrapped around the building's one corner. Coming off vertically, "neon" impressed upon passersby what the signs were. (Courtesy Columbia Historic Preservation Society.)

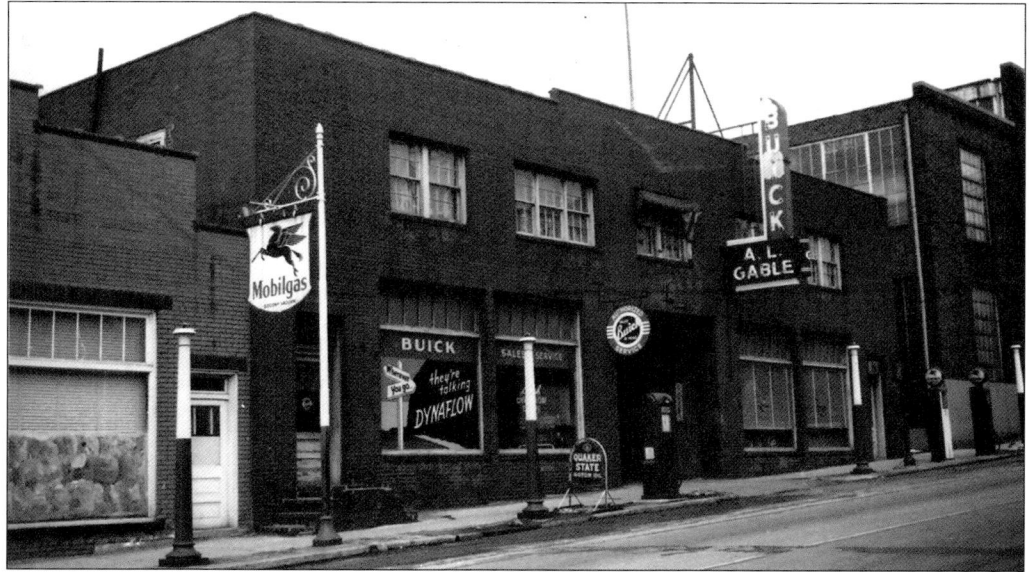

In 1949, A. L. Gable's Buick dealership at 215 Chestnut Street called attention in a window advertisement to the car's Dynaflow automatic transmission, introduced only the year before. A circular overhead sign said the garage was the place for "authorized service." Drivers headed west on the Lincoln Highway could pull over to the curb and fill up with Mobil gas and get a quart of Quaker State motor oil. (Courtesy Columbia Historic Preservation Society.)

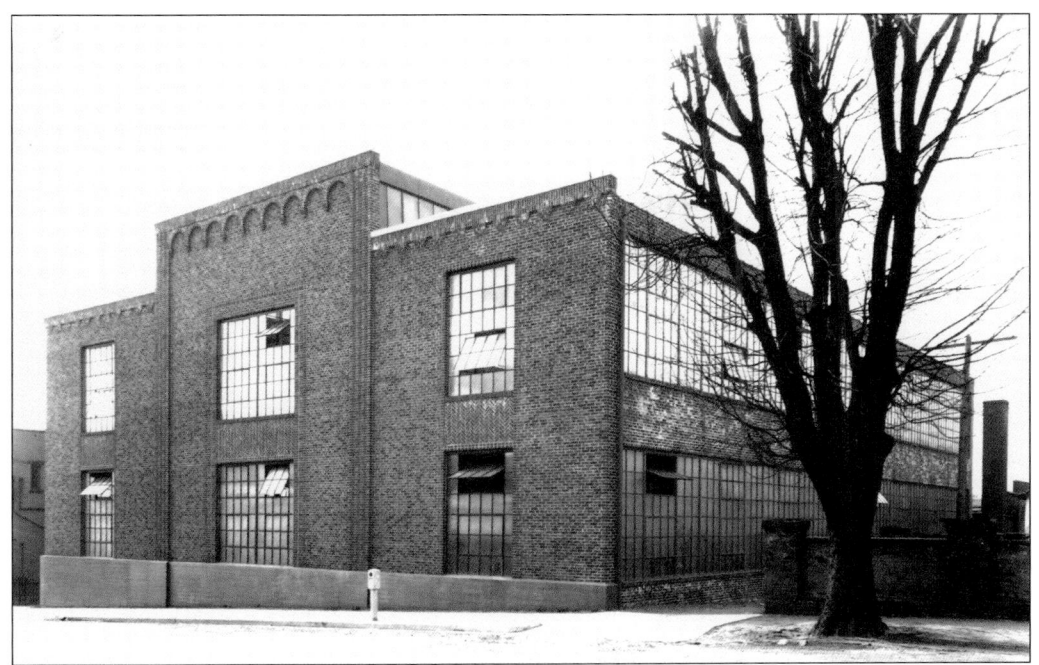

Marietta Silk Company arrived in Columbia decades after the Ashley and Bailey Company built its complex, but it quickly grew to have two mills. One was on South Ninth Street and the other was on North Second Street with a new extension, pictured here, fronting Chestnut Street. The concrete post in front of the building is a marker for the Lincoln Highway. (Courtesy Columbia Historic Preservation Society.)

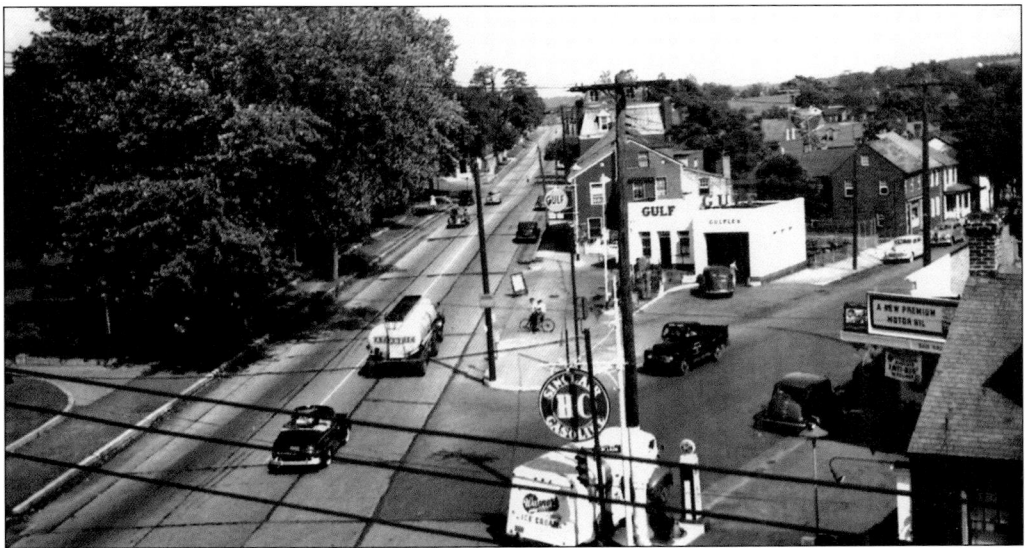

Thomas Hoch photographed much of Columbia from the late 1940s through the 1960s. Often he tried to get high above a location to get a unique photograph. Here on June 6, 1950, he captured Lancaster Avenue proceeding off in the distance, South Fifth Street going off to the right, and the Gulf and Sinclair gas stations. The town square, a park, now occupies the site of this intersection. (Courtesy Columbia Historic Preservation Society.)

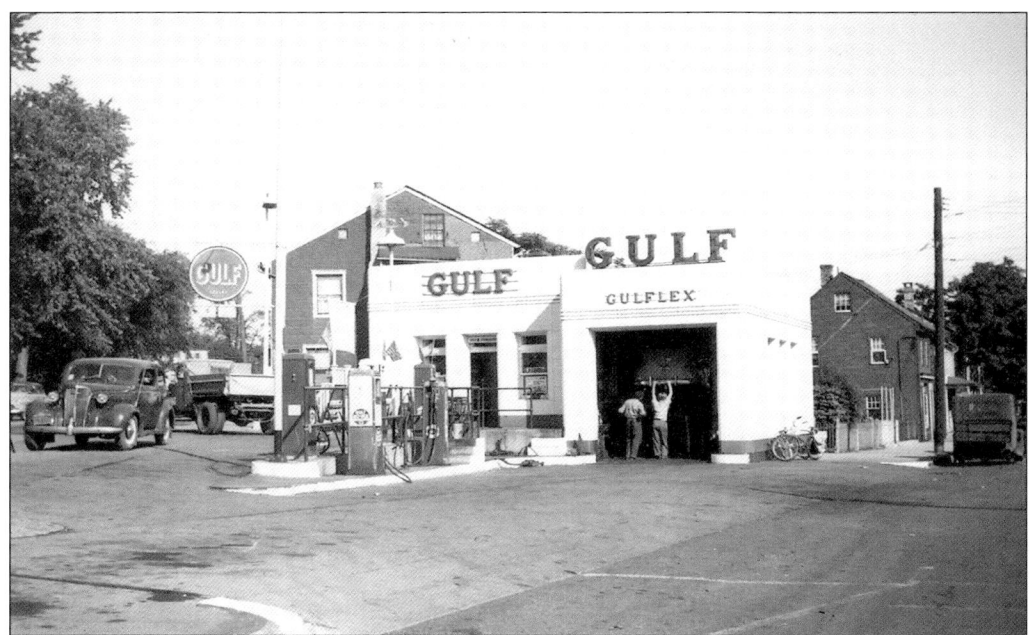

On May 3, 1949, two boys inspect a car up on the lift at the Gulf station at Lancaster Avenue (left) and South Fifth Street (right). Gulf Oil started in 1901, and it had its headquarters in Pittsburgh. Gulflex was the name the company used for its lubrication service and associated products. (Courtesy Columbia Historic Preservation Society.)

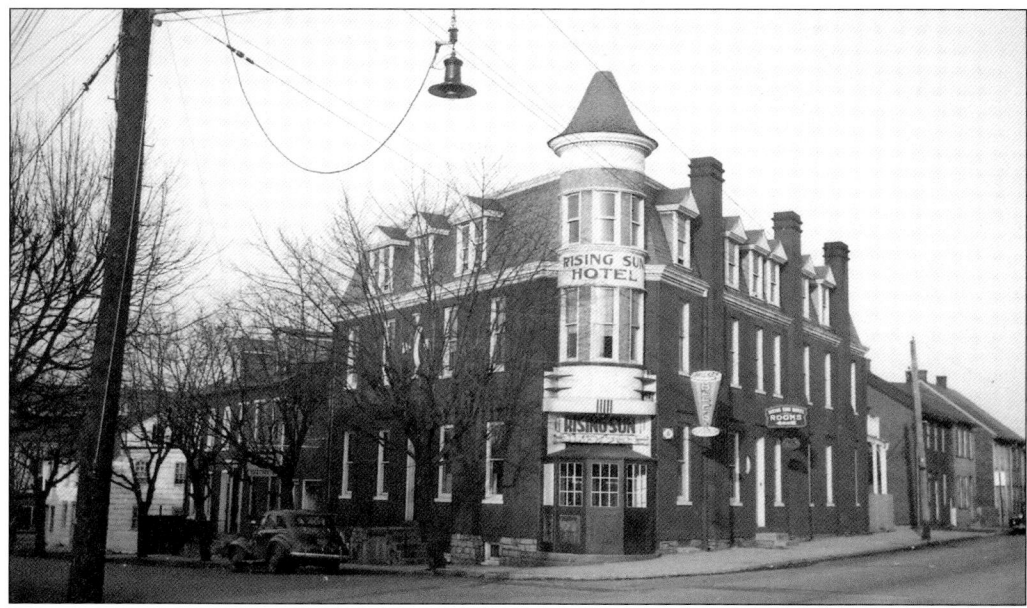

The Rising Sun Hotel, pictured in 1949, has stood on the northwest corner of Lancaster Avenue and Cherry Street since the 1890s. Inside, patrons could get a shifter sandwich, which is like a sub, but on a round roll rather than an oblong one. The local name arose from railroaders who worked the shifting locomotives and wanted a sandwich easy to carry for lunch. (Courtesy Columbia Historic Preservation Society.)

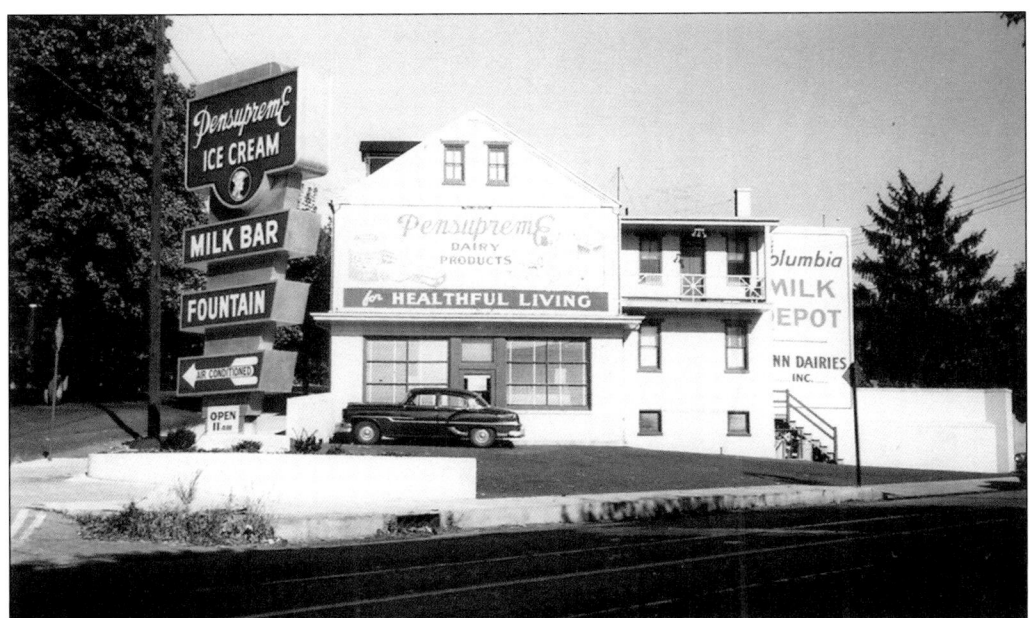

Westbound travelers could easily pull into the Lancaster Avenue parking lot, go into the air-conditioned Pensupreme store, take a break at the milk bar and fountain, and enjoy a hand-scooped Pensupreme ice-cream cone or milk shake. There was a smaller store, to the photographer's back, on the southwest corner, so eastbound patrons would not have to cross traffic. (Courtesy Columbia Historic Preservation Society.)

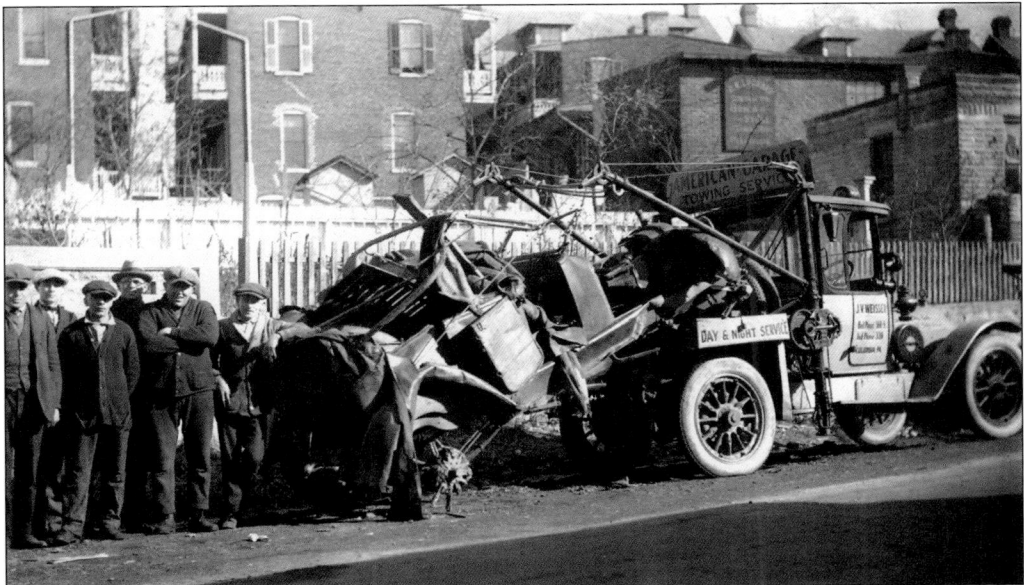

Soon after the invention of the automobile, accidents started happening, necessitating a whole new infrastructure such as garages, tow trucks, stoplights, and gas pumps. Here the tow truck from Joseph V. Weisser's American Garage, located at 138 Lancaster Avenue, removes a wrecked car from Lancaster Avenue near South Sixth Street. The garage offered, "day & night service." (Courtesy Columbia Historic Preservation Society.)

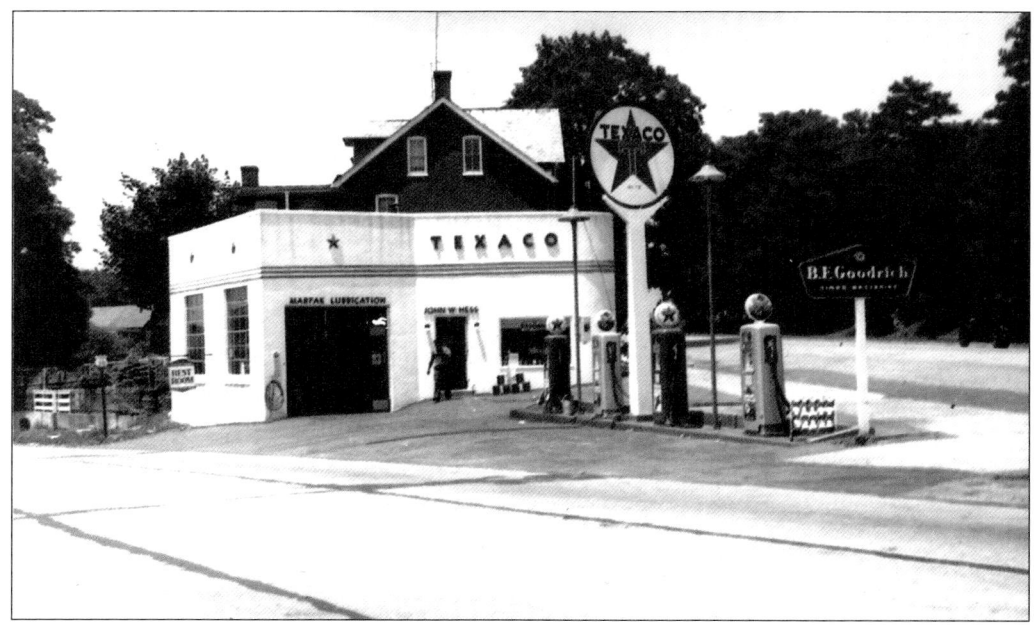

Pictured on June 23, 1953, John W. Hess's Texaco station was at South Sixth Street and Lancaster Avenue. In addition to Texaco Fire Chief gasoline, the station sold B. F. Goodrich tires and batteries. "Marfak Lubrication," seen over the bay, was the name Texaco used to distinguish its lubrication service and supplies from others. (Courtesy Columbia Historic Preservation Society.)

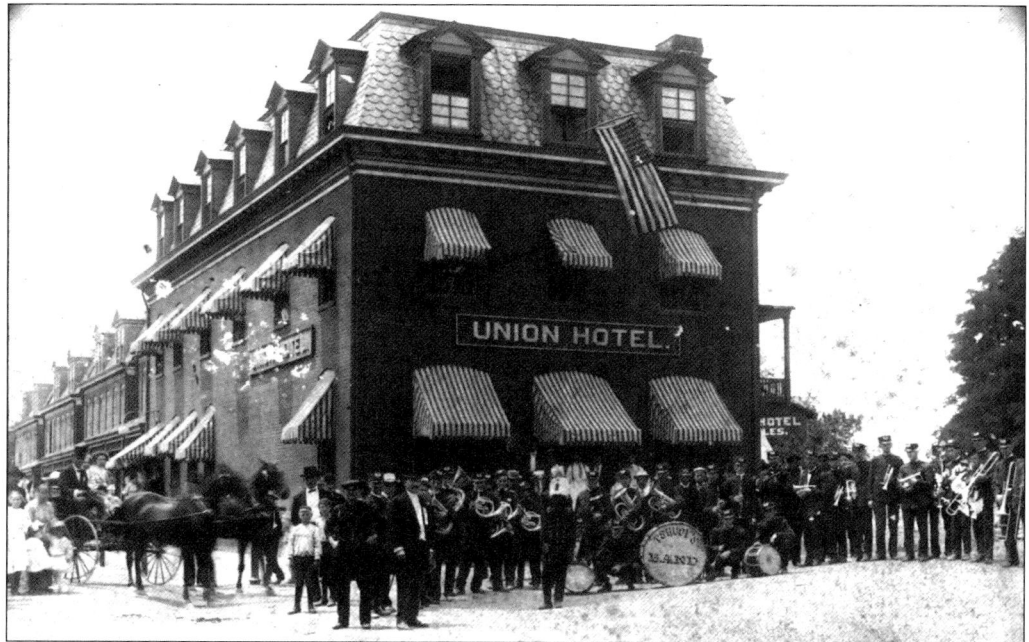

Tshudy's Band gathers for an informal photograph in front of the Union Hotel. Off to the left, by the horse and carriage, runs Union Street, which diverges from Lancaster Avenue in front of the hotel. Lancaster Avenue continues off at a shallow angle to the right through the part in the trees. (Courtesy Columbia Historic Preservation Society.)

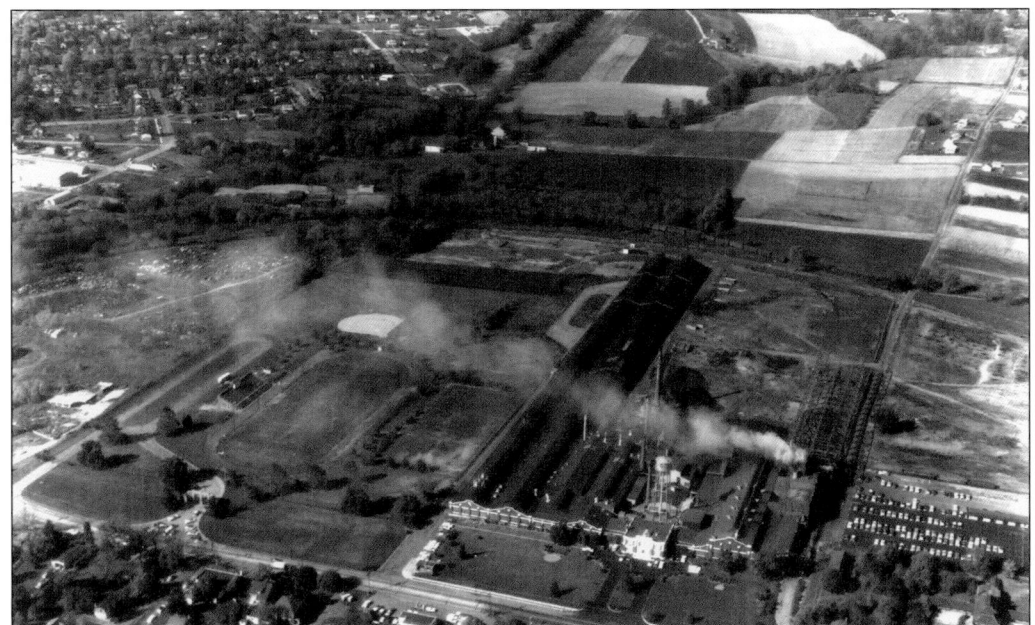

Columbia's largest industry, Columbia Malleable Castings Corporation, acquired by the Grinnell Corporation by 1932 and now Anvil International, moved from North Second and Linden Streets to a new location at Fifteenth Street and Lancaster Avenue. They built a large foundry and plant there, which can be seen on the right. On the left is Glatfelter Memorial Field, opened in 1937. (Courtesy Columbia Historic Preservation Society.)

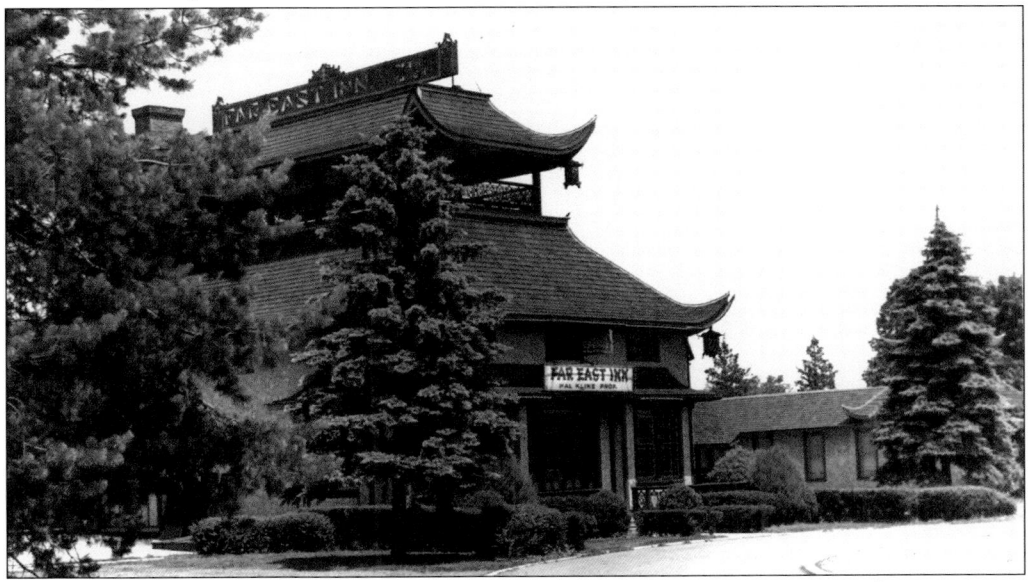

On Lancaster Avenue, east of Fifteenth Street, was the Far East Inn. Lothar R. Zifferer, manager of O.K. Clutch and Manufacturing Company and holder of many patents, started the inn, which with its upturned corners and hanging lanterns, looked oriental. There one could, "bring your friends with full assurance of a delightful hour or two—or a full evening." (Courtesy John Hinkle Jr.)

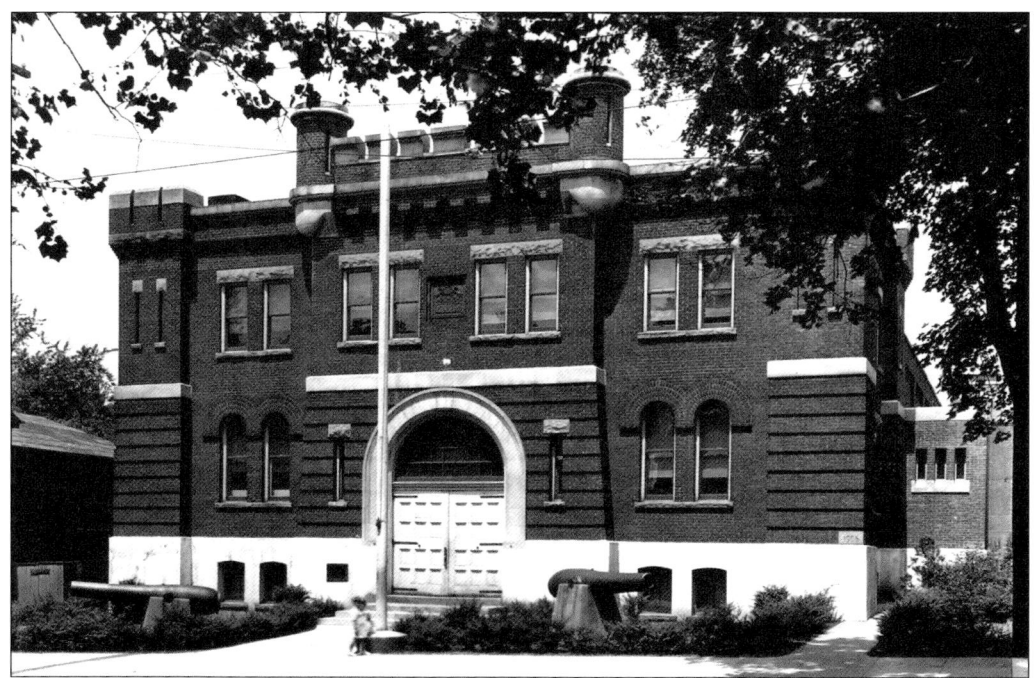

Located at Walnut Street east of North Second Street, the Edward Shannon Armory building replaced an earlier one at the same location. Two muzzle-end loaded cannons guarded the armory and its flagpole. The building, resembling an imposing fort with massive entrance doors, firing ports, and turrets, featured a large inside drill area and offices. (Courtesy Columbia Historic Preservation Society.)

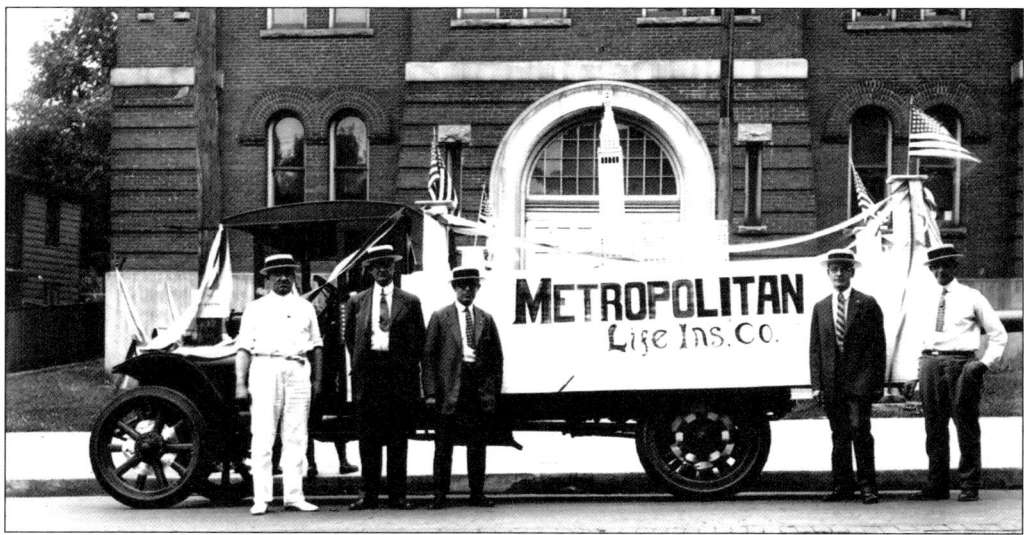

Five men pose in front of a truck decorated with a sign for the Metropolitan Life Insurance Company. In the bed of the truck is a model of the Met Life building in New York City. The company featured the tower in its advertising for many years, calling it "The Light That Never Fails." This picture was taken before 1938, as the Conestoga Traction Company's trolley tracks still run down Walnut Street. (Courtesy Columbia Historic Preservation Society.)

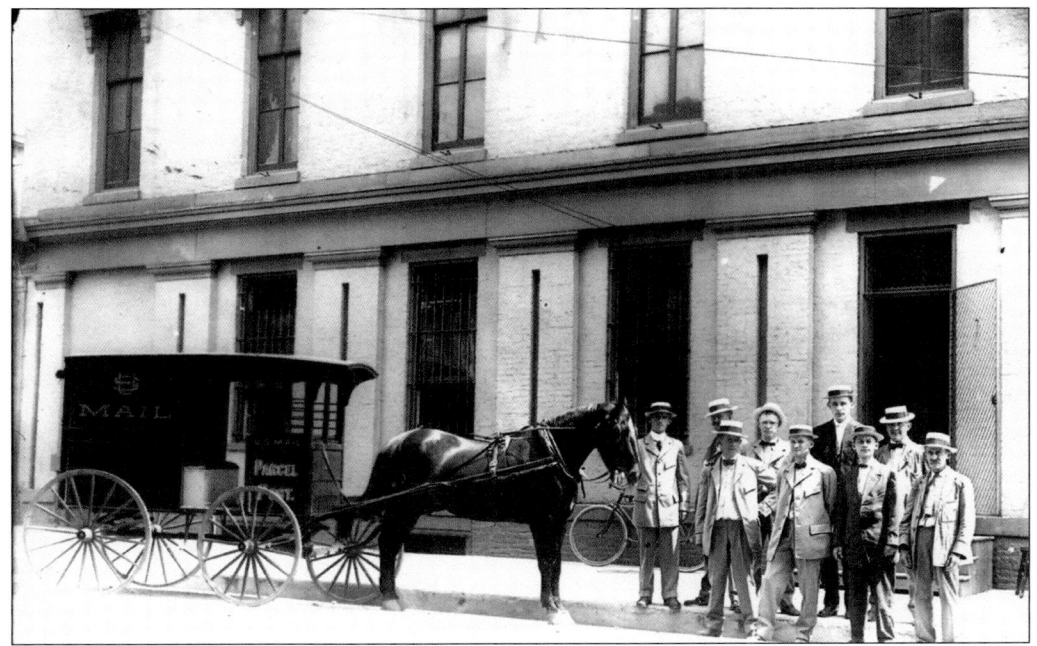

The Columbia Post Office was in the first floor of the Odd Fellows hall at Locust Street and South Second Street. The Odd Fellows hall also at one time had a pharmacy in it. The parcel post delivery horse-drawn wagon sits on South Second Street by the barred windows of the post office. (Courtesy Columbia Historic Preservation Society.)

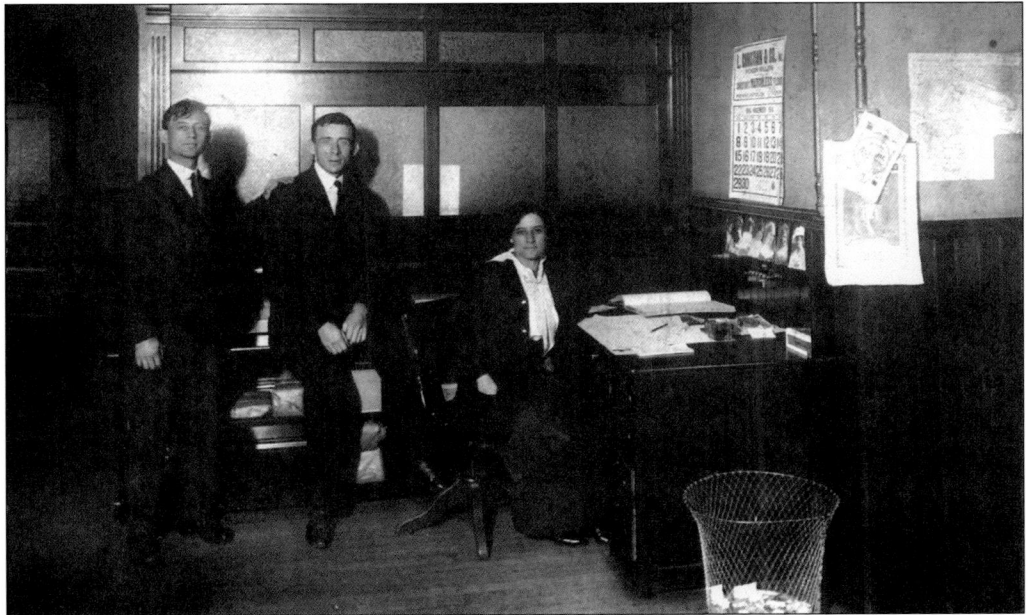

By the calendar on the post office wall at Second and Locust Streets, it is November 1914, and much of the world is involved in the Great War and had been so for around three months. The United States did not declare war for another two and a half years. The man on the left is Charles Eckert, a post office clerk. (Courtesy Columbia Historic Preservation Society.)

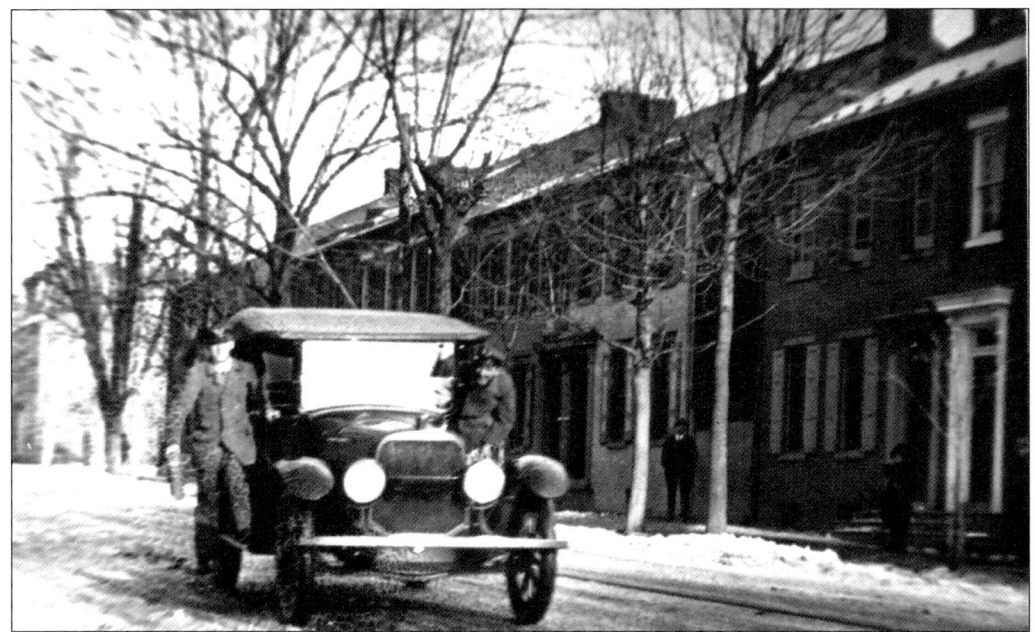

By the year of 1918, the post office was using motor vehicles for some delivery. Here on a dreary winter's day, several employees, with one holding a package for delivery, ride the car's running boards as the car speeds down Walnut Street from North Fifth Street following a light snowfall. (Courtesy Columbia Historic Preservation Society.)

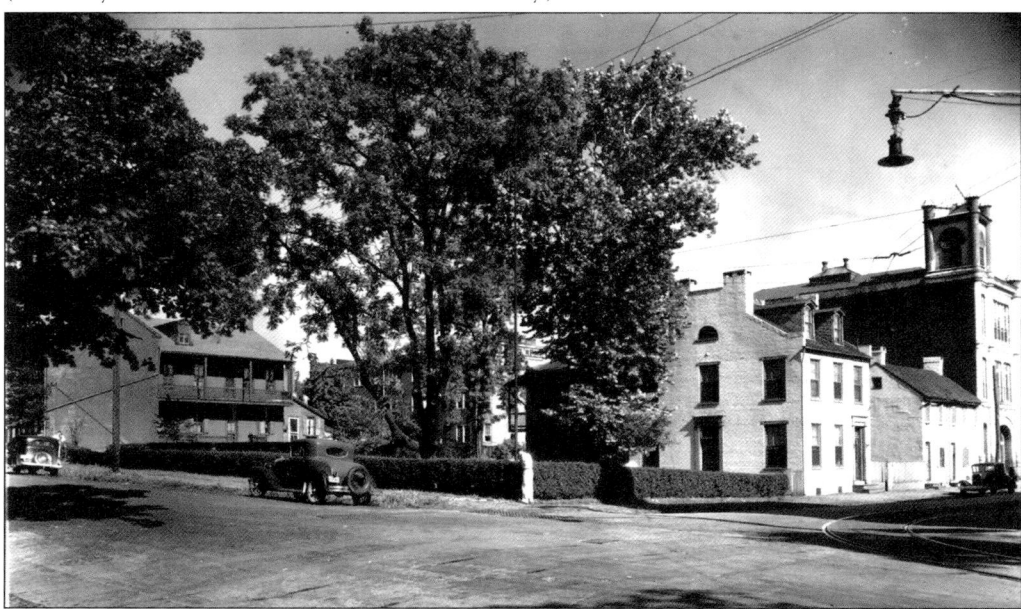

Ultimately, the U.S. post office outgrew the site at Second and Locust Streets and decided to relocate. The government selected a lot at the southeast corner of North Fourth and Walnut Streets and demolished the three houses located there. In the background, on North Fourth Street, is the Keystone Fire Company's building. The trolley tracks curve from Fourth to Walnut Streets. (Courtesy Columbia Historic Preservation Society.)

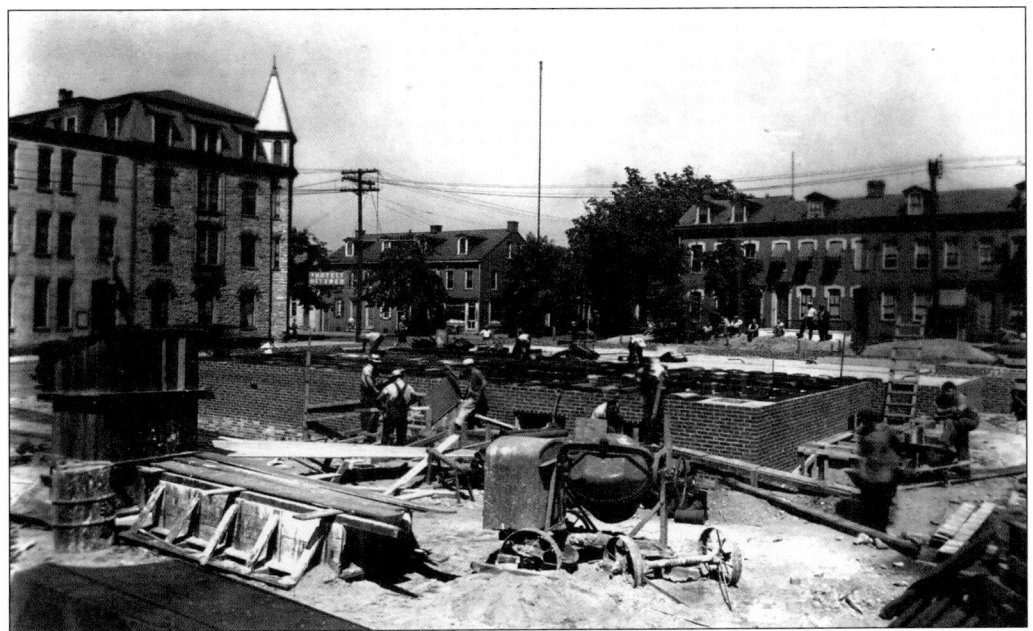

Laying of the cornerstone for the new post office happened in 1930. Workers are almost finished with the basement and are ready to start on the first floor. Hotel Bittner, on the southwest corner of North Fourth and Walnut Streets, lies behind the post office. The row houses, quite common in Columbia, are on the north side of Walnut Street. (Courtesy Columbia Historic Preservation Society.)

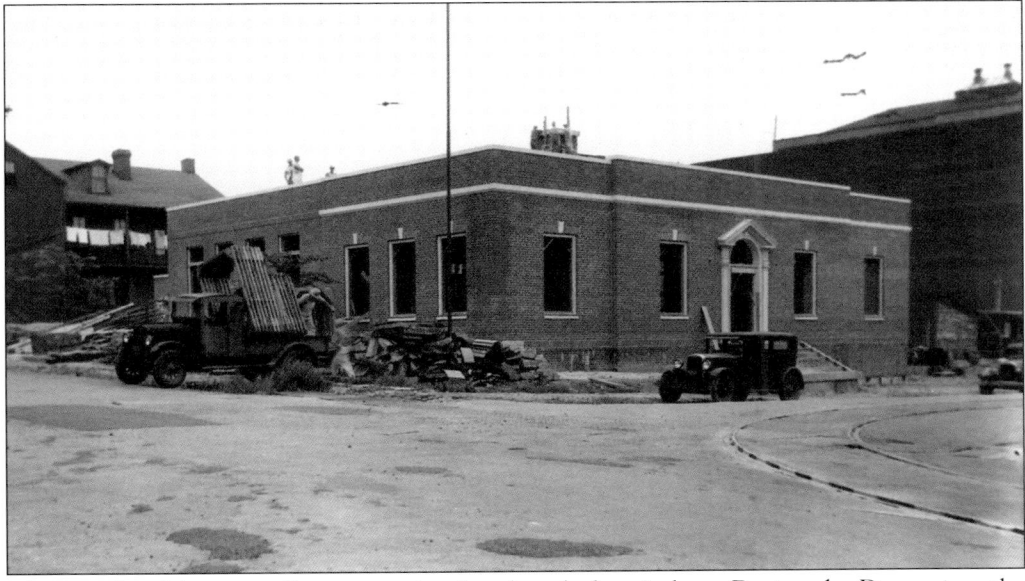

The outside of the post office is completed and ready for windows. During the Depression, the lobby received a large mural showing some of the area's early history from the procurement division of the treasury department as part of the New Deal. Only a few years ago, the post office put up a series of construction photographs like this one. (Courtesy Columbia Historic Preservation Society.)

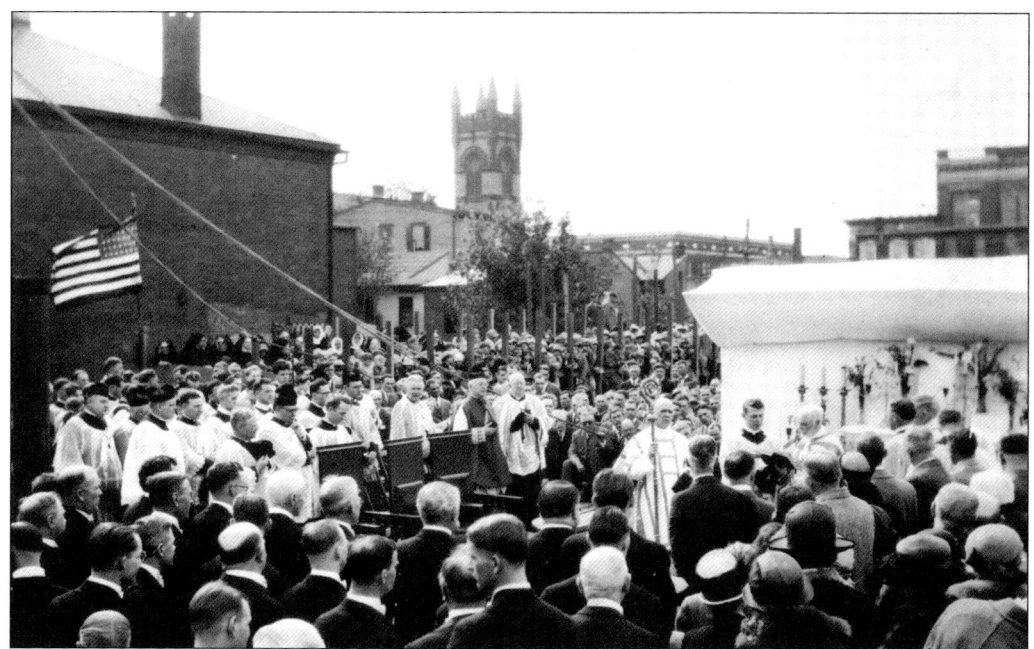

In the mid-1800s, German Catholics felt the need to move from St. Peter's Church and build Holy Trinity where the sermons would be in German. In 1860, they started a new building at South Fourth and Cherry Streets. By the 1900s, the parish had grown so that it needed a new building. On May 1, 1927, Most Reverend Phillip R. McDivett presided at the laying of the cornerstone. (Courtesy Mary C. Wickenheiser.)

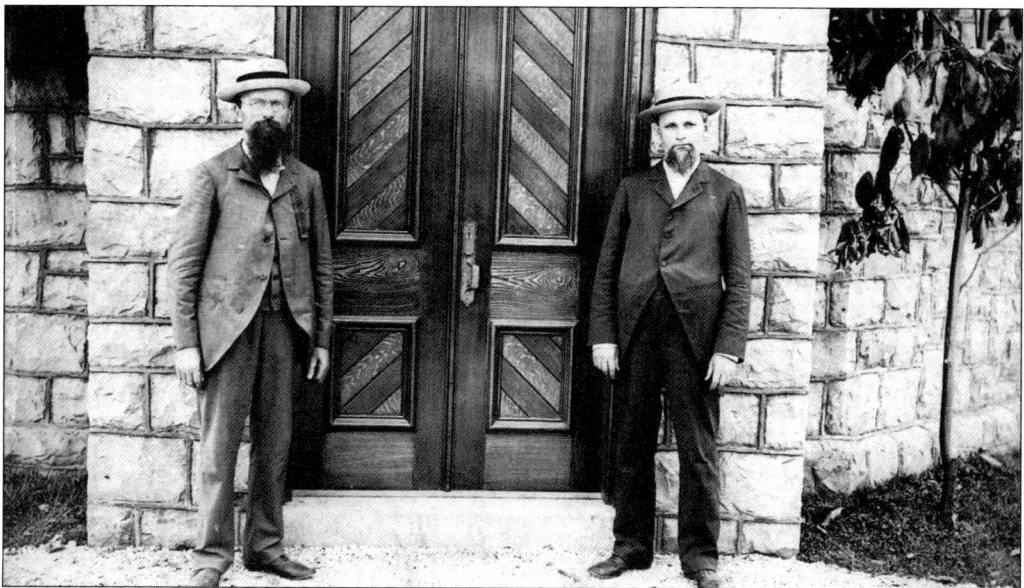

Holy Trinity has a cemetery on South Tenth Street south of Barber Street. Around 1906, Peter Bittner (left) and Joseph Janson flank the cemetery chapel's door. Bittner was the proprietor at Bittner's Hotel. Janson was a cashier at the Columbia National Bank and was president of Janson Iron and Steel Company. (Courtesy Columbia Historic Preservation Society.)

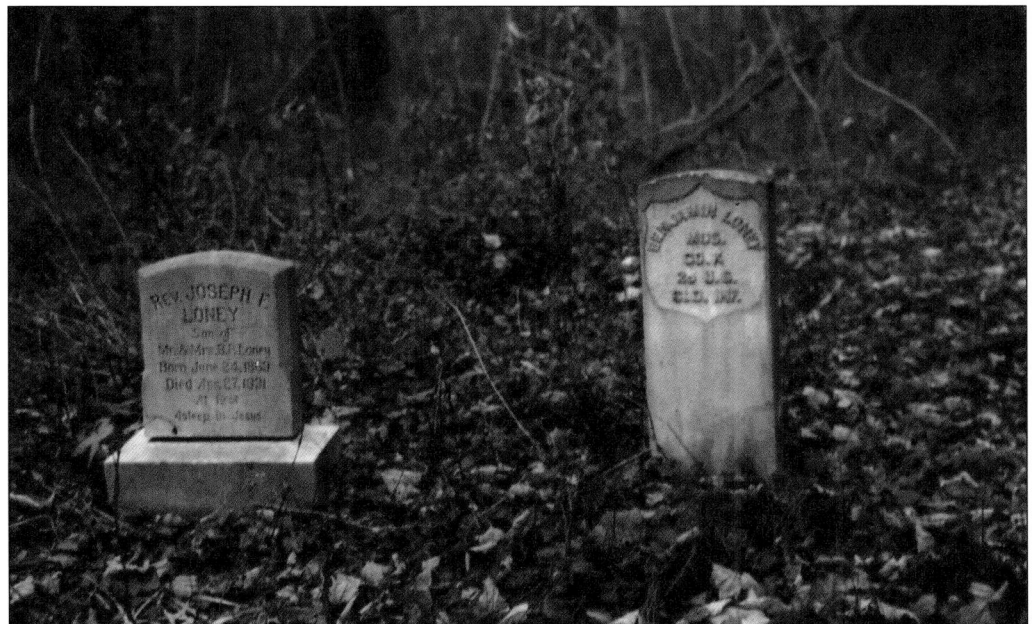

Zion Hill Cemetery is at North Fifth Street and Old Chickies Hill Road. No longer used, many African American citizens are buried there. The tombstone on the right is for Benjamin Loney, who served in the 25th United States Colored Infantry in New Orleans during the Civil War. He went in as a private and came out as a musician. Returning home, he was the choir leader in the African Methodist Episcopal church. (Courtesy Columbia Historic Preservation Society.)

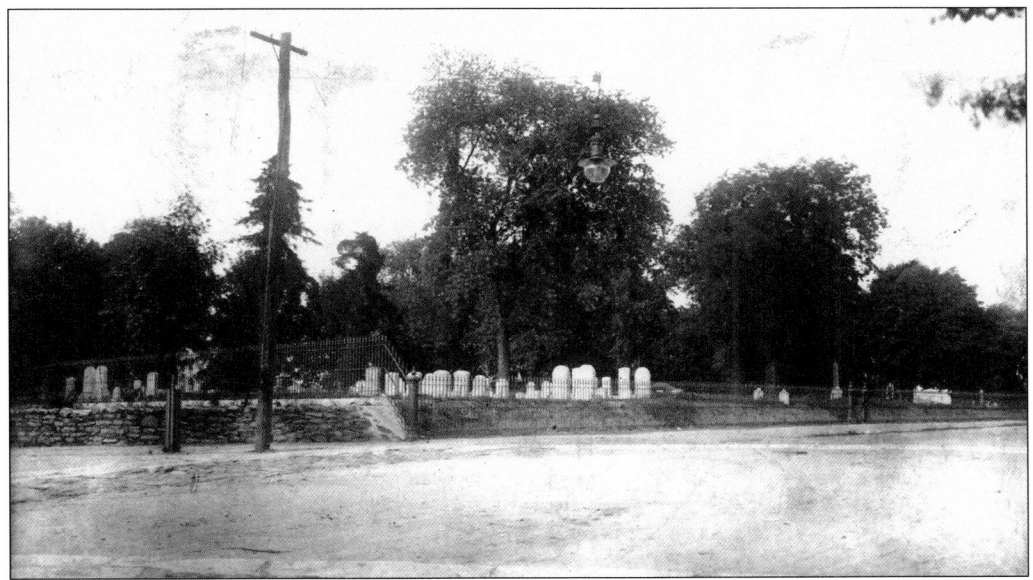

Taking up the better part of a square block, Mount Bethel Cemetery's main entrance is off Locust Street. Here is the southwest corner, which is the oldest part where many of the early Quaker founders are buried in unmarked graves following their custom. The street in the foreground is Cherry Street, but this stretch originally was known as Cemetery Street. (Courtesy Columbia Historic Preservation Society.)

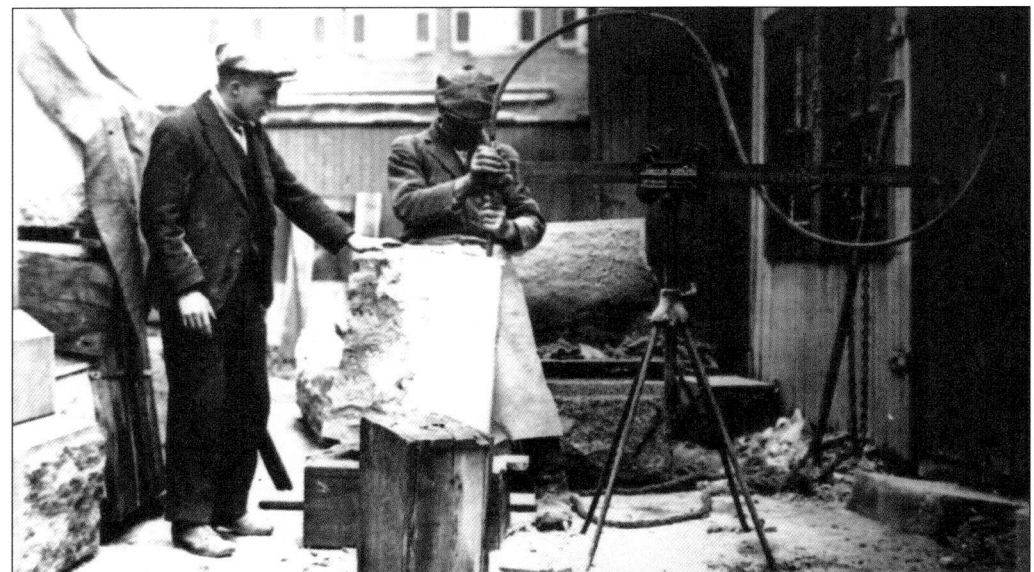

Charles W. Knipe uses a compressed air driven tool to carve a monument. Surrounding him in his outdoor work yard are piles of uncut stones. His business along South Fourth Street had Holy Trinity Catholic Church and its rectory as neighbors just to the east. Homes were all along both sides of the street on this block. (Courtesy Columbia Historic Preservation Society.)

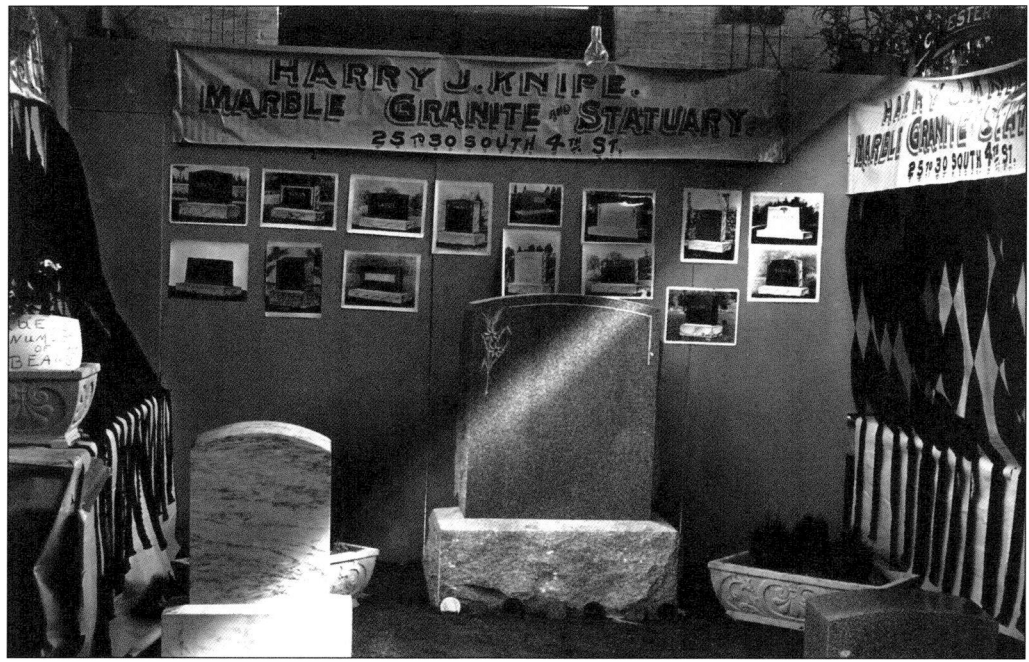

In the early 1900s, Harry J. Knipe had a marble, granite, and statuary business on South Fourth Street and exhibited some examples and photographs of his work in this display. By 1926, Charles W. Knipe, who had been a stonecutter, was taking over from Harry J. Knipe's estate and advertised as a "Manufacturer and Dealer in Artistic Cemetery Memorials." (Courtesy Columbia Historic Preservation Society.)

Columbia Brewing Company was located on South Fourth Street. During Prohibition, agents raided the brewery, accused the operators of brewing beer illegally, and released thousands of gallons down the sewer. When frugal Columbians discovered the beer flowing into a stream, they turned out with containers of all kinds to prevent the waste. Even dogs did their part to stop the pollution, lapping up the beer and becoming drunk in the process. (Author's collection.)

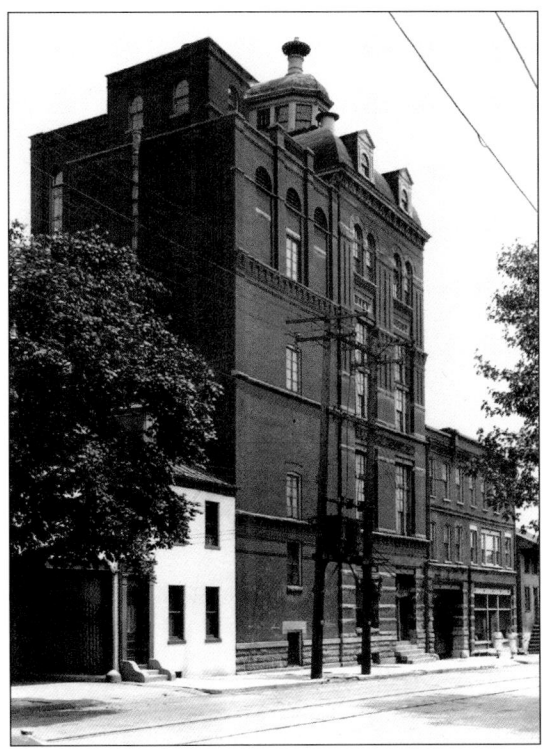

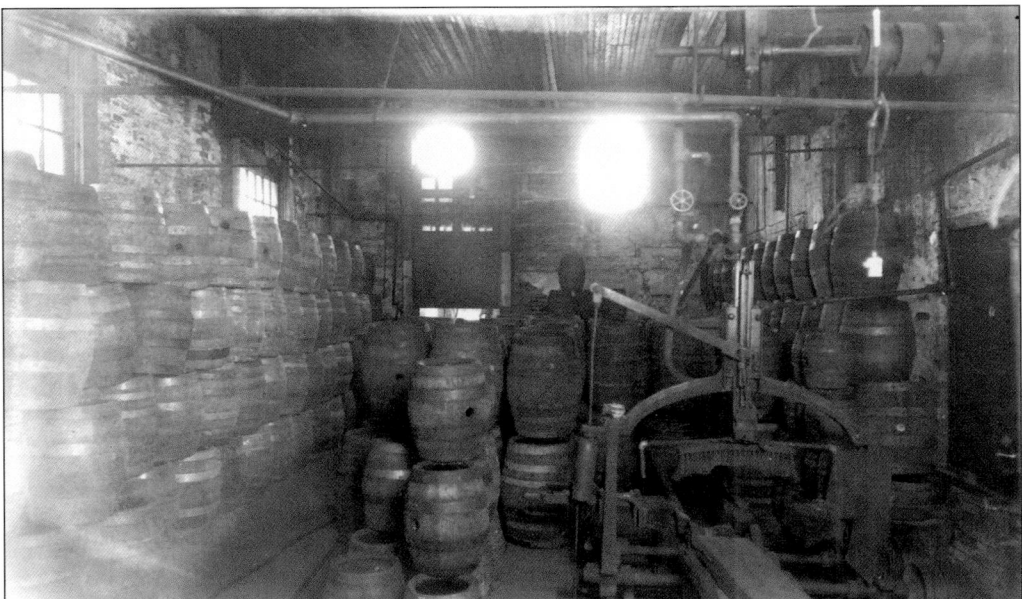

Down in the basement, the beer Columbia Brewing Company made went through the last steps, flowing into wooden kegs and getting a bung stopper driven into the hole to seal it before shipment. Before glass bottles and later cans became popular, this was the normal way breweries packaged their beer, as most of it was sold in bars and beer saloons. (Courtesy Lancaster County Historical Society.)

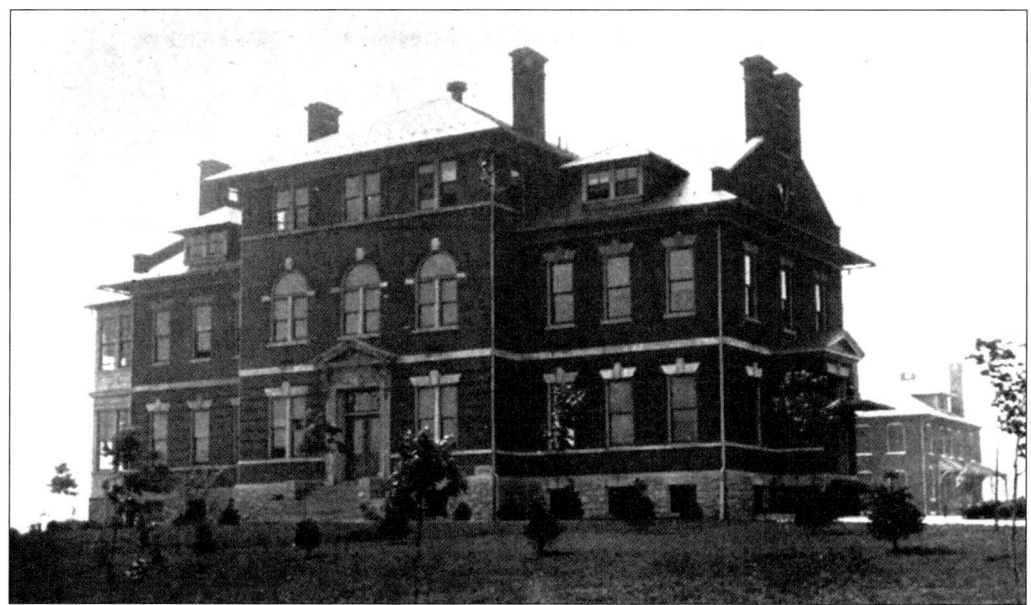

On August 16, 1902, more than 1,000 people gathered on Poplar Street between North Sixth and Seventh Streets to see the laying of the cornerstone for the new Columbia Hospital building that cost $43,000 (about $1 million in current dollars). The new three-story brick building with brown mortar and Indiana limestone trim opened a year later. (Author's collection.)

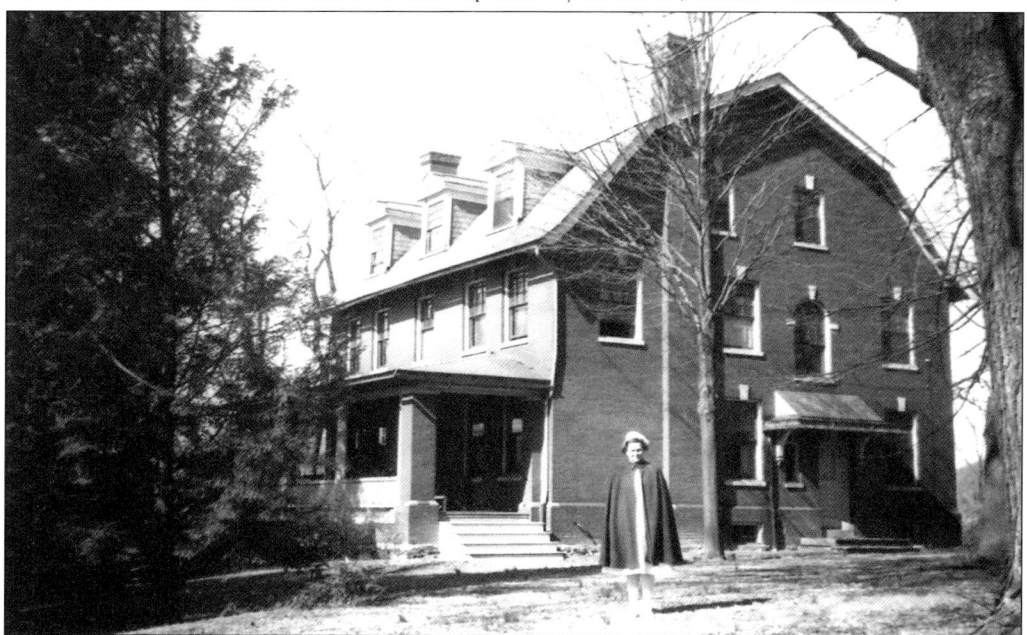

Until the start of the Depression, Columbia Hospital had its own school of nursing. Student nurses stayed in a brick house just west of the hospital. Heat during the winter came from a coal-fired boiler and students dreaded having to stoke it while wearing their white uniforms. Here Lillian M. DeTurick stands by the building after World War II. (Courtesy Columbia Historic Preservation Society.)

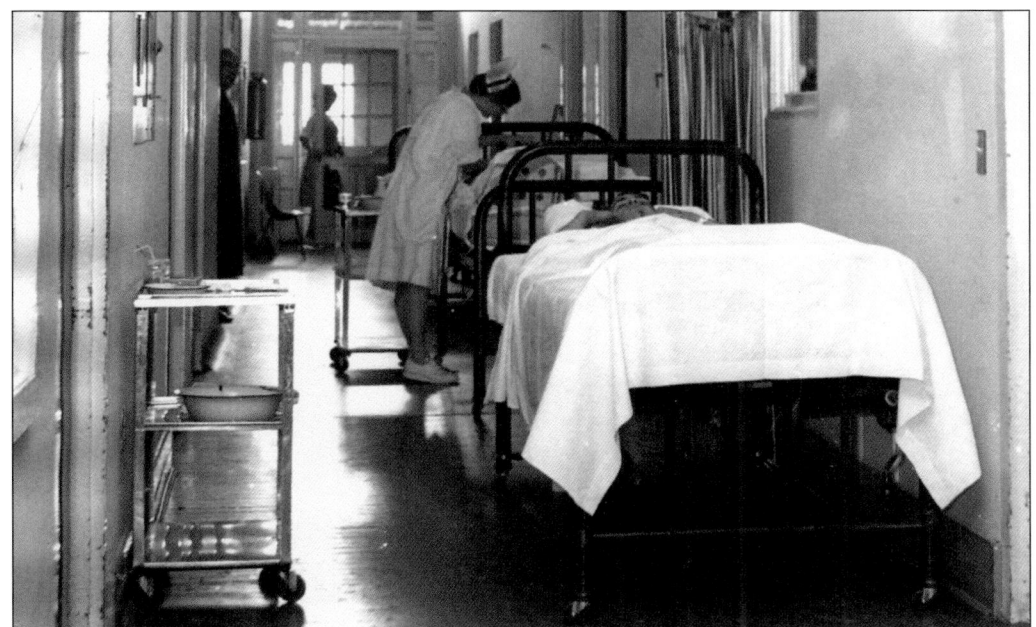

Initially the hospital had a 10-bed men's ward, 9-bed women's ward, 2 children's wards, and a maternity ward. Here, however, the number of patients exceeded capacity and the two patients were in beds in one hall. Later demolition of the nurses' home allowed expansion with a new wing added on to the old building. (Courtesy Columbia Historic Preservation Society.)

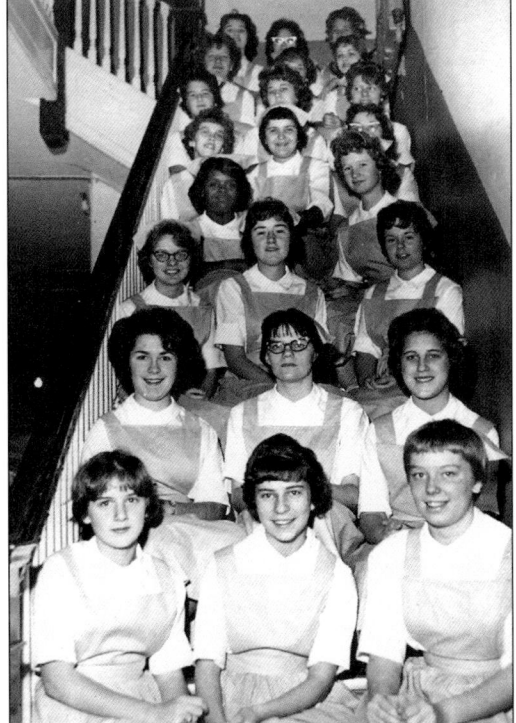

Columbia Hospital always has had strong support from a network of volunteer workers from the community and surrounding area. During the building drive, the hospital auxiliary raised more than $3,000 (over $71,000 in current dollars) in a year. Here 23 junior aides are seated along one flight of stairs in 1962. (Courtesy Columbia Historic Preservation Society.)

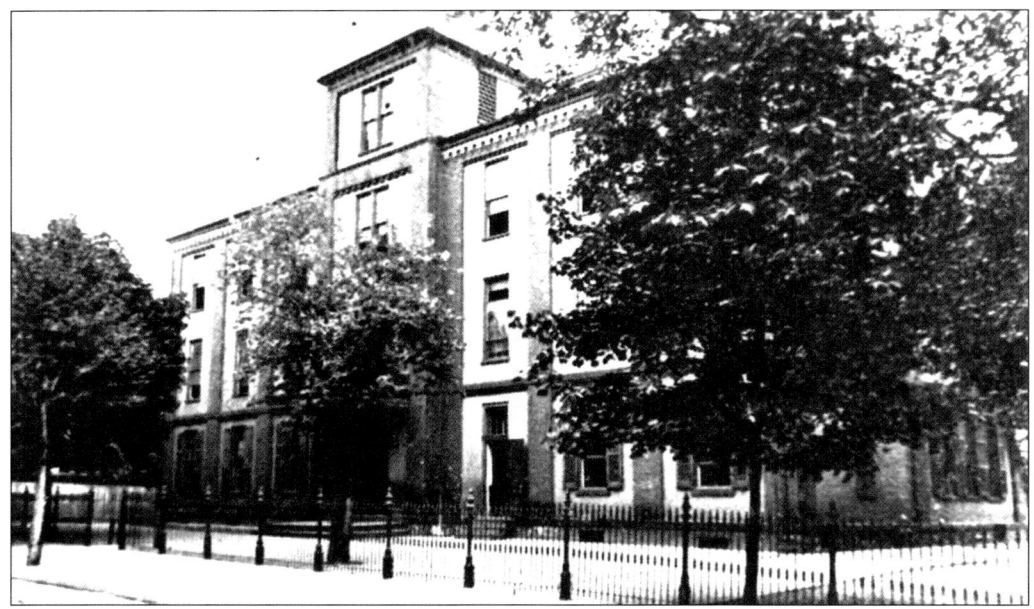

Three-story-high Cherry Street Elementary was located on its namesake street on the south side between Fourth and Fifth Streets. Students went to Cherry from the initially settled parts of the town. Officials demolished the building after a devastating fire destroyed it, and Holy Trinity Catholic Church turned it into a parking lot for its parishioners. (Courtesy Columbia Historic Preservation Society.)

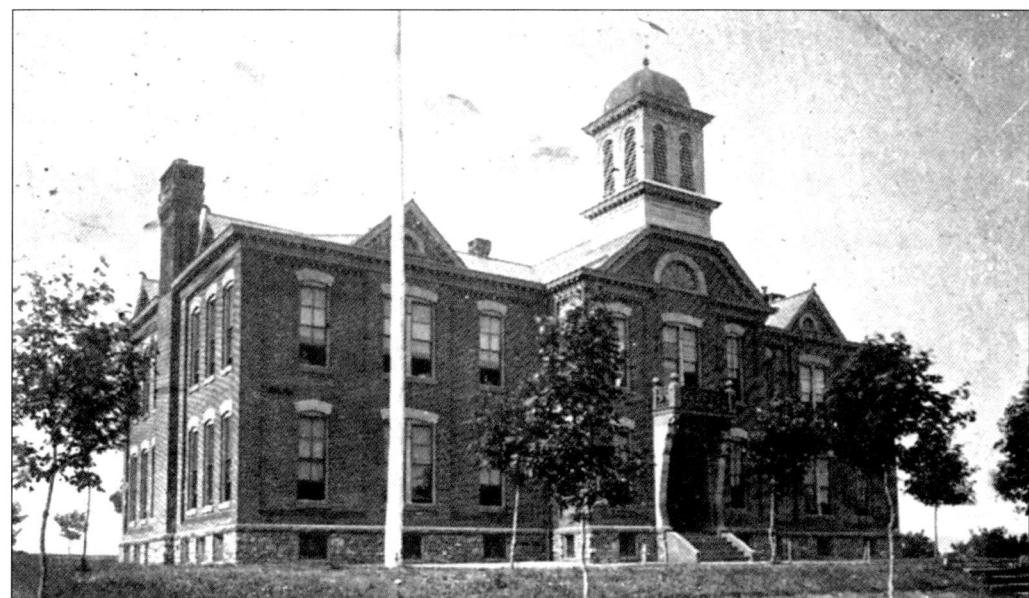

At the end of the 19th century, Columbia's east end south of Lancaster Avenue, centered on Manor Street, began to see substantial growth. To handle it, the school board built a new school at South Tenth and Manor Streets along the trolley route to Lancaster and across Manor from the Susquehanna Fire Company. Apartments now occupy the building. (Author's collection.)

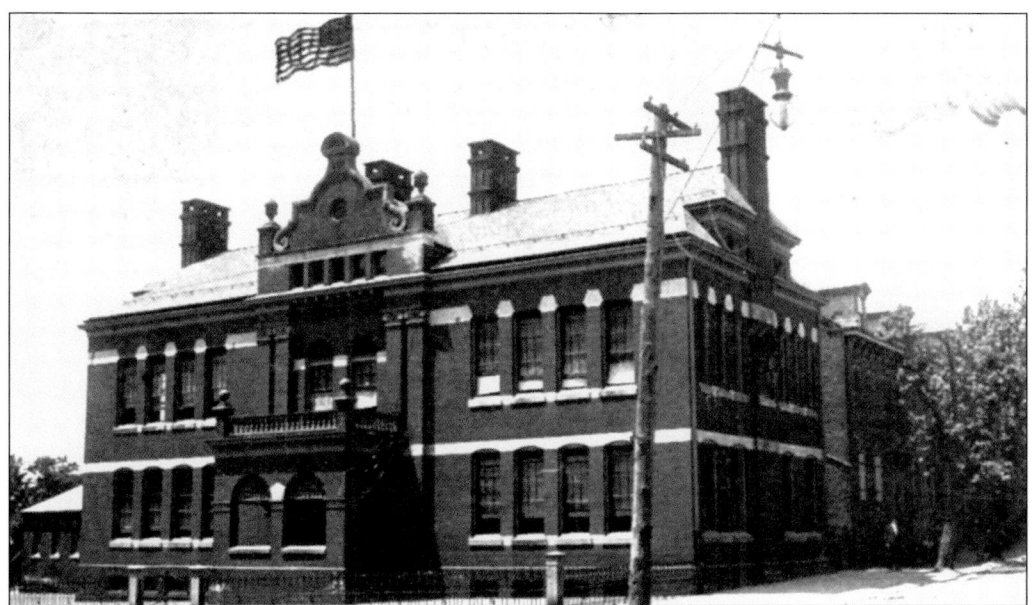

To handle the children from the growing north end of the borough, Poplar Street Elementary was built on the northwest corner of Poplar and North Third Streets. Typical of schools built in urban settings at the time, the building occupied almost the entire parcel it sat upon. An art studio now uses the building. (Author's collection.)

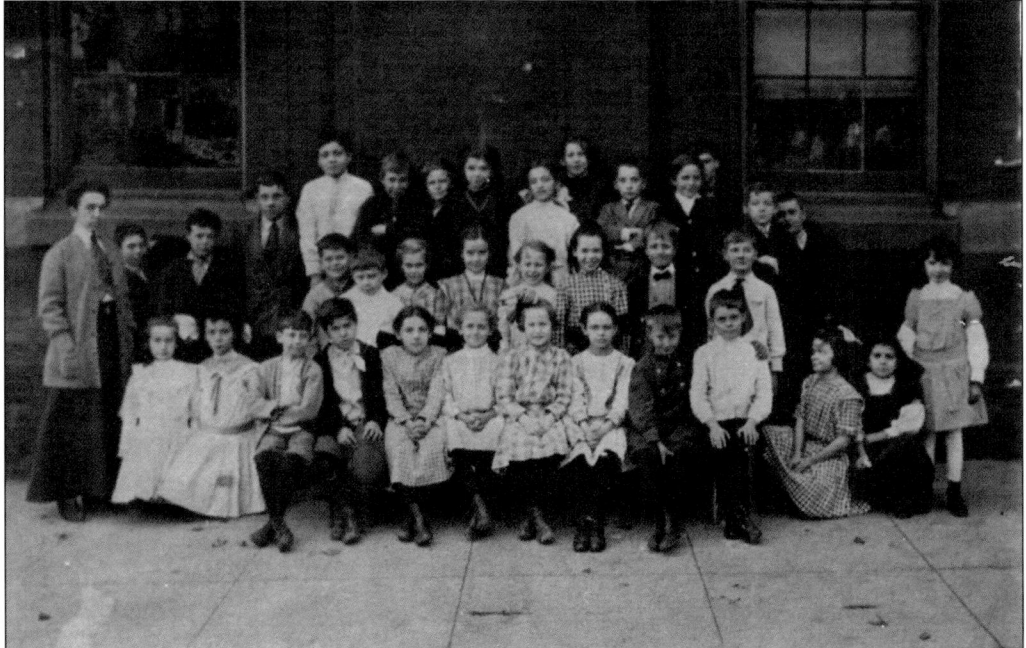

A class from an unknown grade poses in 1911 for a photograph with the Poplar Street School as the background. The teacher, to the left, and her 35 students face the camera. It is probably early fall or late spring as the teacher needed her sweater, but the students did not need coats. (Courtesy Columbia Historic Preservation Society.)

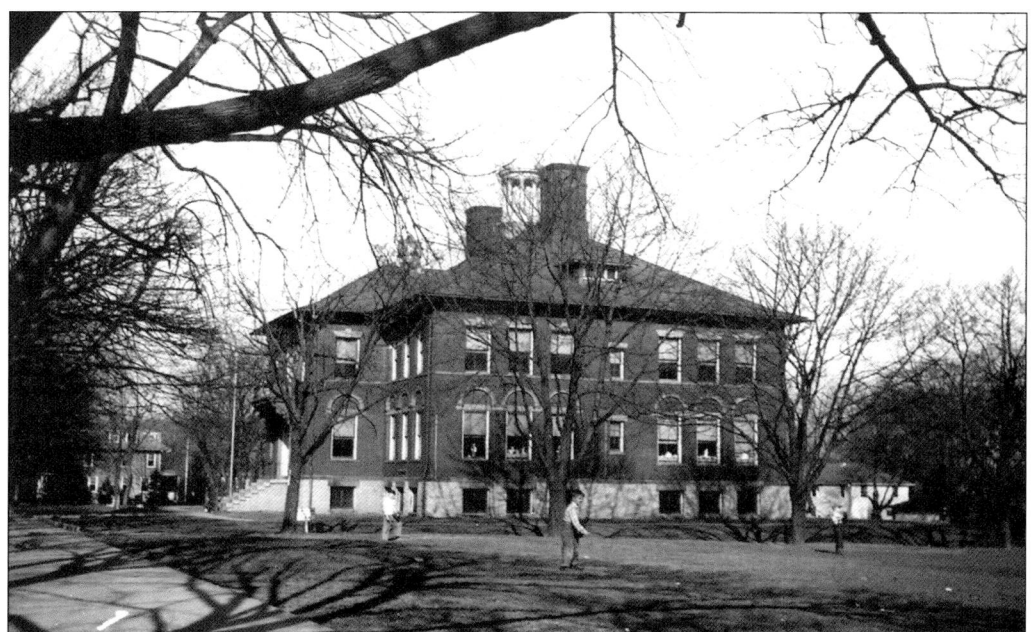

In 1905, the school board built the last elementary school until the mid-20th century. Named for Dr. William G. Taylor, board president who died at the time of construction, the school was for east end children north and east of the Lincoln Highway. A replacement bearing the same name took the place of the original school, and it is seen here in 1949. (Author's collection.)

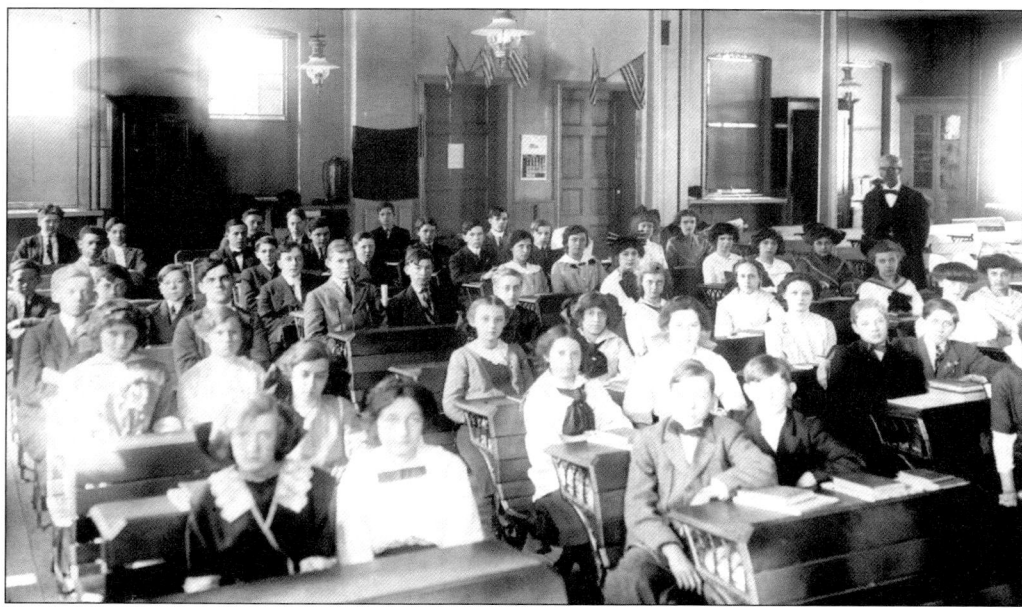

Students in Taylor School sat two to a desk with the seat back being part of the desk behind. The calendar in the photograph is unreadable, but the one flag appears to have the 45-star arrangement adopted when Utah became a state in 1896. The 46-star flag came in 1907, when Oklahoma joined the union. This time frame dates the photograph as being near Taylor's opening. (Courtesy Cleon G. Berntheizel.)

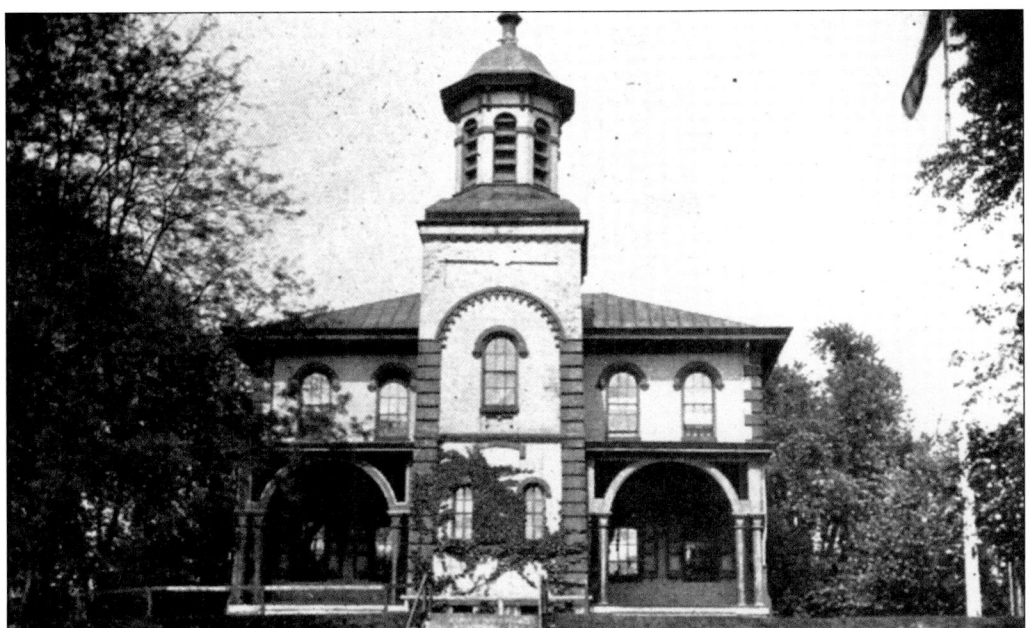

The photographer was standing near Lancaster Avenue looking east to take this 1913 photograph of Columbia High School a block away on top of Locust Street Park Hill. South Sixth Street is on the other side of the building. When built, the school was quite modern, but by this year it was starting to show its age. Ultimately demolished, the building stood where Park Elementary does today. (Author's collection.)

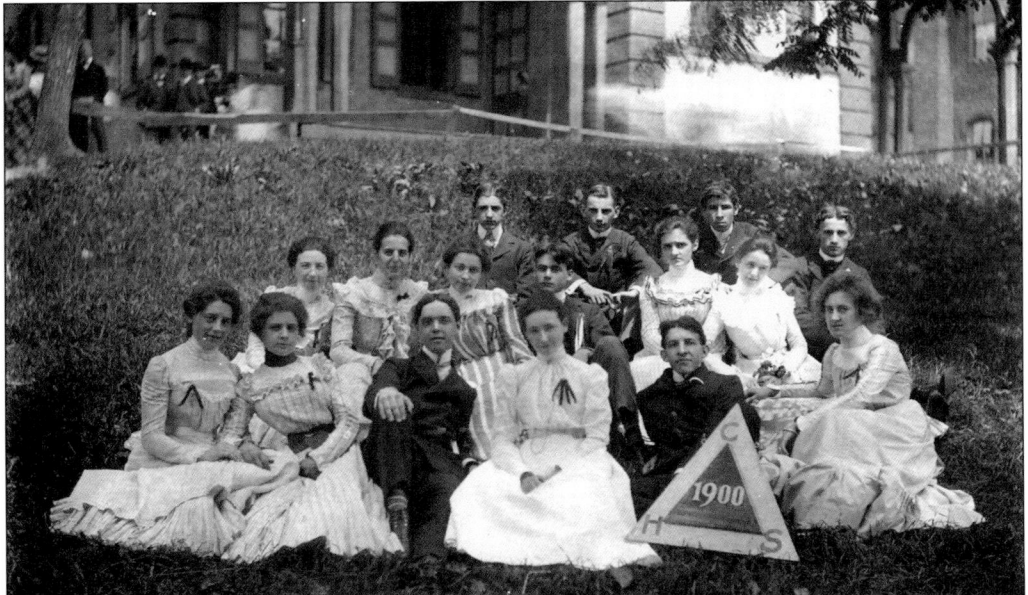

The small class of 1900 poses on the hill in front of Columbia High School on South Sixth Street. While dressed up, the nine girls and seven boys still mange to seem to be relaxed as they prepare to graduate in the last year of the 19th century. Hovering in the background by the school are perhaps teachers or proud parents. (Courtesy Columbia Historic Preservation Society.)

55

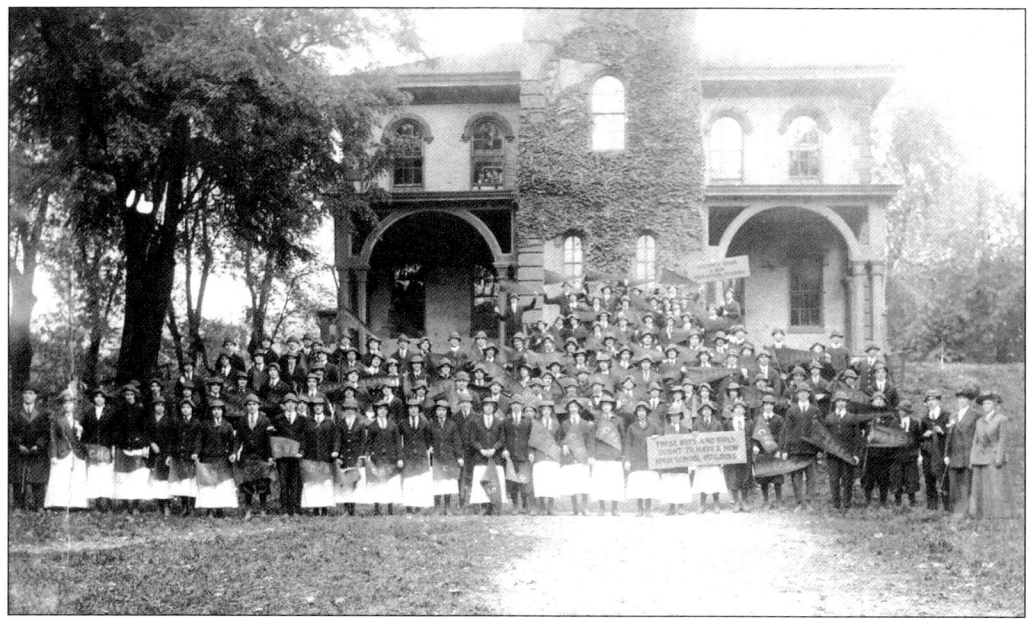

In 1916, judging by the banners some carry, Columbia High School students, flanked by a man and woman to the left and two women to the right, rally to get a new high school building. One large sign proclaims, "These boys and girls ought to have a new high school building." Another said, "Columbia needs a new high school building." (Courtesy Columbia Historic Preservation Society.)

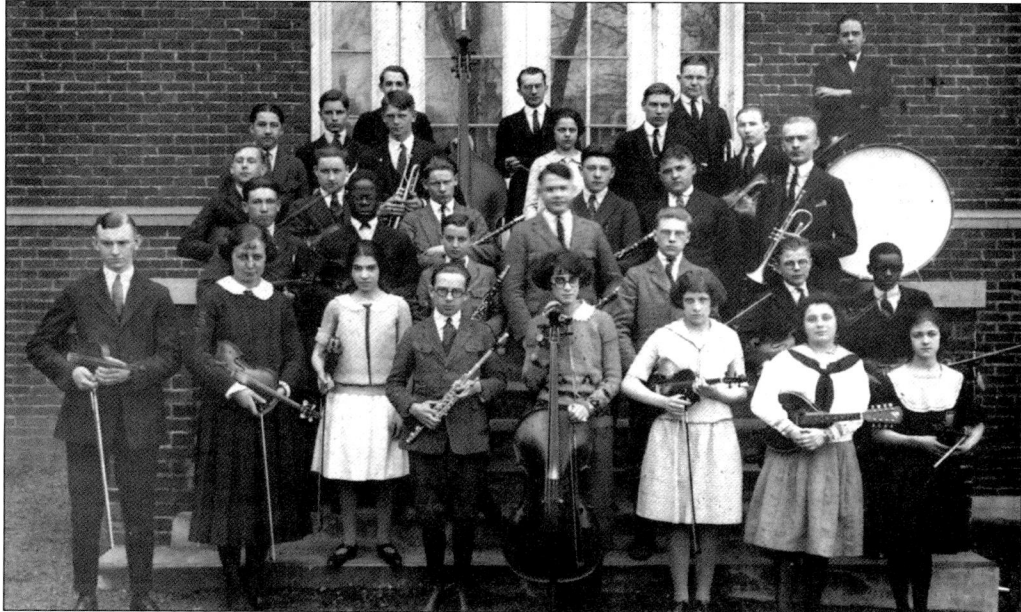

In 1922, Columbia High School had an orchestra. On the day of the photograph, the orchestra's 32 members lined up on the high school steps with their instruments, which included violin, cello, mandolin, clarinet, bass, and drum. The boys wore coats, white shirts, and ties, while the girls were more varied in their attire. (Courtesy Columbia Historic Preservation Society.)

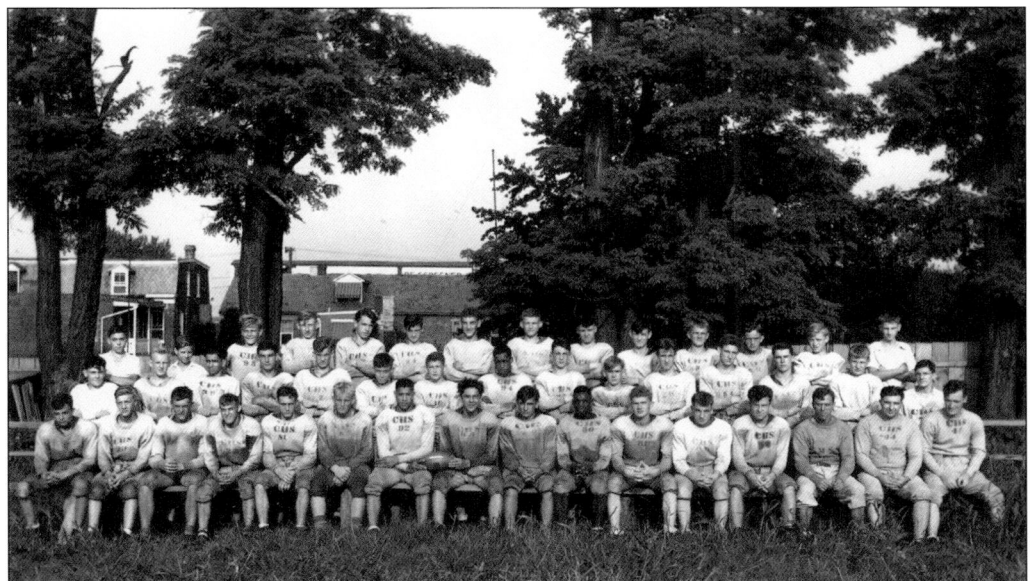

Football has always been a much-followed and supported sport at Columbia High School. Judging by their uniforms' appearances, members (probably from a 1940s-era team) pose after practice at Janson field about one block from the high school. South Eighth Street homes are in the background; peeking above them is the top of Kiehl's Coal Yard silos. (Courtesy Columbia Historic Preservation Society.)

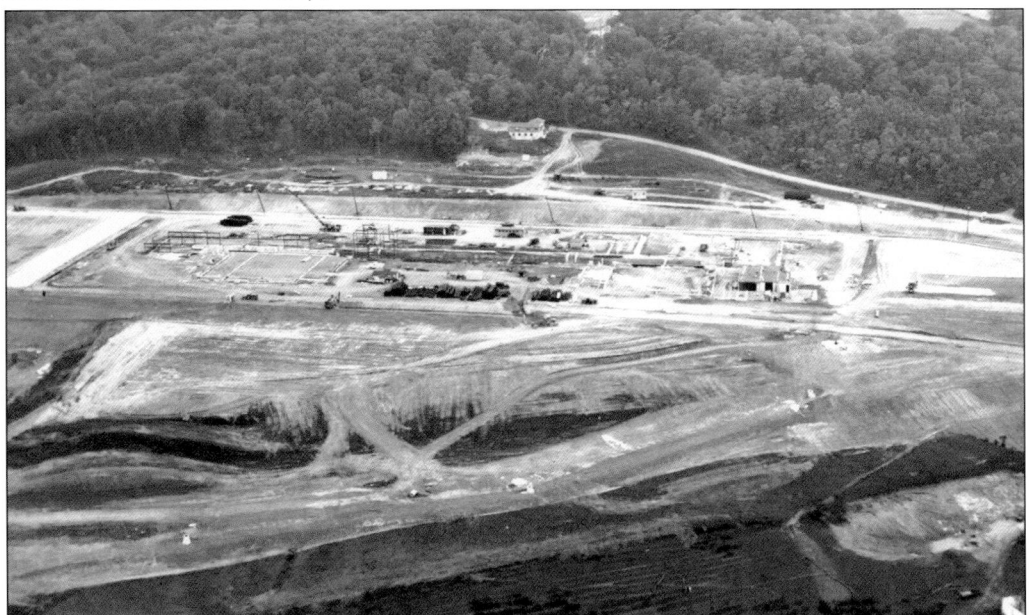

In the 1950s, Columbia again needed a new school building, this time for a junior-senior high school. Locust Street Park did not have sufficient room so officials chose to build on a farm on the north side of town. Construction crews leveled the top of the farm's hill and built access roads to the new school by extending to North Ninth Street and to Kinderhook Road. (Courtesy Columbia Historic Preservation Society.)

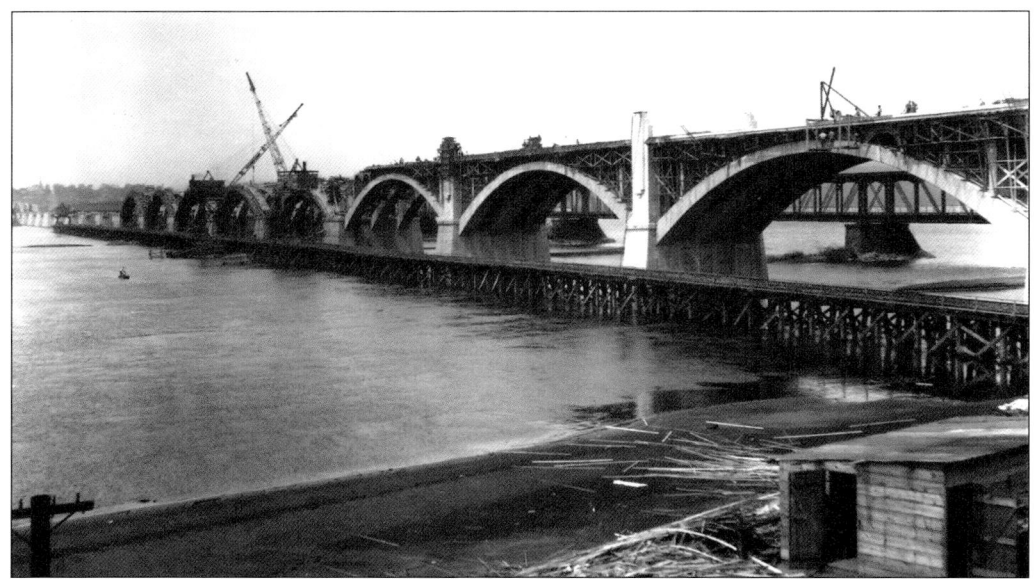

Construction is well under way on the new concrete arch highway bridge in this view looking west from the Columbia shore toward Wrightsville. Cranes traveled along the low wooden temporary bridge in the foreground and moved forms for the arches and supplies to where workers needed them. Behind the new bridge and upstream is the 1897 Pennsylvania Railroad steel bridge. (Author's collection.)

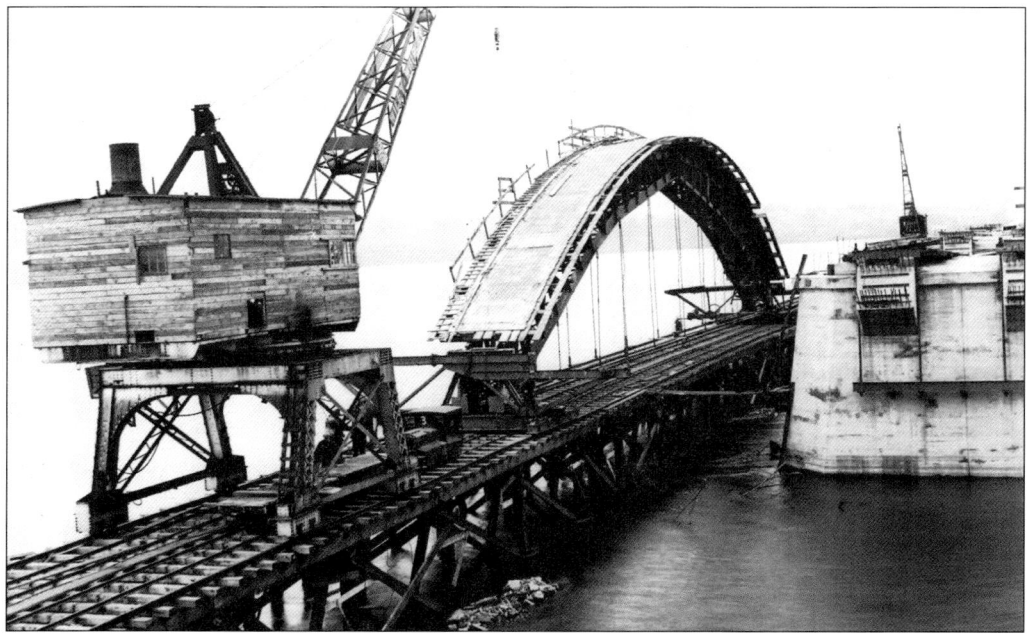

Here a form for the main arches is on the temporary wooden bridge that allowed workers to easily shift it away from a completed arch and over to a set of piers awaiting arches. Notice the small gasoline-powered engine with a flatcar; this arrangement allowed rapid movement of supplies from the shore to a point where the crane could pick them up and position them where needed. (Courtesy Columbia Historic Preservation Society.)

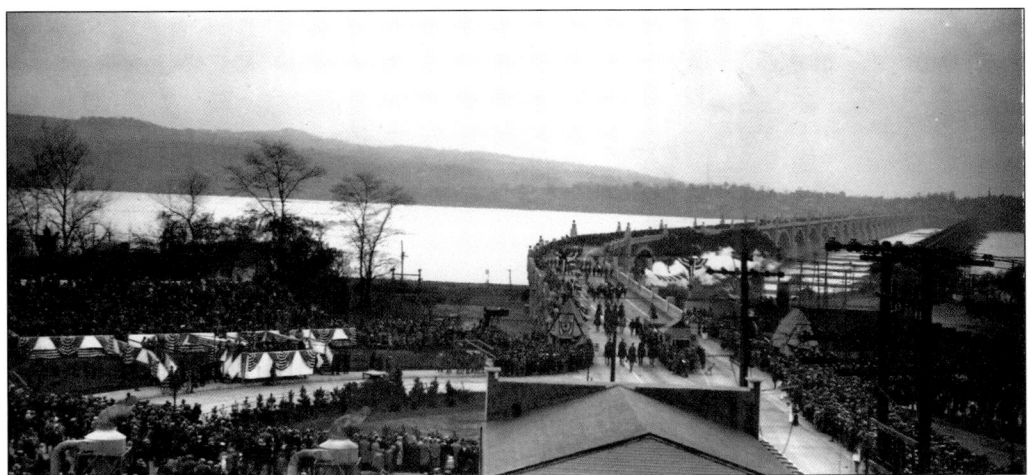

The Lancaster–York Intercounty Bridge opened Armistice Day 1930 with a parade and dedication program. The parade started on the Wrightsville end, with participants marching across the mile-and-a-quarter-long bridge with its approaches to the Lancaster County shore and a reviewing platform set up on the downstream approach to the bridge. (Courtesy Columbia Historic Preservation Society.)

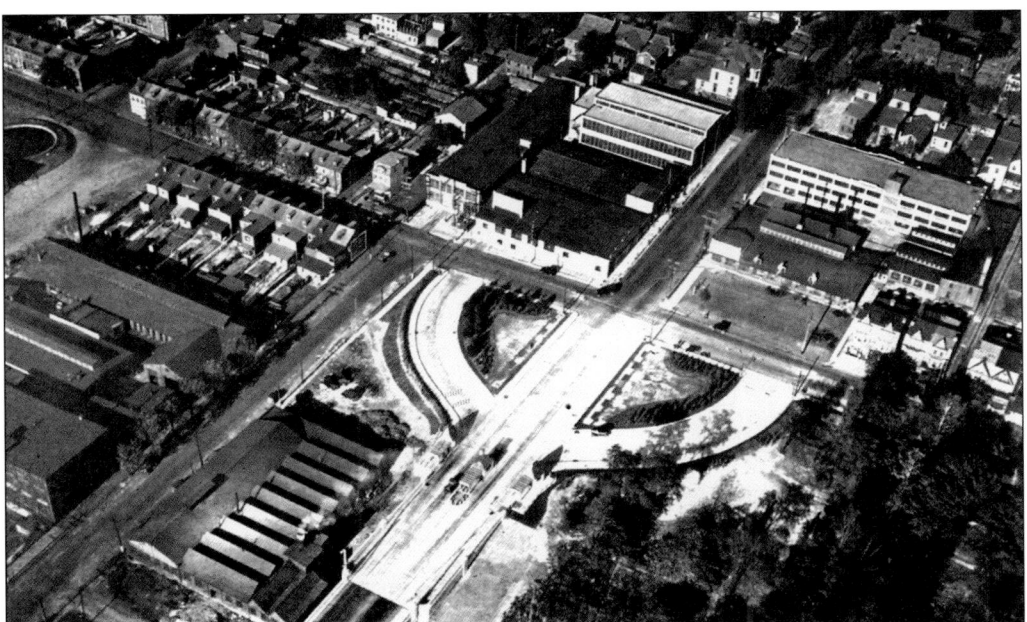

This aerial view shows the Columbia approach to the new bridge carrying the Lincoln Highway west. Chestnut Street with the Marietta Silk Mill (among other industries) to the left or north and Keeley Stove Company enameling complex to the right connects with the bridge. The two curved entrances end on North Second Street. The two curved and straight entrances converged on the tollbooths. (Author's collection.)

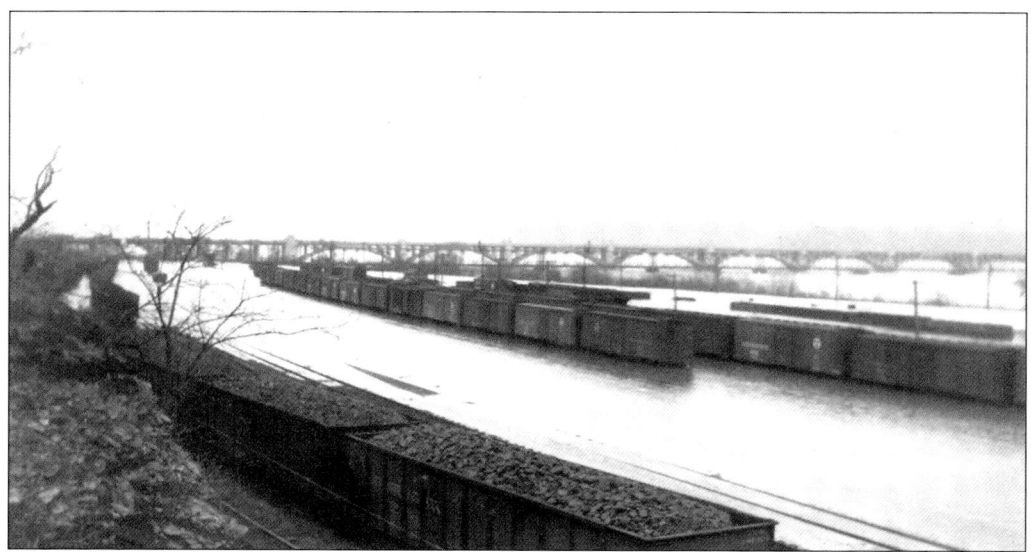

The 1936 Susquehanna River flood covered much of the PRR's Columbia yard. Floodwaters have risen to the axles of the freight cars in the middle of the yard, as seen from Cedar Street. Only the loaded hoppers that are on a higher track are unaffected. In the distance are the railroad and highway bridges. (Courtesy Columbia Historic Preservation Society.)

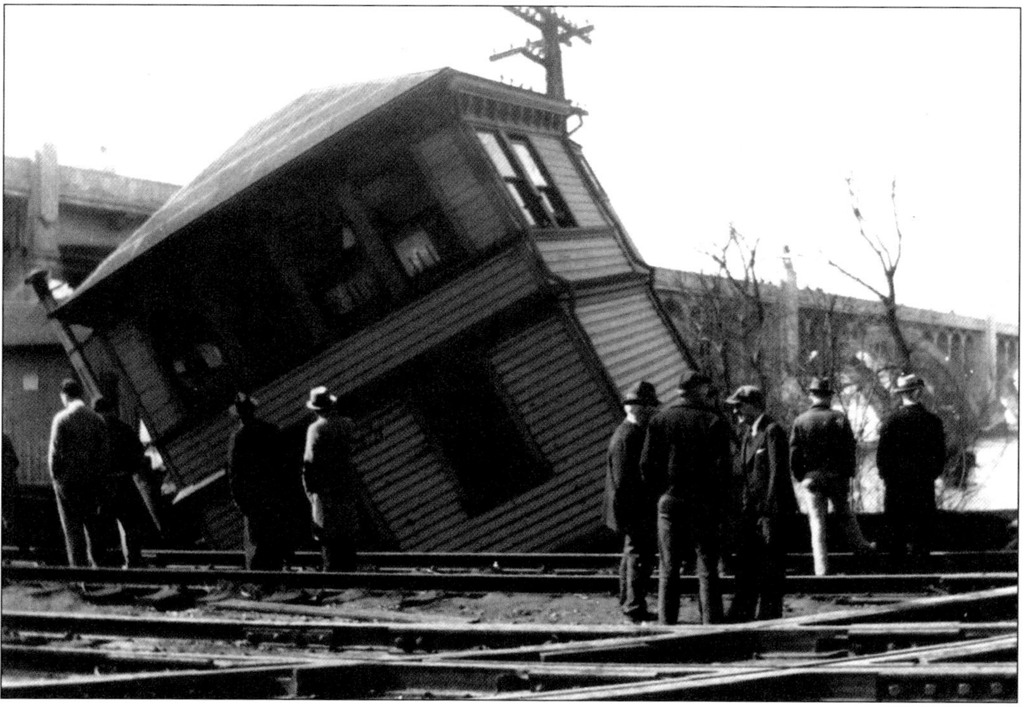

So strong was the force of the floodwaters that it knocked over the railroad tower that controlled the area's switches. Known as LG-42, an identifier for the PRR's Atglen and Susquehanna Branch or low grade, people along the tracks could see the levers used to throw switches still in position behind the windows. (Courtesy Columbia Historic Preservation Society.)

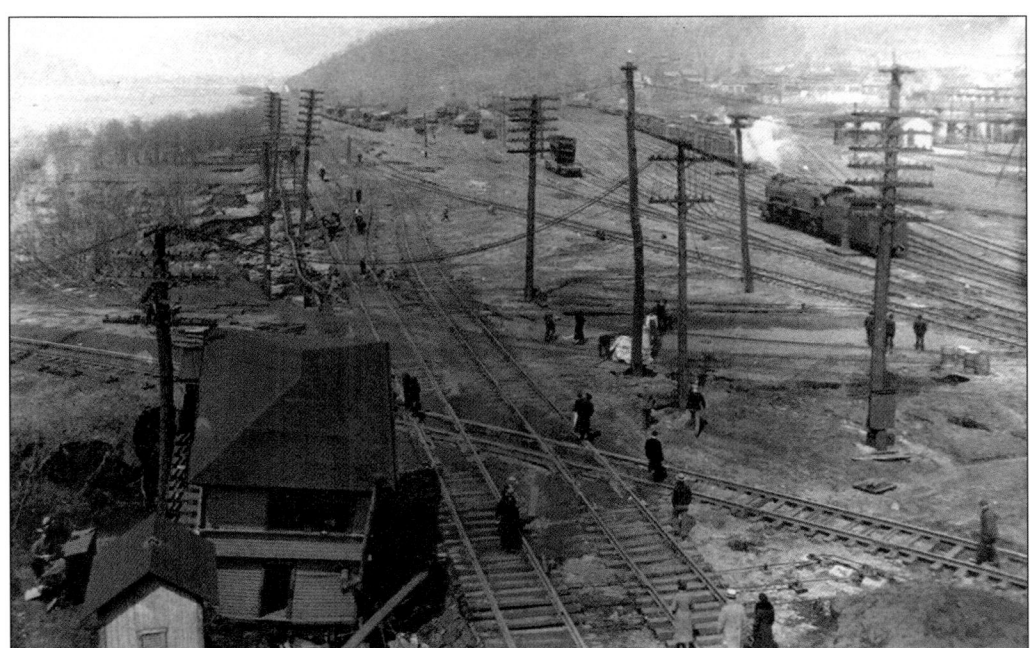

Shot from the 1930 bridge, this photograph captures the badly damaged LG-42 railroad tower and people out inspecting the damaged PRR tracks and yard. (Courtesy Columbia Historic Preservation Society.)

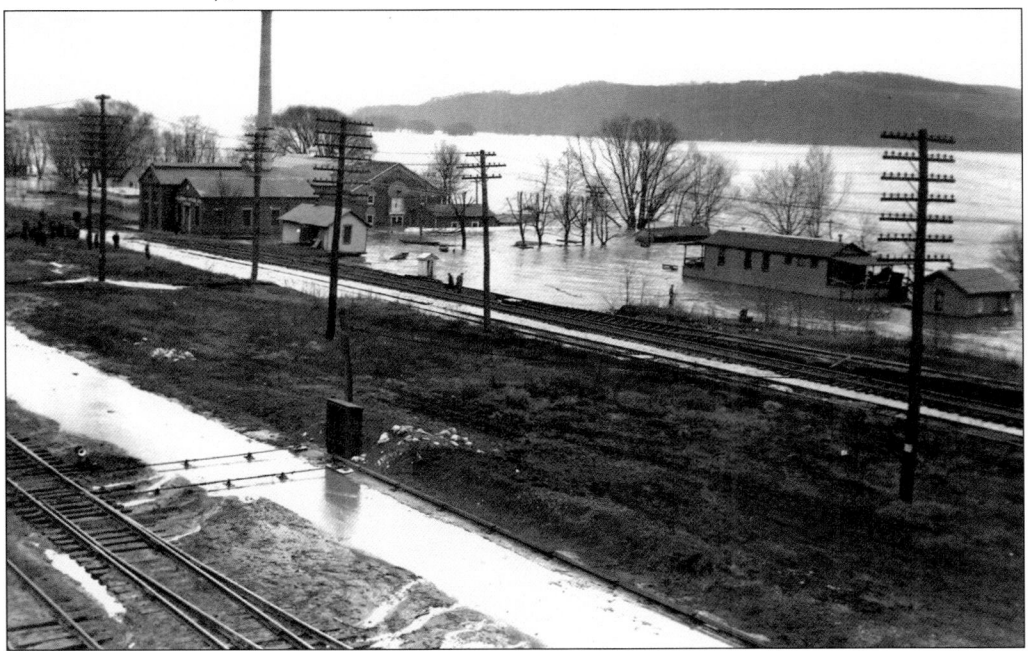

From the south side of the new Lincoln Highway Bridge the photographer had a good vantage point to see the Susquehanna River downstream. To the right, water covers buildings in Columbia's river park. To the left, the waters flooded out Columbia Water Company's pumping station at the foot of Locust Street. (Courtesy Columbia Historic Preservation Society.)

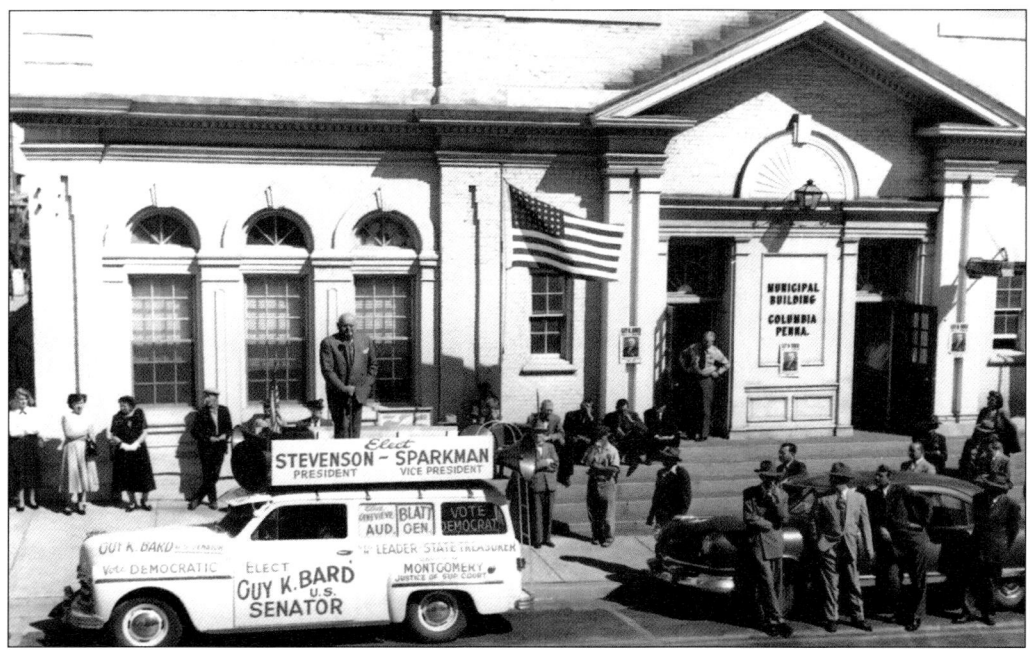

On September 27, 1952, Guy K. Bard gave a stump speech in front of the municipal building on South Third Street. Bard had resigned as judge for the U.S. District Court for the Eastern District of Pennsylvania to run as the Democratic candidate for the U.S. Senate. He was unsuccessful in his bid, losing to incumbent Edward Martin. Bard died the following year. (Courtesy Columbia Historic Preservation Society.)

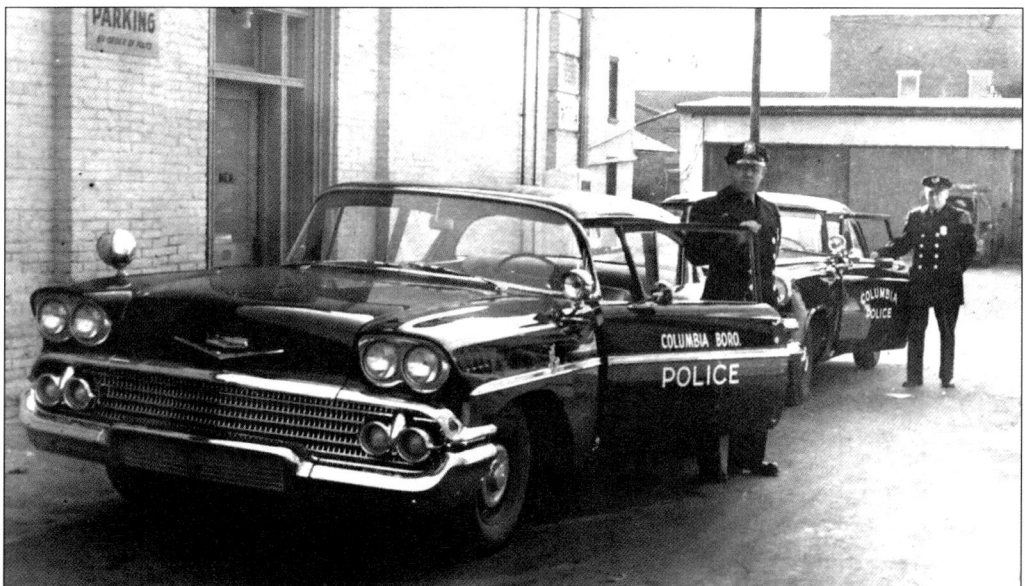

Columbia Borough police officers Schlossman and McManus stand beside two police cruisers parked on the north side of the Market House in 1958. In the back is South Third Street. The police station is out of the photograph to the right in the municipal building, which the town built out of the ruins of the opera house. (Courtesy Columbia Historic Preservation Society.)

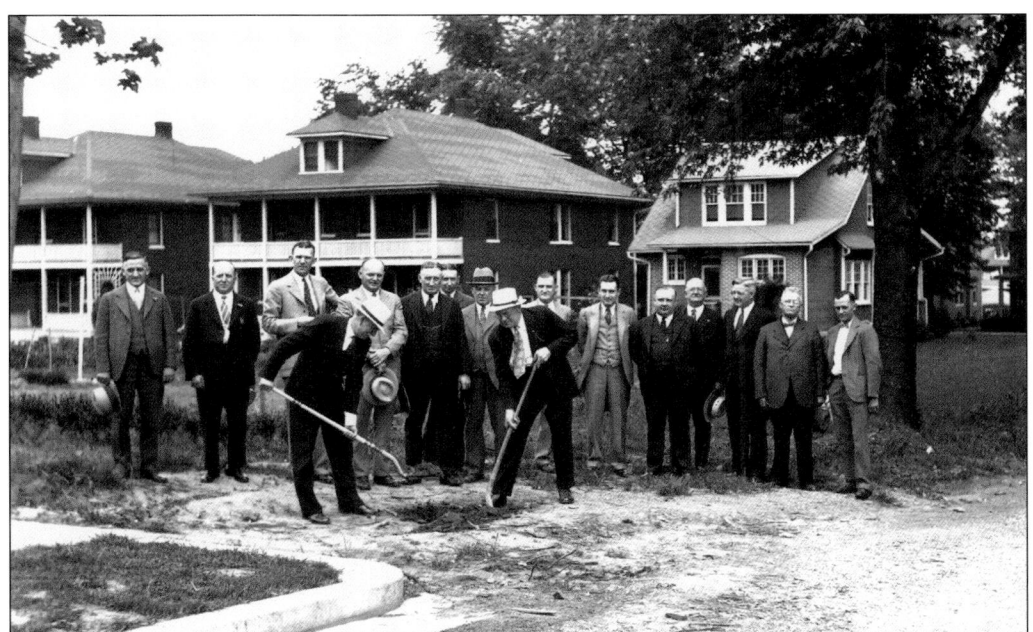

In May 1932, Gen. Edward C. Shannon and Burgess D. K. Lockard use shovels to break ground for sanitary sewer lines on North Tenth Street between Walnut and Chestnut Streets. With this addition of important infrastructures, home and business owners could connect into sewers and do away with inconvenient and unsanitary outhouses. (Courtesy Columbia Historic Preservation Society.)

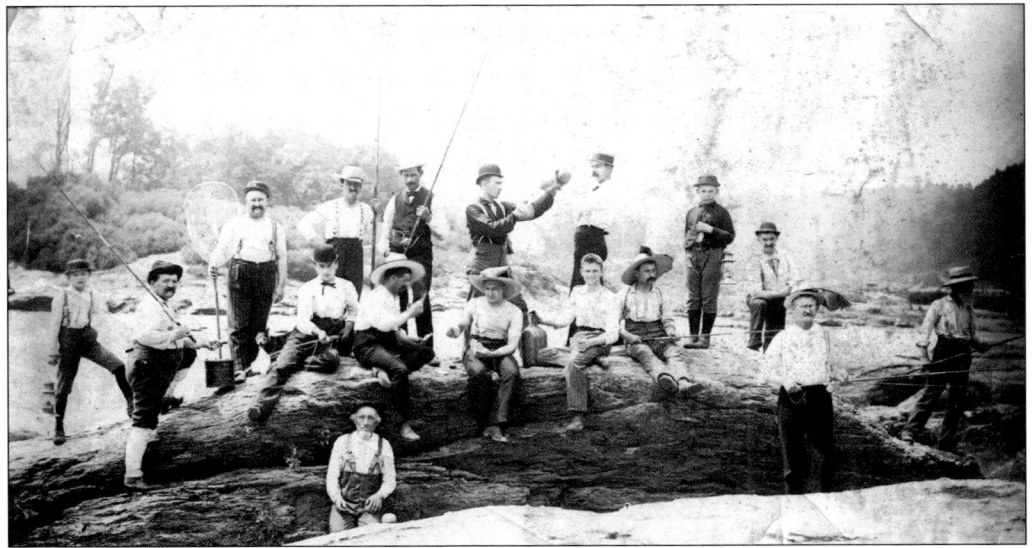

Before construction of Holtwood Dam on the Susquehanna River well downstream of Columbia, shad and eels freely spawned each spring, swimming upstream from the Chesapeake Bay. That migration and the year-round population of fish in the river supported enough people that certain Columbia neighborhoods came to be known as "Shadtown" and "Fishtown." In 1891, this group of local fisherman poses and clowns around for the photographer. (Courtesy Columbia Historic Preservation Society.)

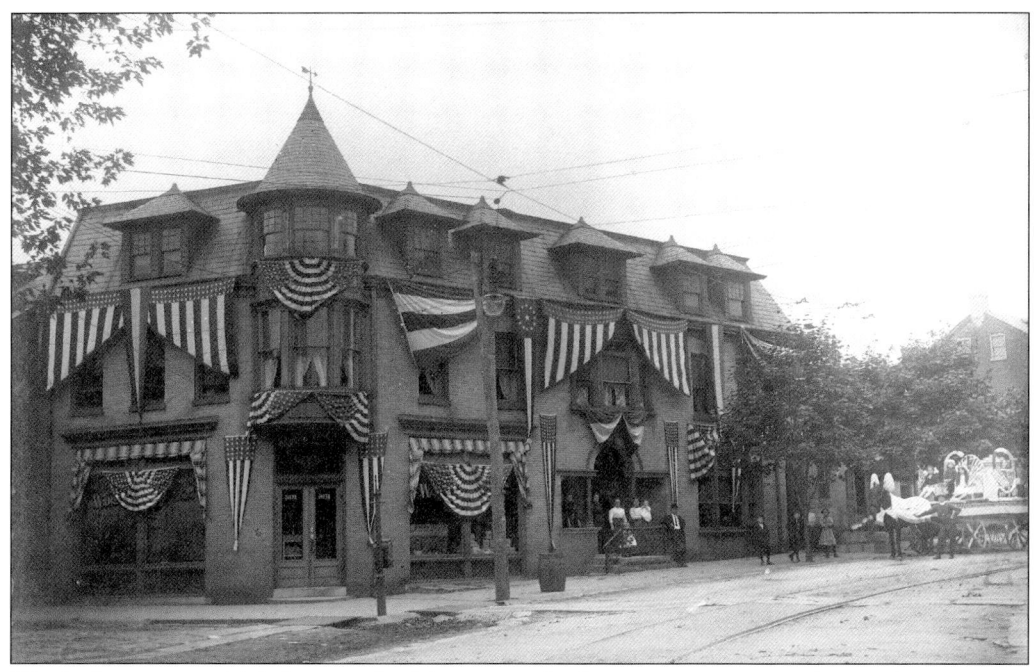

Warden's grocery, which later evolved into a confectionary store, was on the northeast corner of South Third and Union Streets. At one time, such confectioneries were common across town; even in 1930 during the Depression there were 16 listed under "Confectionary and Ice Cream—Retail." A parade may be forming, judging by the float to the right. (Courtesy Columbia Historic Preservation Society.)

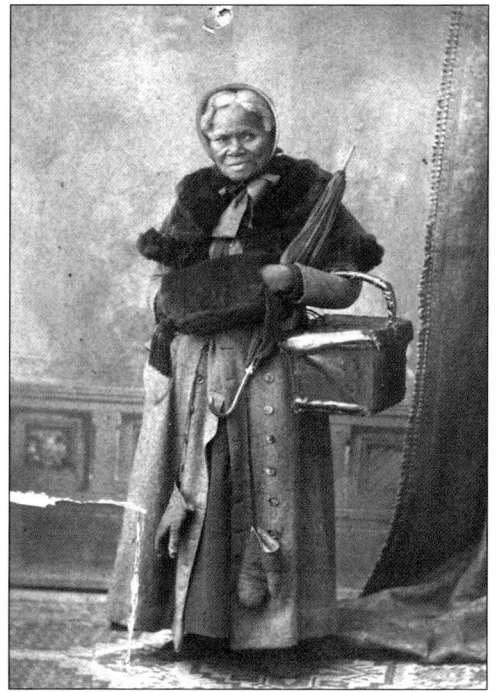

Hannah Bosley was born a slave in Maryland in 1812. She and husband Thomas Prosser bought their freedom and moved to Columbia in 1841. After Prosser died, Hannah married Isaac Bosley. She was a chiropodist, or corn doctor. She carried a basket, which may have held her medical supplies, for this c. 1880 portrait. She lived to be 83 and was survived by 4 children, 10 grandchildren, and 1 great-grandchild. (Courtesy Lancaster County Historical Society.)

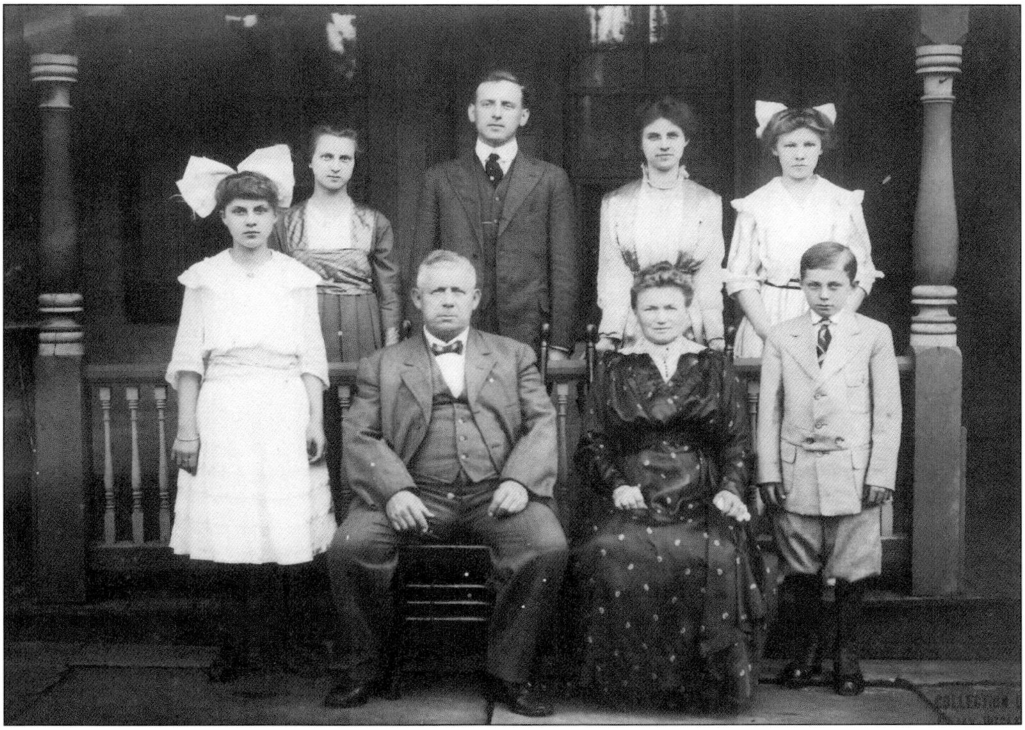

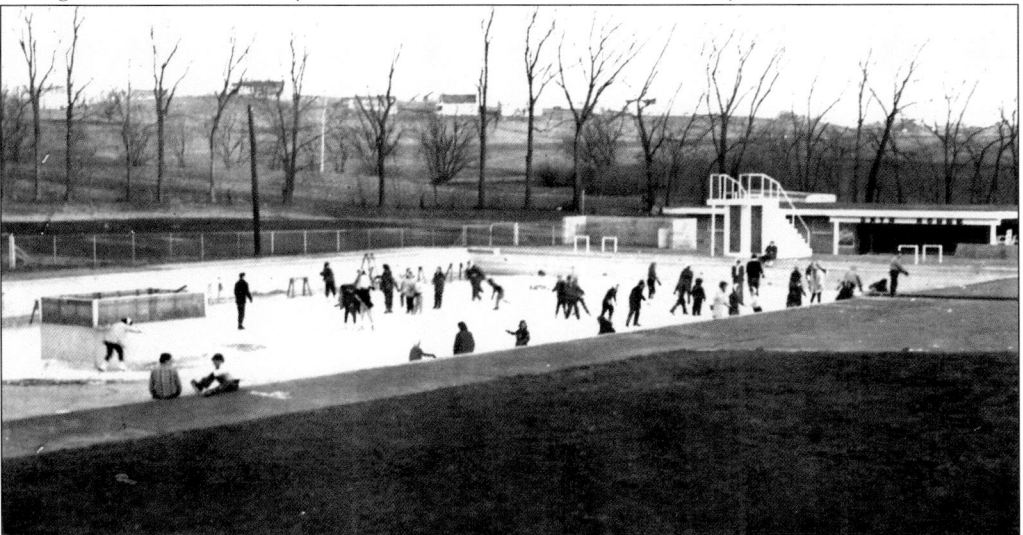

William Herbert, seated with his wife Barbara, had a coal yard and ice plant along Mill Street in back of their home at 302 South Fourth Street. Surrounding them are their children. Herbert was one of several coal dealers to delivered coal to homes, merchants, and business for heating during the winter. (Courtesy Columbia Historic Preservation Society.)

Locust Heights, at the east end of Locust Street, is Columbia's swimming pool. Filled with adults and children in summer, the pool usually stands deserted over the winter months. But at least once owners had a small amount of water at the pool's bottom and allowed ice-skaters to have a go. (Courtesy Columbia Historic Preservation Society.)

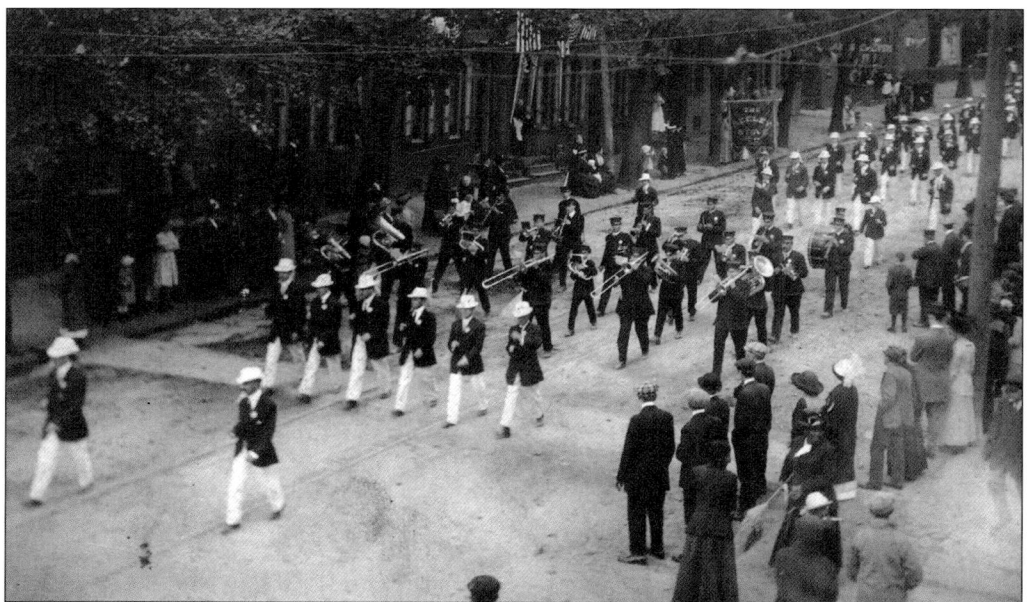

The fire companies and many larger industries often had marching bands eager to participate in parades. Here everyone uniformed and marching in step is associated, as the held-up high banner says, with the Keeley Stove Company. While most spectators stand, a few have brought chairs on which to rest in comfort. (Courtesy Columbia Historic Preservation Society.)

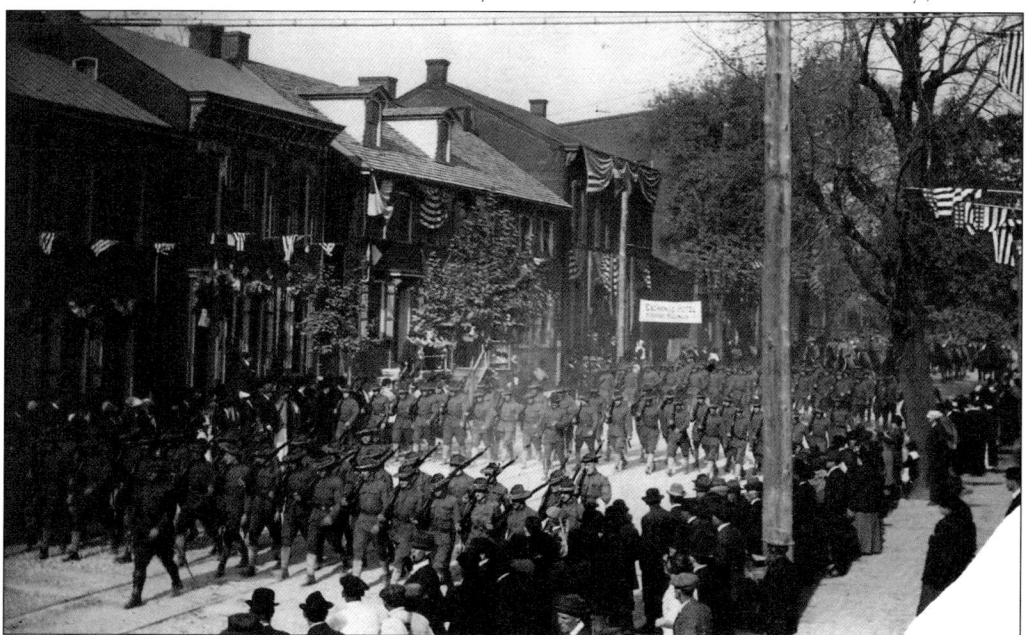

Soldiers—rifles on shoulders, leggings above their shoes, and campaign-style hats on their heads—march west along Walnut Street and the trolley tracks toward North Third Street with spectators three deep lining both sides of the route. The white banner is for the Exchange Hotel, 313–315 Walnut Street, Joseph H. Desch, proprietor. (Courtesy Columbia Historic Preservation Society.)

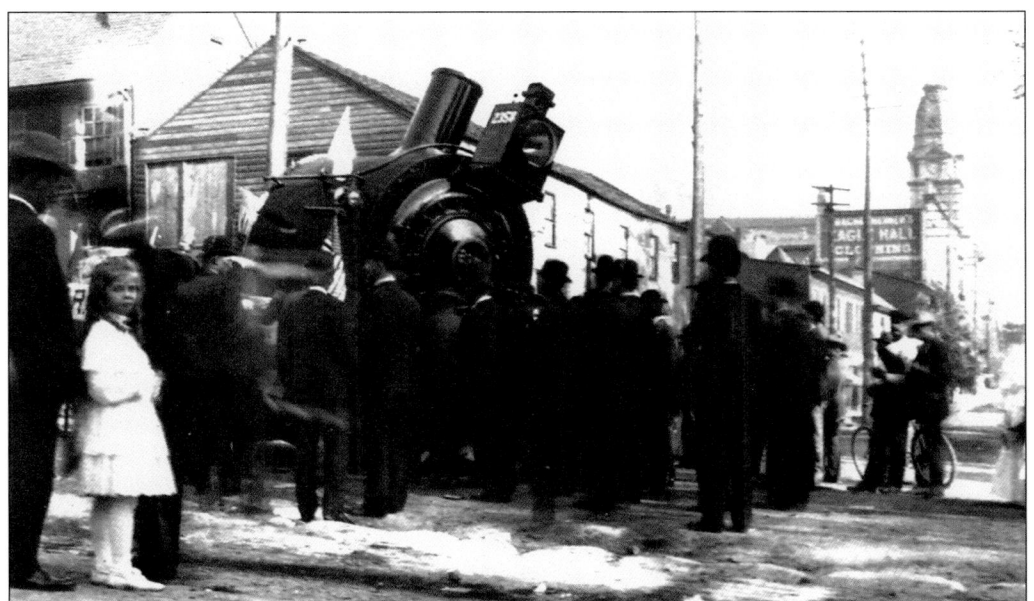

At first glance, this may appear to be a locomotive that derailed. Closer inspection shows it seems to be just the front end. PRR employees in the Columbia Shops built a replica of an engine's front end, brought it along for an Old Home Week parade, and marched along with it. (Courtesy Columbia Historic Preservation Society.)

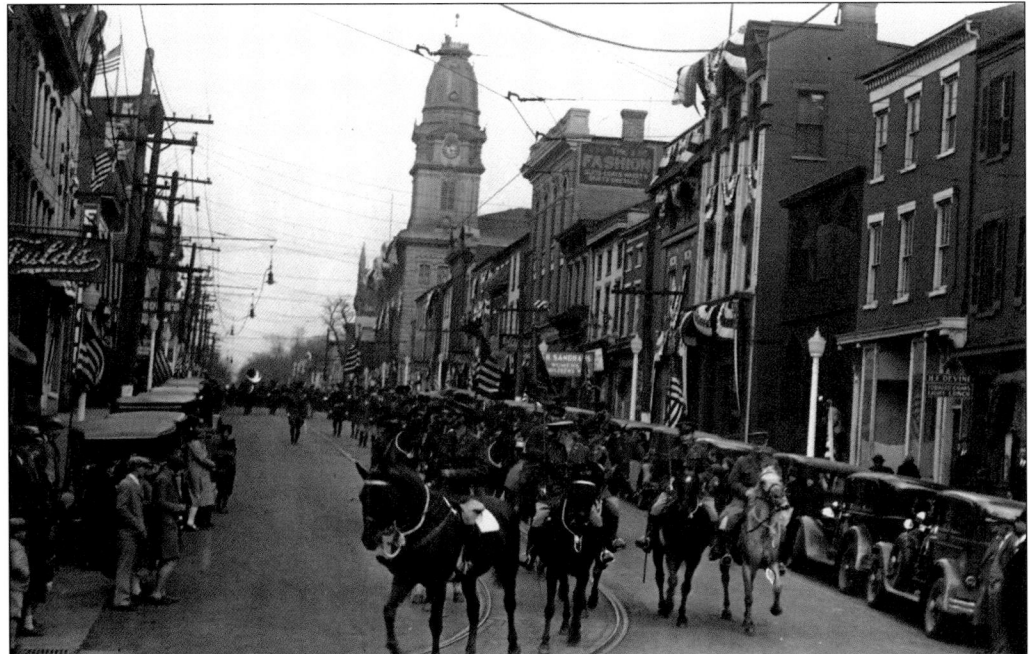

Columbia has, throughout its history, had a long tradition of parades. Here the horses are following the trolley tracks off of Locust Street on to North Second Street. The woman on the left standing in the street has her camera positioned ready to capture the moment. In the distance is the opera house. (Courtesy Columbia Historic Preservation Society.)

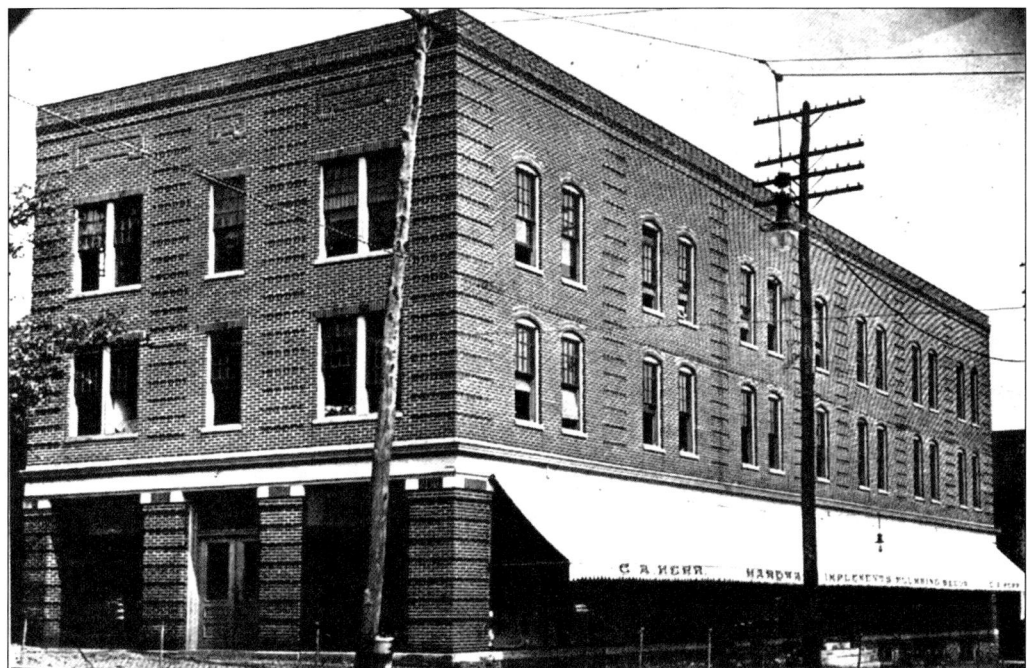

Seen here in 1913, this building at North Third and Walnut Streets had many owners and uses during it life. Occupants included a wagon shop (with painting done on the second floor), a second-hand furniture store and agricultural implement shop, the Standard Underwear and Embroidery Company, C. (Cal) A. Herr's Hardware store and his successor, and an antique co-op. (Author's collection.)

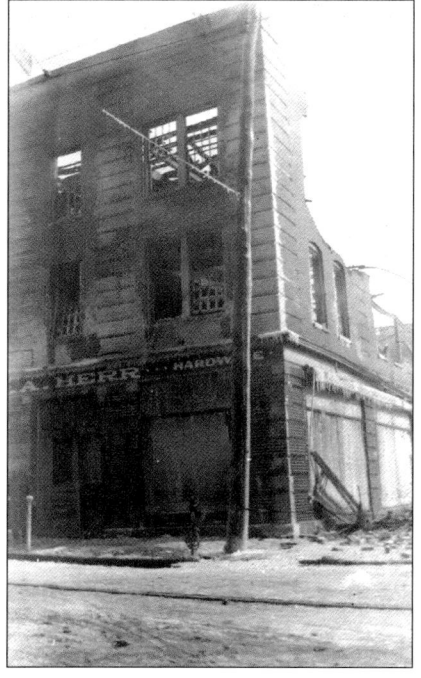

While it was Cal Herr's hardware, a bad winter fire ravaged the building. Much of the interior fell in, floors gave way, walls buckled and collapsed, and most steel beams warped. Ice coated everything in the aftermath. Despite the damage, Herr rebuilt his hardware store but without the third floor. (Courtesy Columbia Historic Preservation Society.)

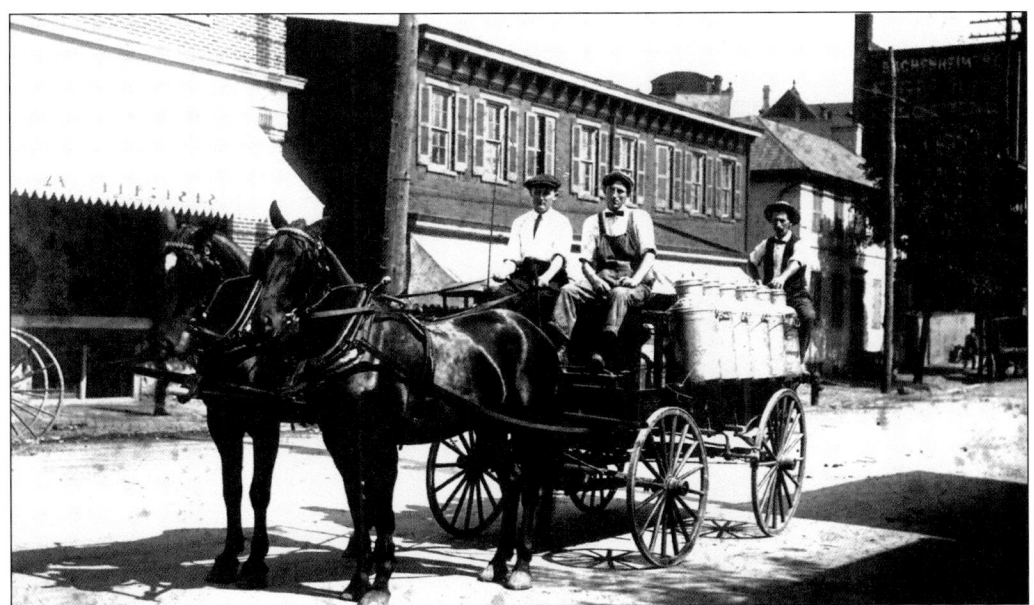

This driver has reined in the pair of horses who wait patiently as the photographer captured them and the wagon they pulled, loaded with milk cans, on film. The wagon is on North Third Street between Locust and Walnut Streets. On the left is Cal Herr's hardware store. The building on the right is Bachenheimer's Eagle Hall, which sold men's clothing. (Courtesy Cleon G. Berntheizel.)

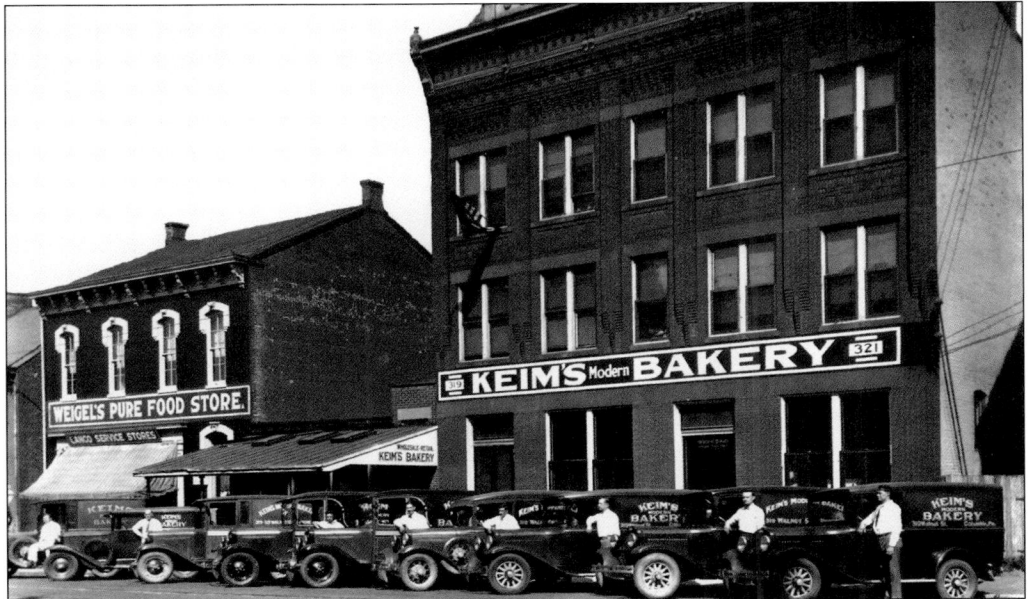

Drivers proudly pose with their bread delivery trucks at Keim's Modern Bakery at 319 Walnut Street. Cornelius J. Keim's bakery offered bread both for the wholesale and retail and trade. A 1926 advertisement said that it "is immaculate clean always open for inspection" and that it was the "Home of Keim's Honey Bread." Wesley J. Weigel's Pure Food Store was just to the west at 313 Walnut Street. (Courtesy Columbia Historic Preservation Society.)

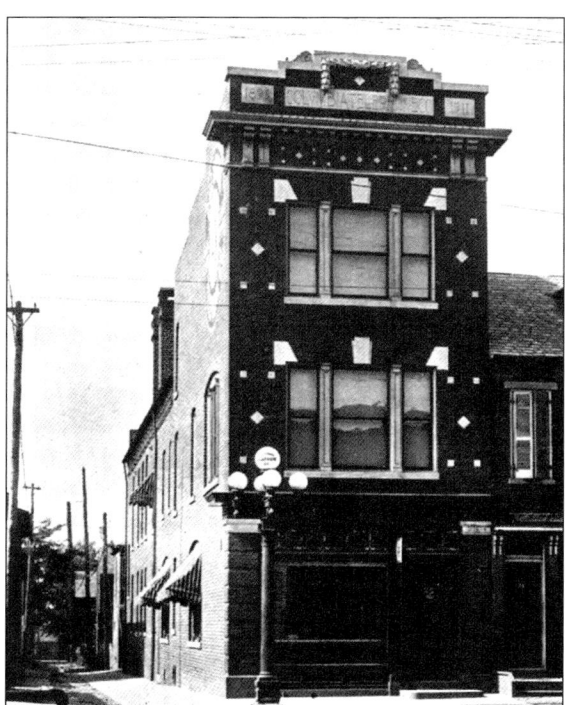

After Columbia Telephone Company got well established as an independent phone company, it constructed a narrow building at 22 North Third Street in 1895 and 1911, as indicated at the top of the building. In 1927, the company ran an advertisement saying "What is home without a telephone." Years later, Stover's News Agency expanded to include this building. (Author's collection.)

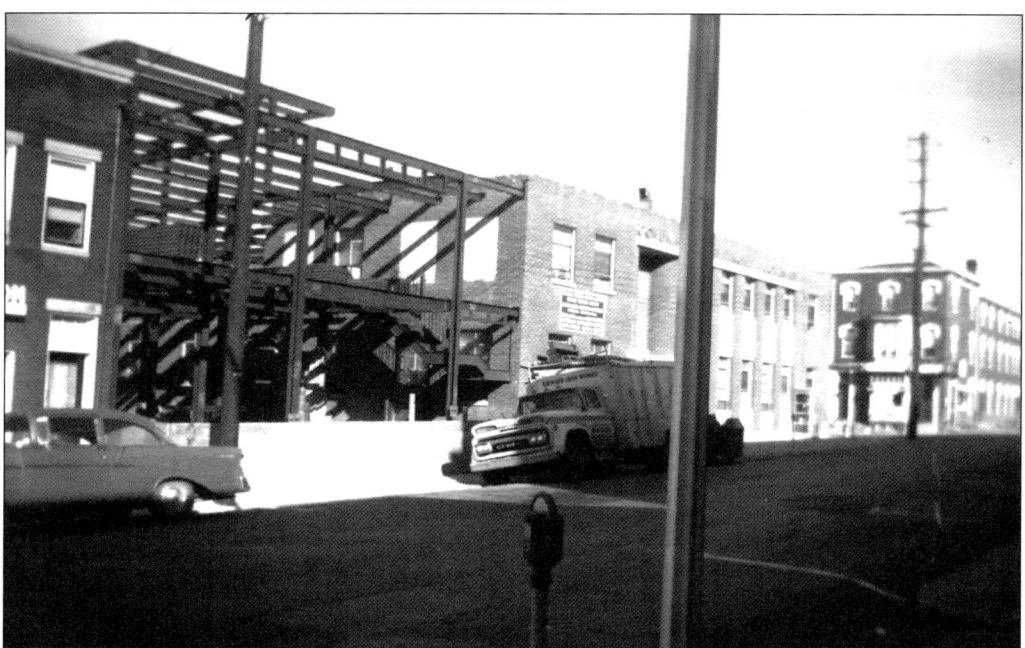

In 1947, following World War II, the Columbia Telephone built a new central office building to hold its equipment, operators, and staff on the southwest corner of North Third and Walnut Streets. By the mid-1960s, the company started an expansion, whose steelwork frame is seen here. A successor company replaced this building with a new, much smaller one in 1982 on North Second Street. (Courtesy Columbia Historic Preservation Society.)

The *Columbia News* printed for a century from 1888 to 1988. During its later years, its office and printing was at 341 Chestnut Street and it published six days per week. In addition to the paper, the company did commercial and job printing. Here a linotype operator sets the type for printing. (Courtesy Columbia Historic Preservation Society.)

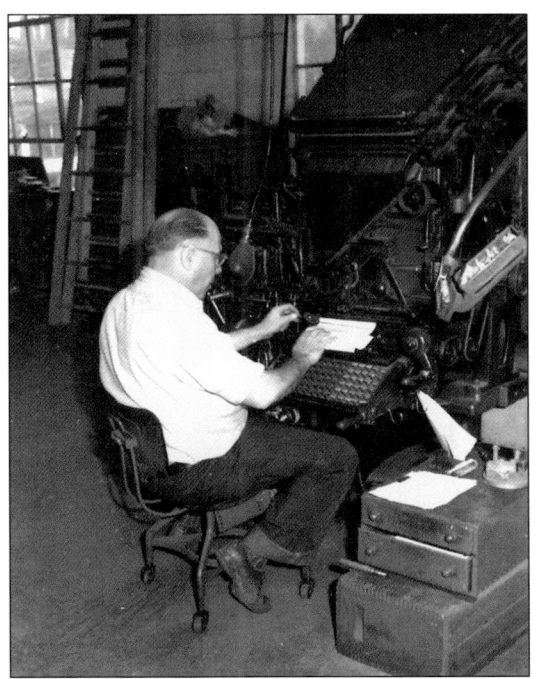

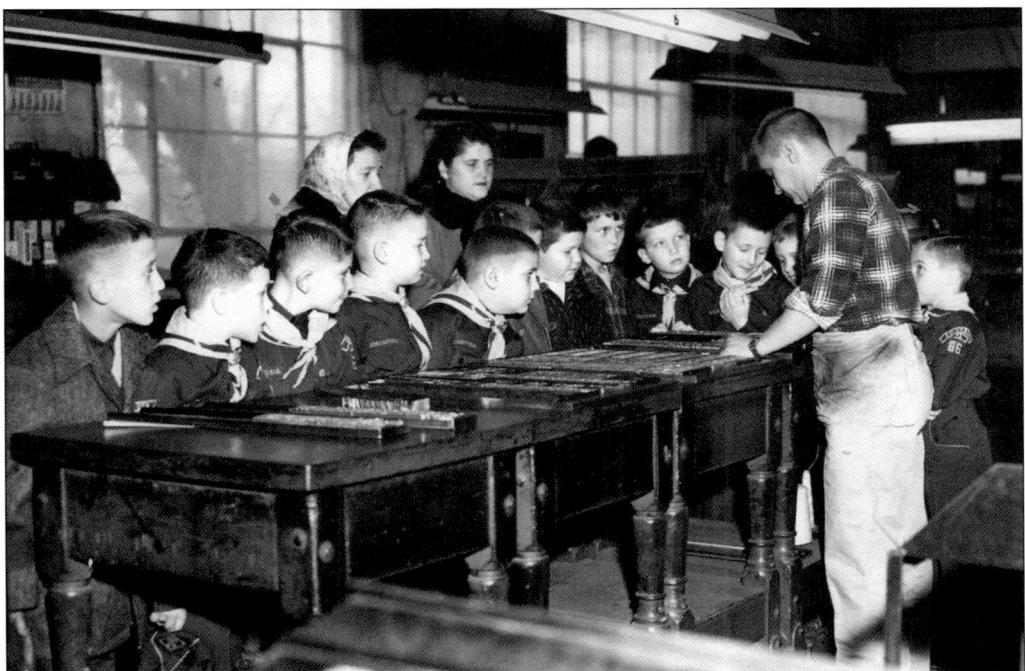

On a visit to the Columbia News, these Cub Scouts, den mothers behind them, found themselves enthralled by an employee who explained how printers went about their jobs. He could have explained that small letters in the trade were called lowercase. More frequently used, they occupied a place conveniently near the typesetter as opposed to capital letters or uppercase, whose name designated a position farther away. (Courtesy Columbia Historic Preservation Society.)

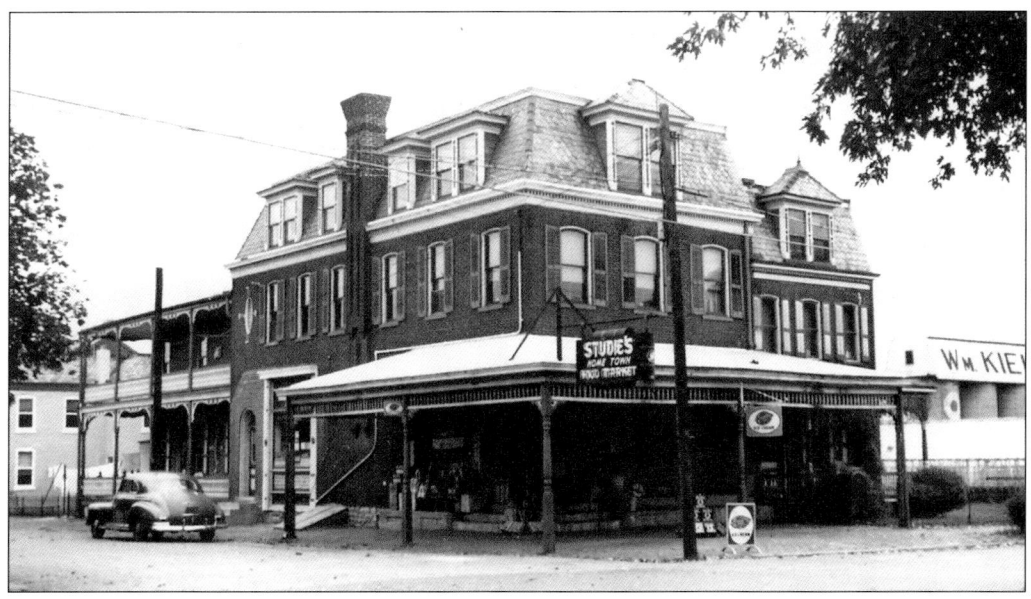

The first word in Studie's Home Town Food Market, pictured in October 1949 at South Eighth and Blunston Streets, is pronounced "stoo-dees," short for Studenroth, the owner's last name. Until replaced by chain convenience stores, corner grocery stores were common around town. To the right rear are the silos of William Kiehl's coal yard on Wright Street. (Courtesy Columbia Historic Preservation Society.)

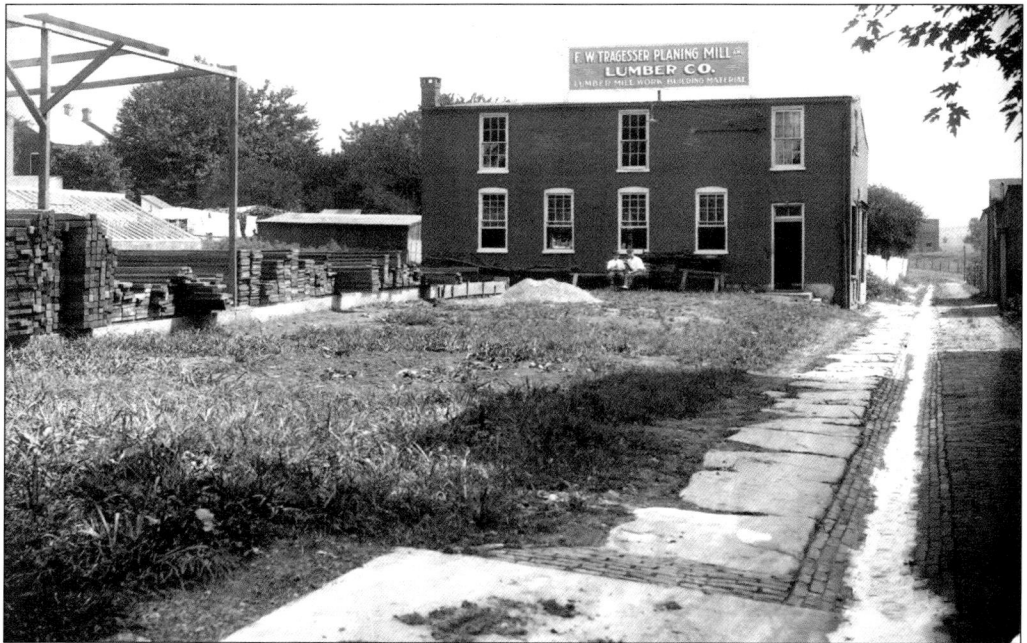

Following his return from World War I, Frank Tragressor operated a planning mill and lumberyard on the north side of Avenue S between South Eighth and South Ninth Streets. On a warm day, employees had the windows open on the Eighth Street side of the business, whose sign offered lumber millwork and building material. (Courtesy Columbia Historic Preservation Society.)

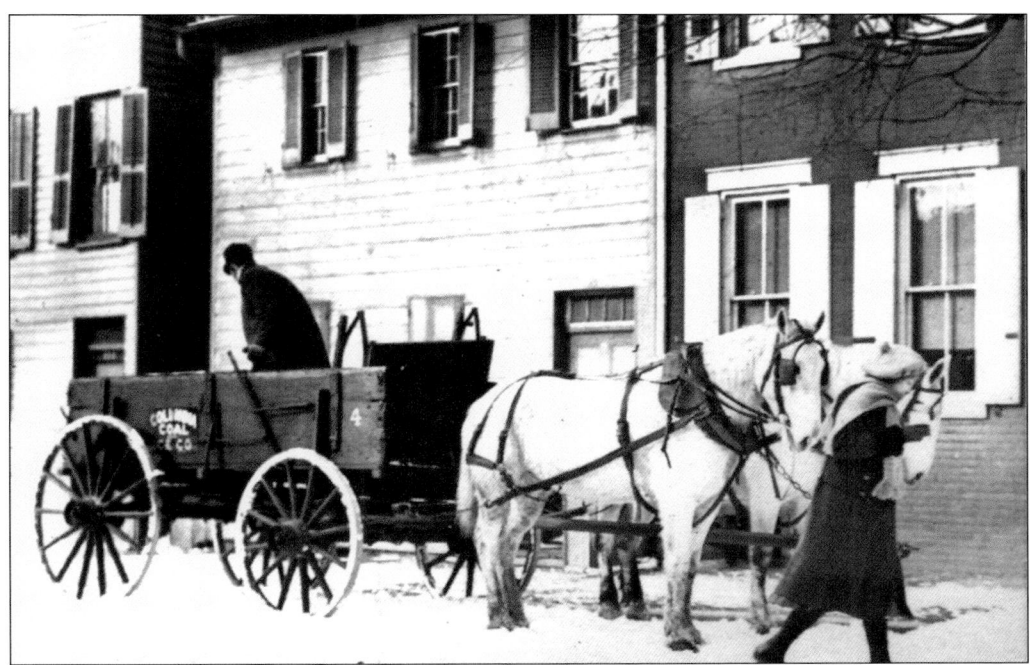

The team pulling the Columbia Coal and Ice Company No. 4 delivery wagon waits patiently as the driver delivers a load of coal to a home on a snow-covered Walnut Street. The company had two coal yards; one was on North Second Street between Maple and Linden Streets and the other was at South Ninth and Blunston Streets. (Courtesy Columbia Historic Preservation Society.)

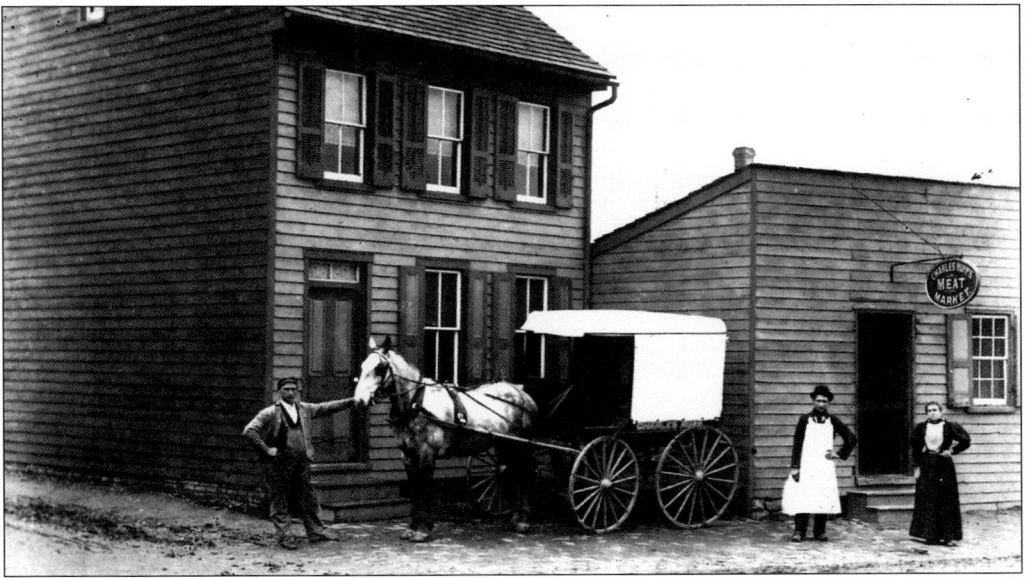

Charles Rupp's Meat Market proclaims the oval sign while the wagon simply has the label Charles Rupp between the white side and the rear wheel. Butchers who traveled about town stopping outside of customers' homes were common until the 1960s. They often would work out of a central shop, but they would wait to do the final cutting until they could find out what their customers desired. (Courtesy Columbia Historic Preservation Society.)

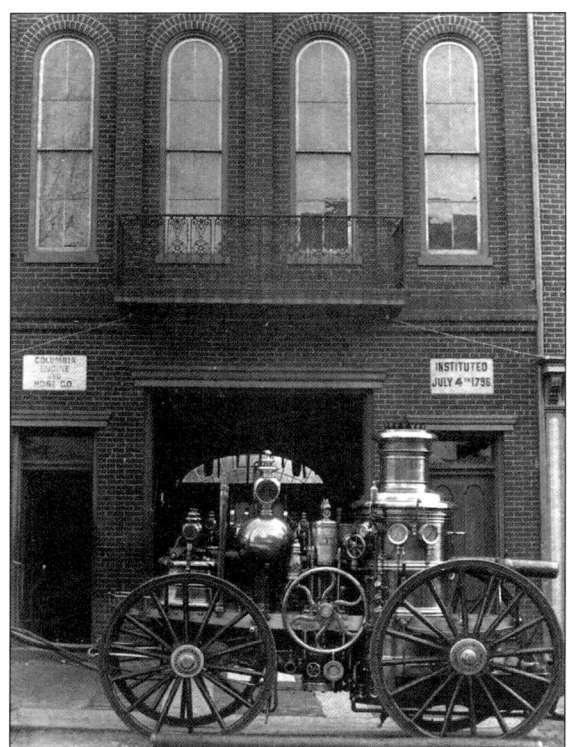

The stone above the left door says "Columbia Engine and Hose Company," and the one above the right says "Instituted July 4, 1796," the company's founding date, which was only about six years after the town's layout. Now known as Columbia No. 1, the company has had several homes through its long history. Here its horse-drawn, steam-powered pumper sits outside 268 Locust Street. (Courtesy Columbia Historic Preservation Society.)

It is almost difficult to recognize this as the home of Columbia No. 1, as covered as it is in bunting, flags, and streamers. Decoration of fire companies, businesses, and homes was quite common for the Fourth of July (especially significant for No. 1 as it is the founding date for the company) and other patriotic occasions. (Courtesy Columbia Historic Preservation Society.)

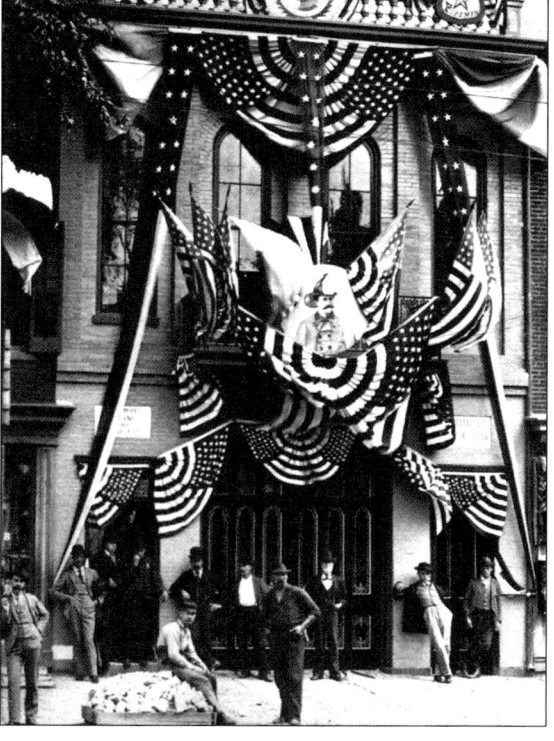

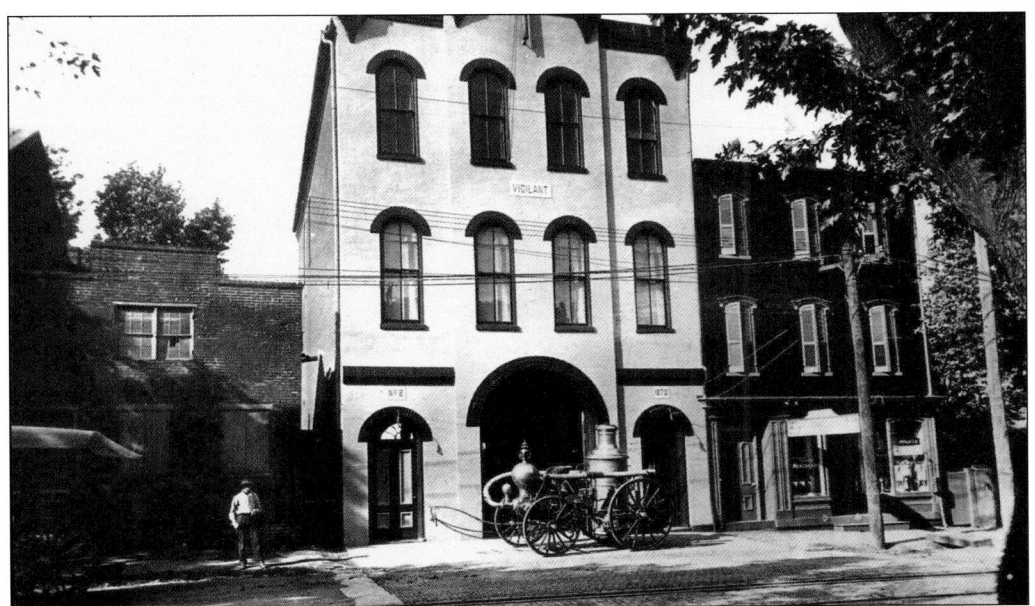

The Vigilant Steam Fire Engine Company, as it was known formally in 1916, was Columbia's second-oldest fire company. For many years the Vigies, as they were called, had their station at 24 North Second Street. The three stones said "Vigilant" at the center of the building between the second and third stories, "No 2," the company's number over the left door, and "1870," the cornerstone over the right. (Courtesy Columbia Historic Preservation Society.)

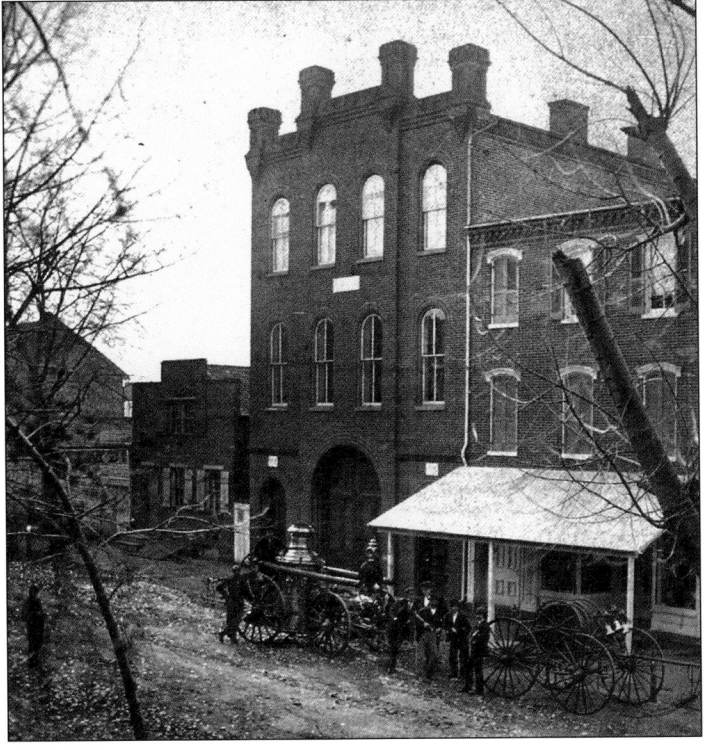

North Second Street is still unpaved in this early view of the Vigilant Fire Company with its steam-powered pumper and hose wagon in front of the station and its elaborate brickwork at the top. Vigilant, Shawnee, and Keystone merged into the Columbia Consolidated Fire Company with its station on South Tenth Street. (Courtesy Columbia Historic Preservation Society.)

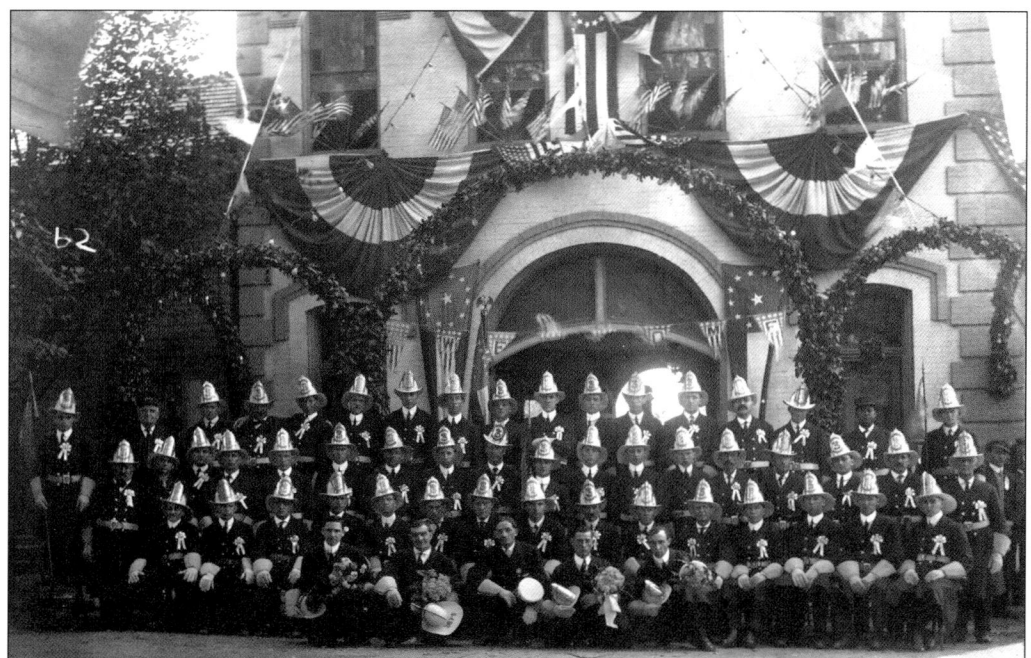

The photographer's long exposure caused some of the individual letters in the "Welcome" over the station to blur as he took the Shawnee Steam Fire Engine Company members' formal portrait. Dressed in coat and tie, members either wore or carried a helmet emblazoned with 3, the company's number and stood in front of decorated station building at 518–522 Union Street. (Courtesy Columbia Historic Preservation Society.)

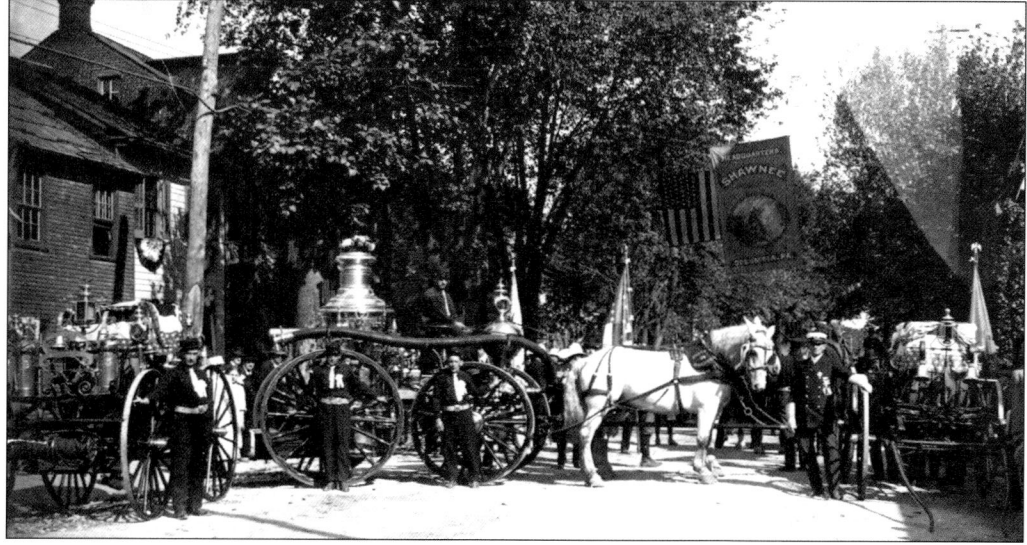

Attired in dark hats, shirts, and pants with white ties, members pose on Union Street at their headquarters, as named in the one overhead flag, by three of their pieces of equipment. The centerpiece is the steam-powered pumper drawn this day by a matched pair of white horses. On the right, an officer wears a dark coat and pants and a white cap. (Courtesy Columbia Historic Preservation Society.)

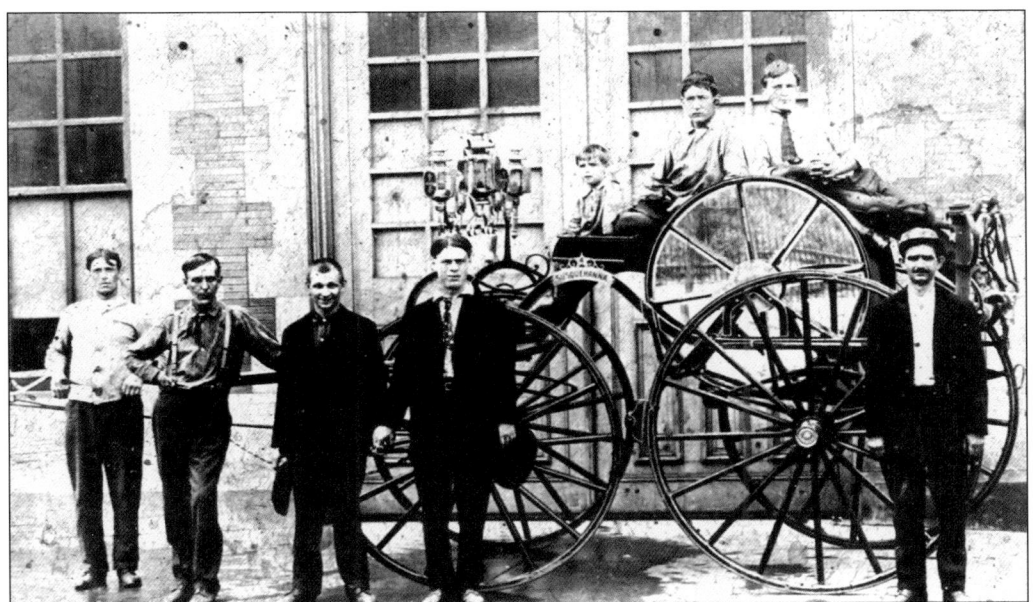

Formed in 1896, Columbia's fourth fire company's name in 1916 was the Susquehanna Steam Fire Engine and Hose Company. The Hambones, as the company was nicknamed, built its station at Manor Street near South Tenth Street. Pictured here in front of the station is a hose engine with "Susquehanna" on the curved plate beneath the seat. (Courtesy Susquehanna Fire and Rescue Company No. 4.)

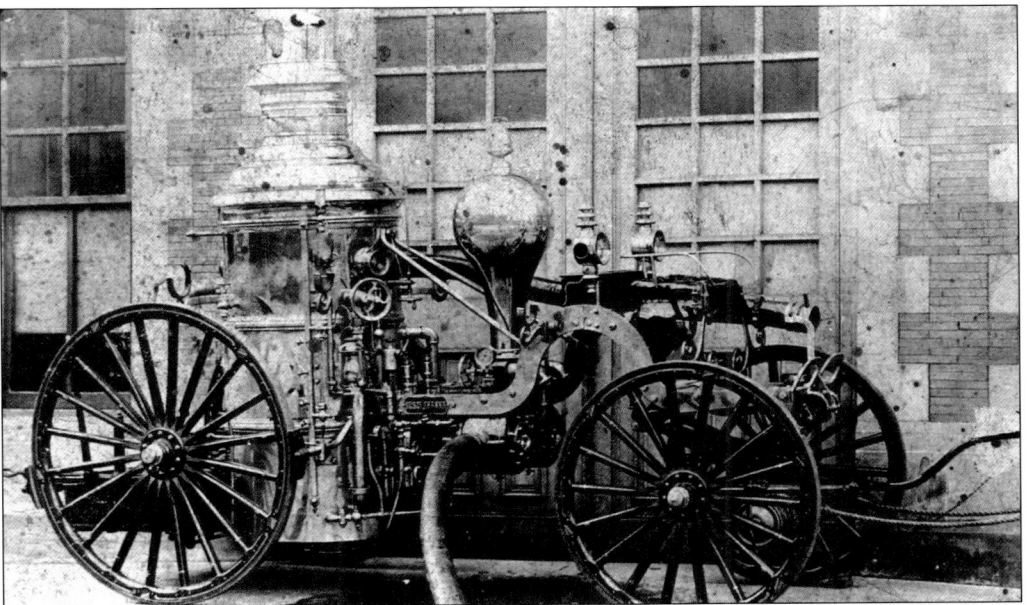

Here is Susquehanna's steam-powered pumper outside Susquehanna's station at the east end of Columbia. The horizontal plate above the hose says "Susquehanna" on it. Unlike the much larger railroad steam engines, the ones fire companies typically owned had vertical boilers that helped to keep the weight down and the vehicle maneuverable. (Courtesy Susquehanna Fire and Rescue Company No. 4.)

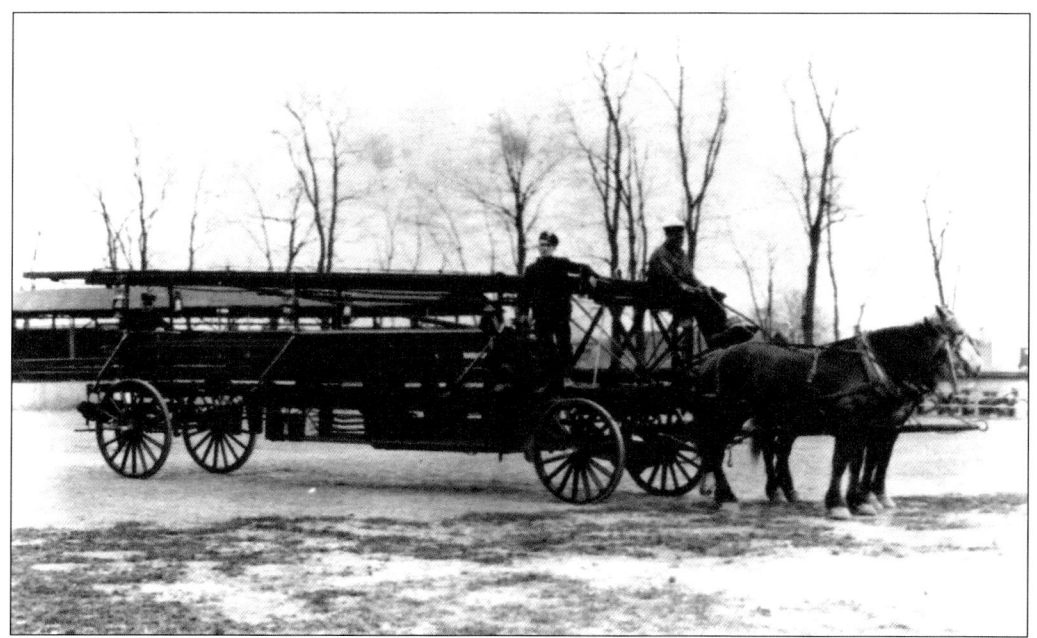

In 1902, Columbia's youngest fire company, No. 5 in sequence, had the name of Keystone Hook and Ladder Company (nicknamed Hookies). By 1916, the company had changed its name to Keystone Truck and Chemical Company, reflecting its change to motor-powered vehicle and specialization in fighting certain fire types with chemicals. Pictured is Keystone's ladder wagon, drawn by a pair of horses. (Courtesy Columbia Historic Preservation Society.)

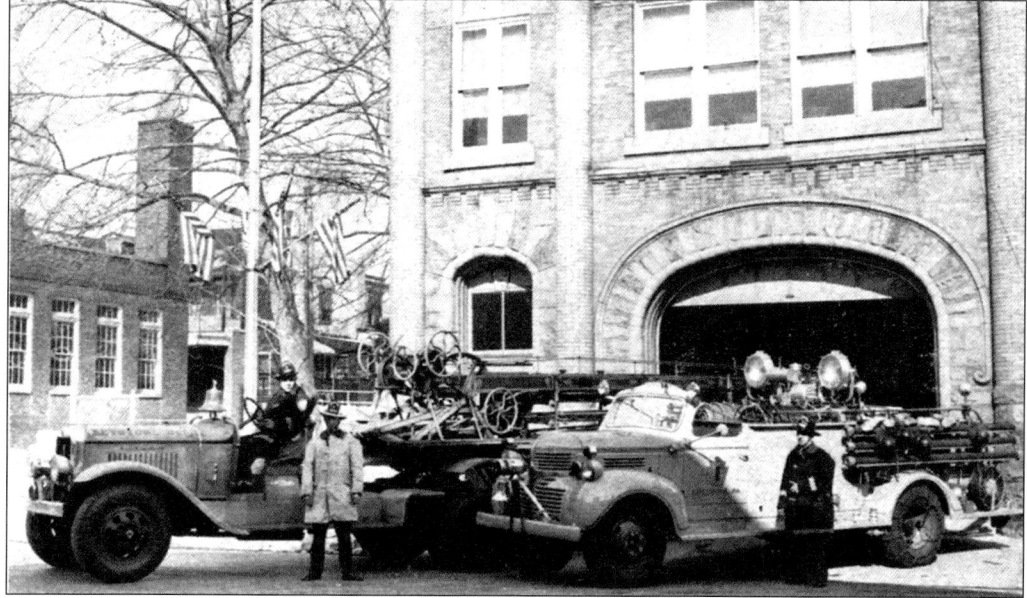

In 1965, Keystone posed its units in front of its station at North Fourth Street. On the left is its ladder truck. On the right is a unit that the Owen-Roanoke company built in Virginia as a "first-due" eight-person self-contained unit with a 400-gallon water tank and a 60-gallon-per-minute, 800-pounds-per-square-inch pump. (Courtesy Susquehanna Fire and Rescue Company No. 4.)

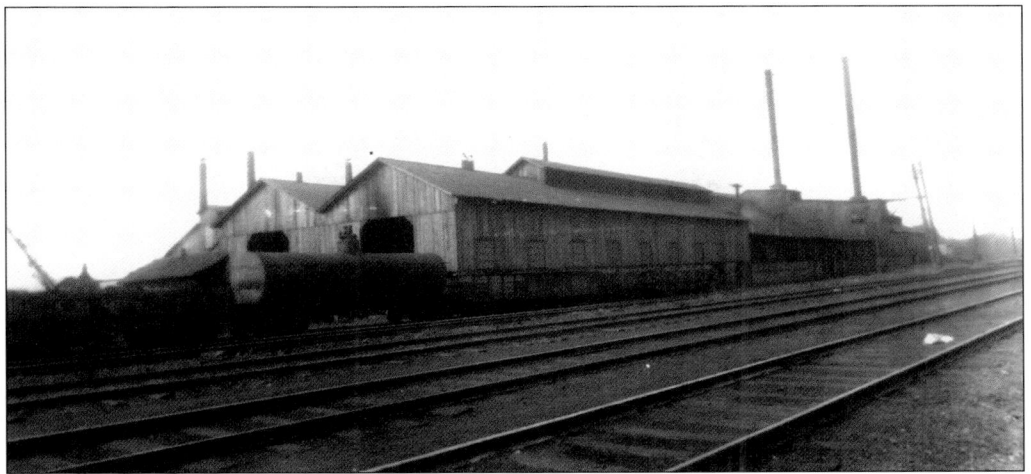

The Susquehanna Iron Company, commonly known as the Rolling Mill, had its operation at South Front and Mill Streets. To the west was the Susquehanna River and to the east, in the foreground, was the Pennsylvania Railroad. Established in 1865, the complex had 12 puddling and 3 heating furnaces and three train rolls. The 100 to 150 workers could produce 10,000 tons of iron bars per year. (Courtesy Columbia Historic Preservation Society.)

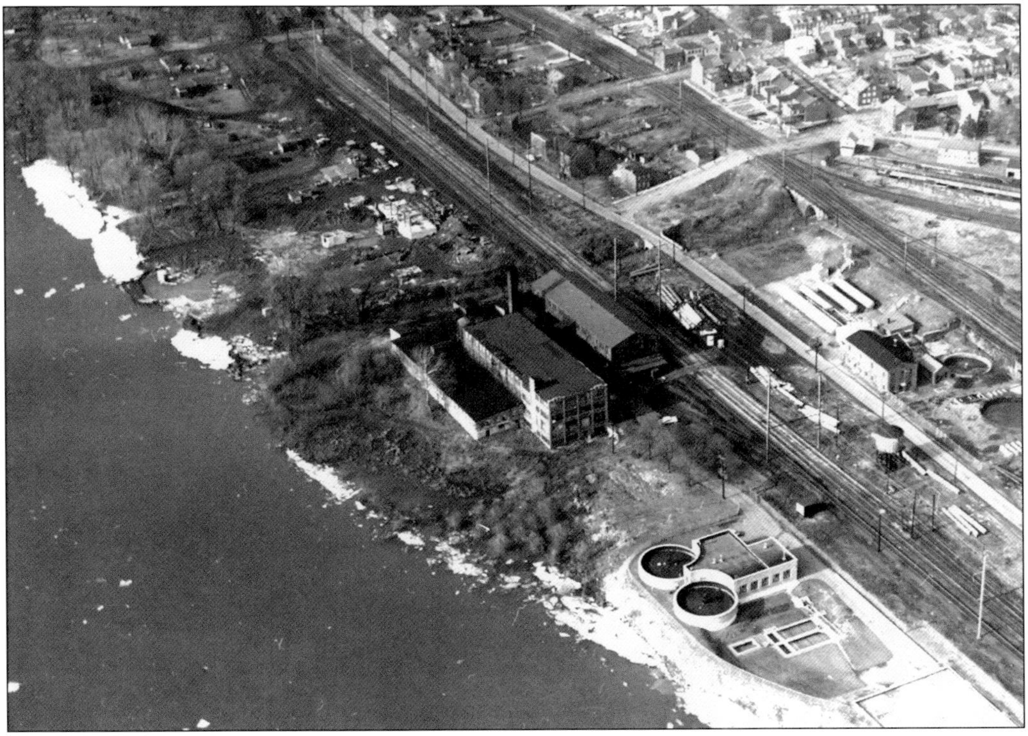

By the time a Scottish family, the Clelands, decided to build the Lace Mill, land along the river was scare. However, Shawnee Furnace had been disposing its solid waste into the river, which created an artificial parcel, a perfect site for the mill. The mill and subsequent expansions resulted in the complex in the center. Columbia's sewer plant with the two circular treatment tanks is downstream. (Courtesy Columbia Historic Preservation Society.)

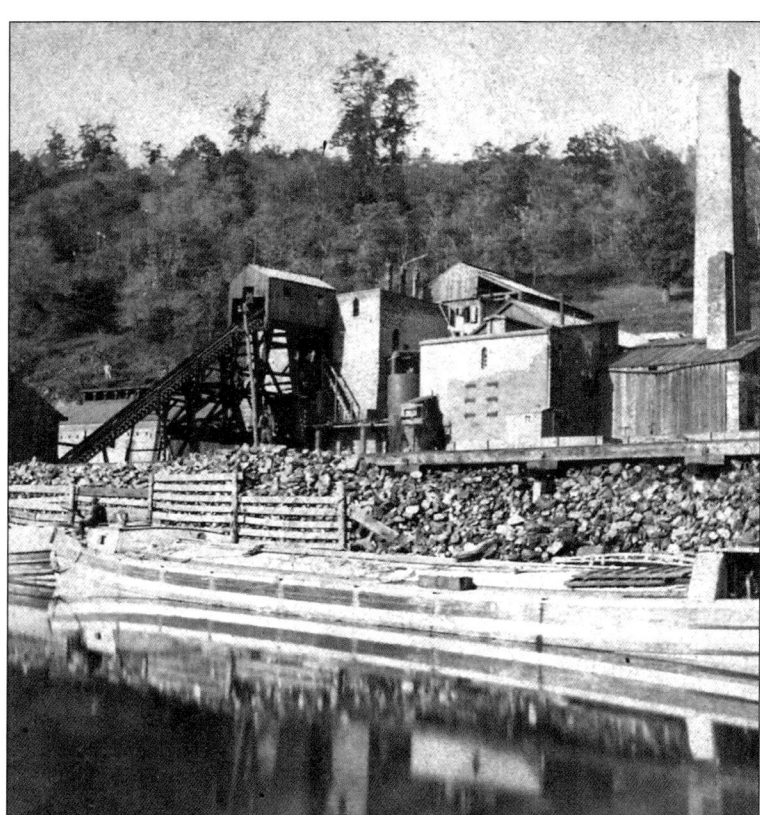

St. Charles Furnace was at the north end of Columbia by the Pennsylvania Canal and the PRR. The furnace was one of several in the area that took advantage of nearby iron ore and the canal and railroad that could bring anthracite coal in and ship iron and its products out. Reflected in the canal is a boat tied up by the furnace. (Courtesy Columbia Historic Preservation Society.)

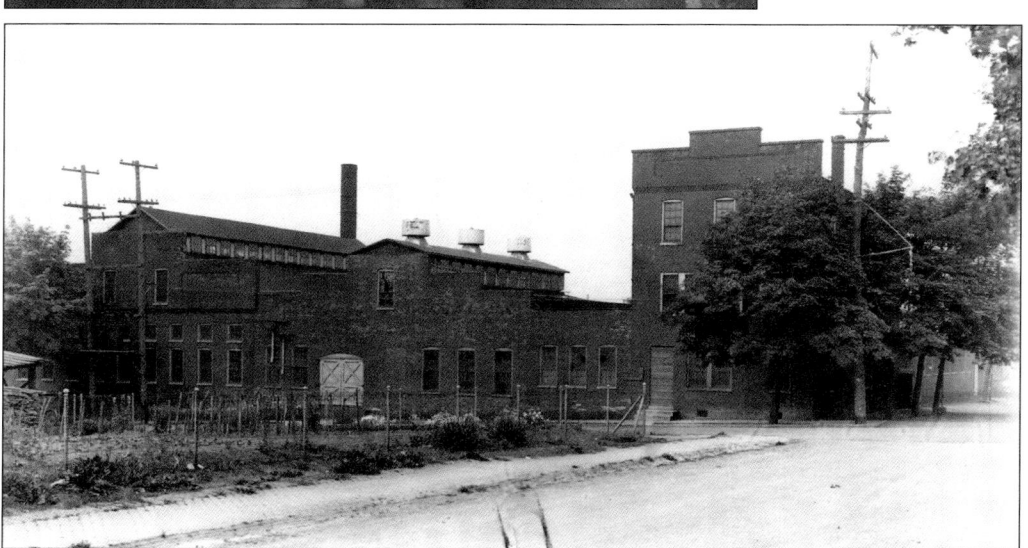

The Columbia Malleable Castings Corporation, through the first three decades of the 20th century, operated under several names—for example, Columbia Grey Iron Company and Columbia Malleable Iron and Steel Company—on the west side of the intersection of Second and Linden Streets. Inside this complex was the location for the cover photograph for this book. (Courtesy Columbia Historic Preservation Society.)

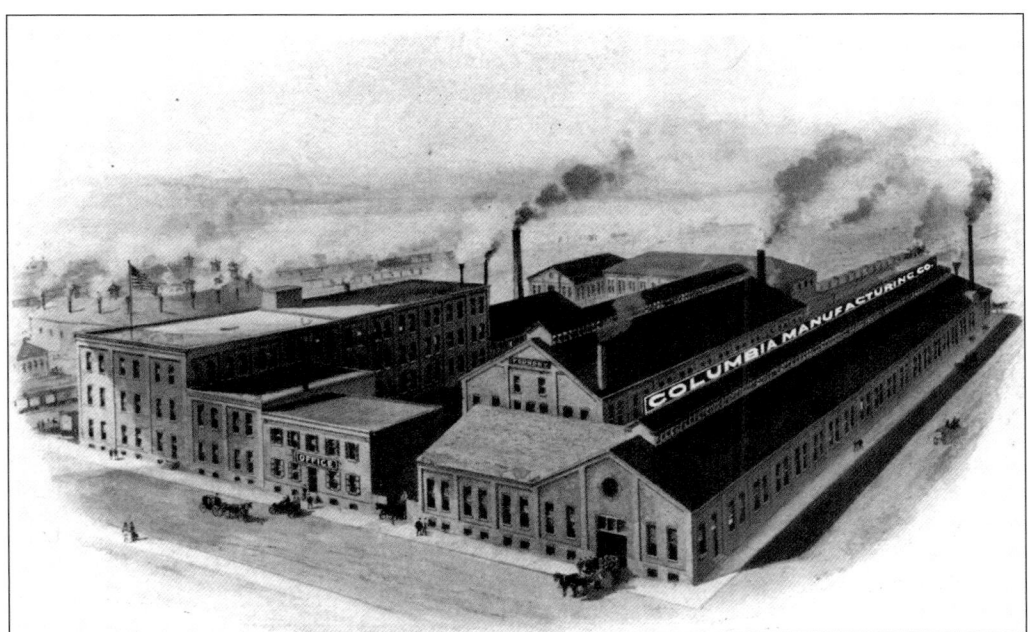

The Columbia Manufacturing Company was located at the northwest corner of North Second and Bridge Streets. The company produced "a very extensive line of high-grade laundry machines and other supplies." To make this equipment, the company had a pattern shop and storage, foundry, machine shop, paint shop, and office within its complex. (Author's collection.)

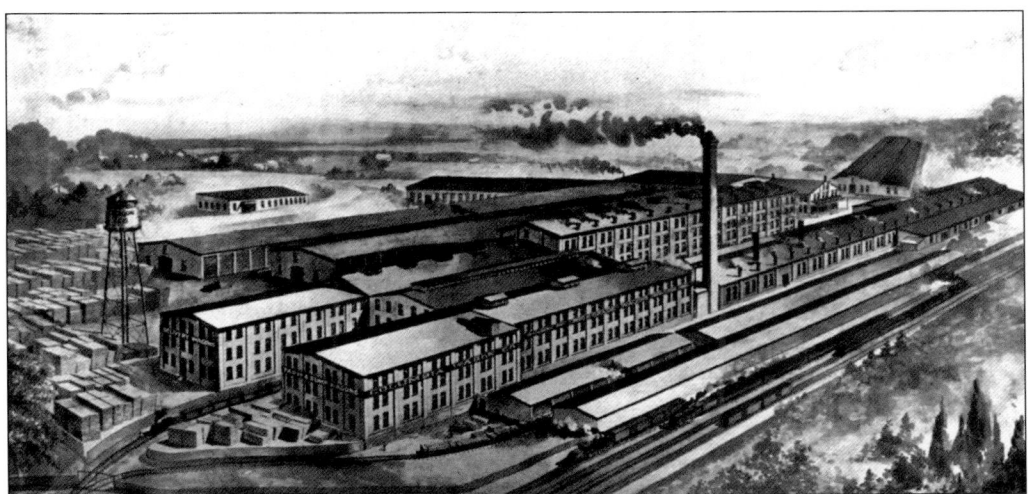

Columbia Wagon Company built a complex on Plane Street by PRR's Columbia Branch. The company built wagons, buggies, and sleighs. Later Columbia Body Company tried building customized truck bodies in the facility. Then after the Depression, the American Tobacco Company used the complex for storage. Now it is the Columbia Wagon Werks Apartments. (Author's collection.)

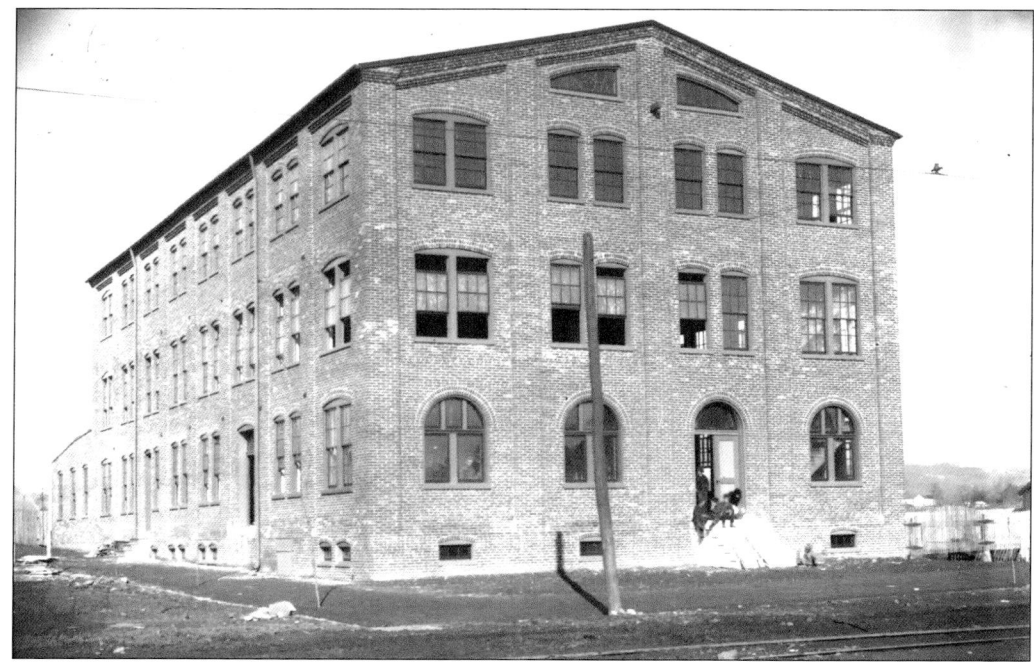

By 1899, three companies under the umbrella name of Triumph had relocated at a new building at Twelfth and Manor Streets from a previous site at Fourth and Union Streets. Moving in were the Triumph Shirt Company, Triumph Embroidery Company, and Triumph Steam Laundry. Out in front in the center of muddy Manor Street were the trolley tracks. (Courtesy Columbia Historic Preservation Society.)

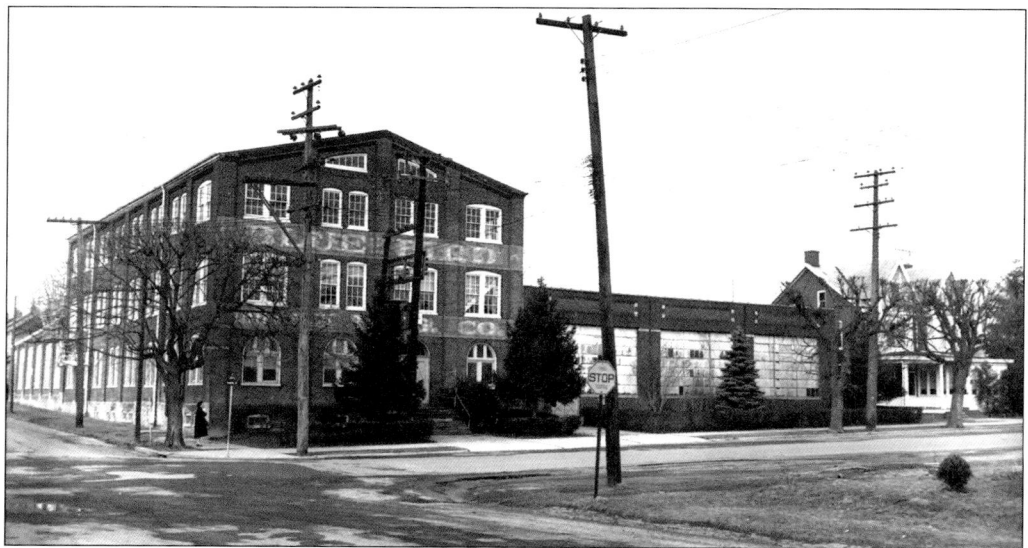

By 1940, the Blue Bird Silk Manufacturing Company had set up in the building on the northeast corner of Twelfth and Manor Streets. A new one-story extension to the east joined the original building. The Conestoga Traction Company had abandoned service to Columbia in 1938, and it pulled up its tracks including those along Manor. (Courtesy Columbia Historic Preservation Society.)

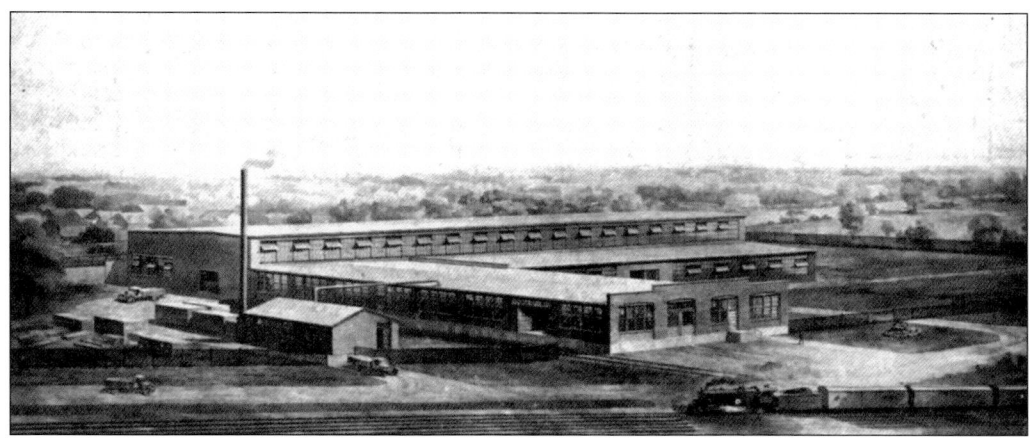

After getting its start on Bridge Street near Second Street and outgrowing the plant, the O.K. Clutch and Machinery Company built a larger facility by 1926 at Florence and Mill Streets. There the company had access to not only roads but also to a spur of the Reading Railway that allowed shipment of its products nationwide. (Author's collection.)

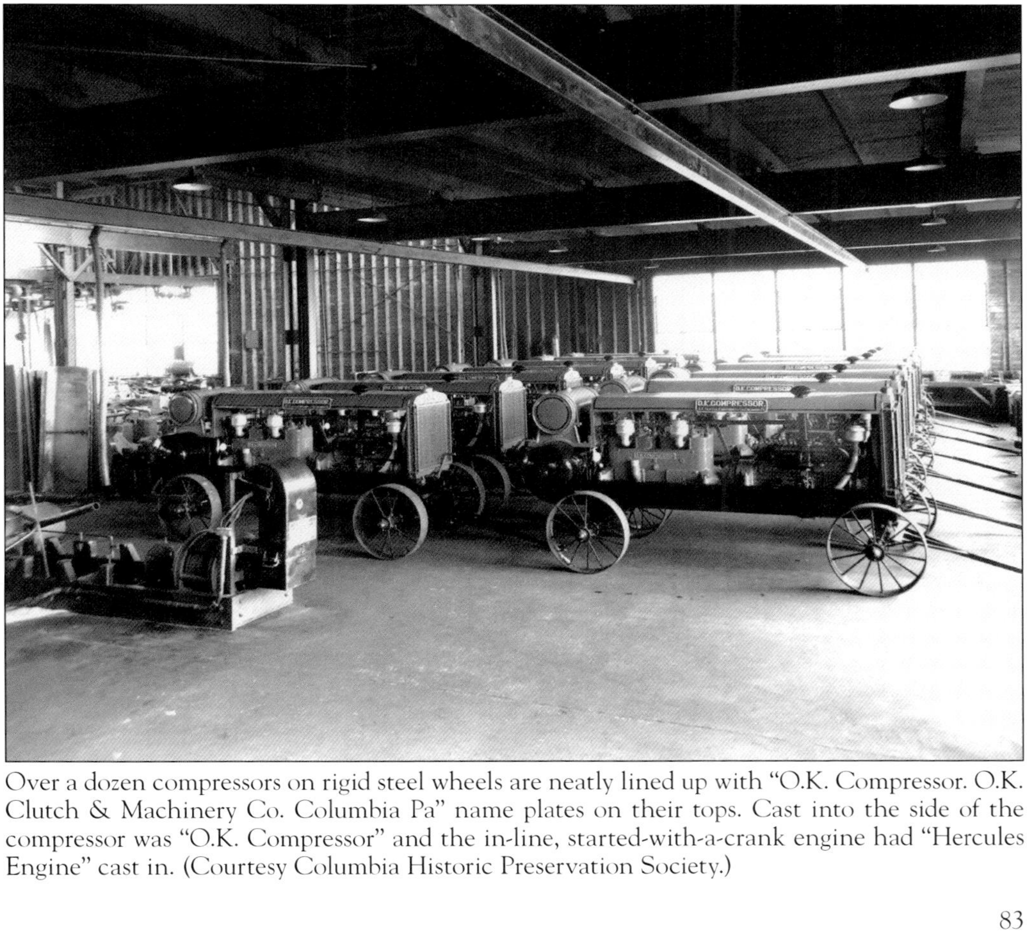

Over a dozen compressors on rigid steel wheels are neatly lined up with "O.K. Compressor. O.K. Clutch & Machinery Co. Columbia Pa" name plates on their tops. Cast into the side of the compressor was "O.K. Compressor" and the in-line, started-with-a-crank engine had "Hercules Engine" cast in. (Courtesy Columbia Historic Preservation Society.)

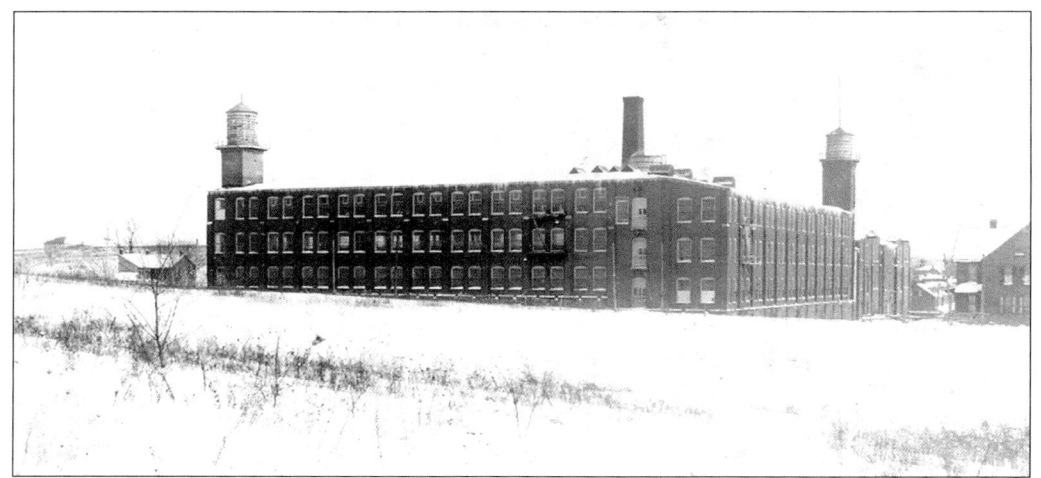

Dwight Ashley and Peter Bailey formed a silk mill company in Patterson, New Jersey, in 1873. In the later 1890s, they built, opened, and operated a silk mill in Columbia at North Third and Cedar Streets. Here is the three-story building after a snowstorm that left icicles hanging from the eves. (Courtesy Columbia Historic Preservation Society.)

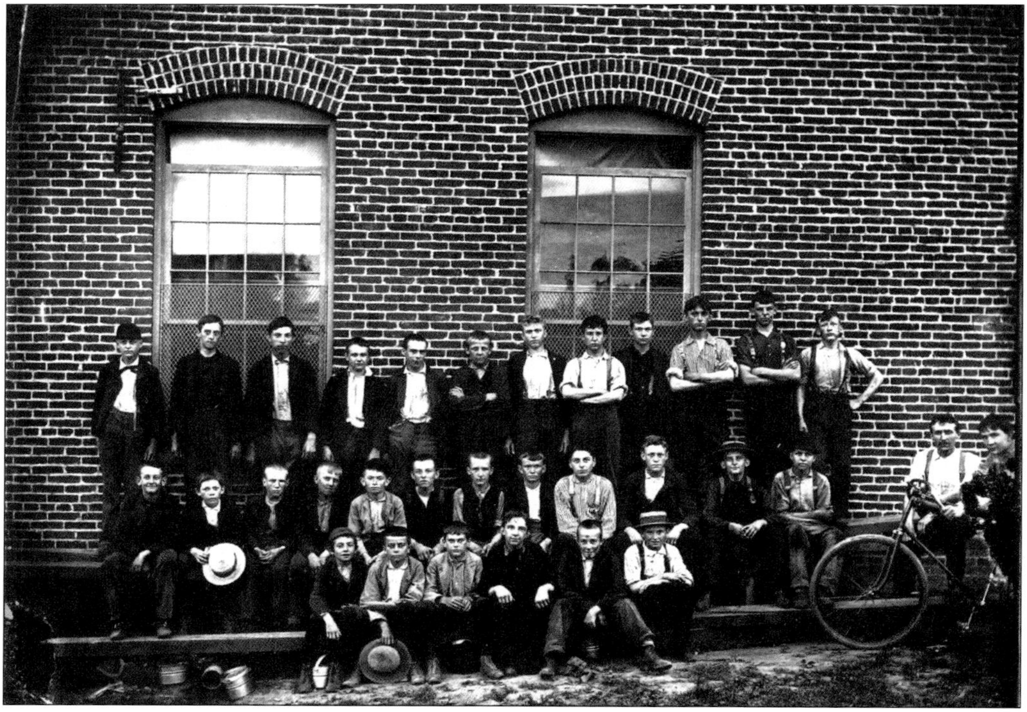

The Ashley and Bailey silk mill, as was typical of that kind of factory, was labor intensive, employing many men, women, and young people before the country adopted stricter labor laws. In 1894, some mill workers lined three deep along a south facing outside wall for a photograph. The large windows assured good natural light in the mill. (Courtesy Columbia Historic Preservation Society.)

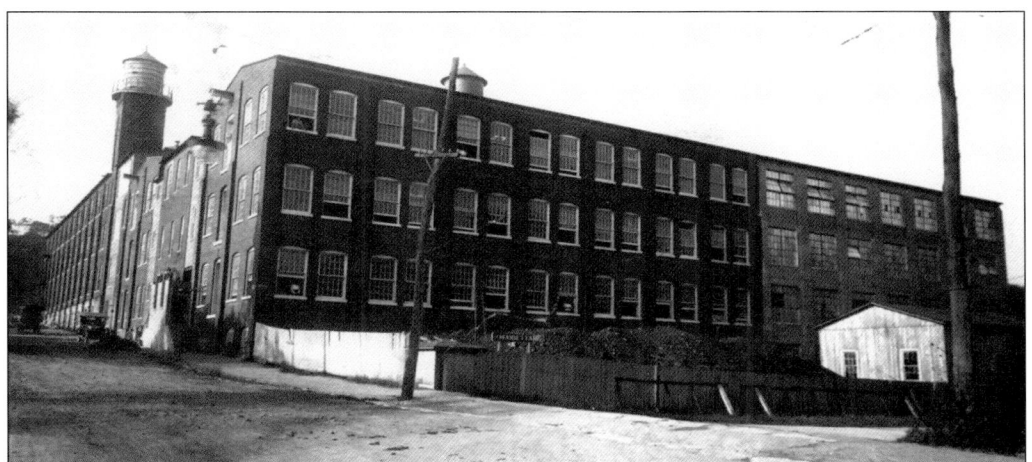

By 1916, the Schwarzenbach-Huber Company, a Swiss company, had taken over the Ashley and Bailey plant in Columbia. By that time, Schwarzenbach-Huber had plants in New Jersey, Pennsylvania, and Virginia and was the largest silk operation in the world. The company made major expansions to the Columbia mill, such as the one that went up where the dirt pile is at North Third and Linden Streets. (Courtesy Columbia Historic Preservation Society.)

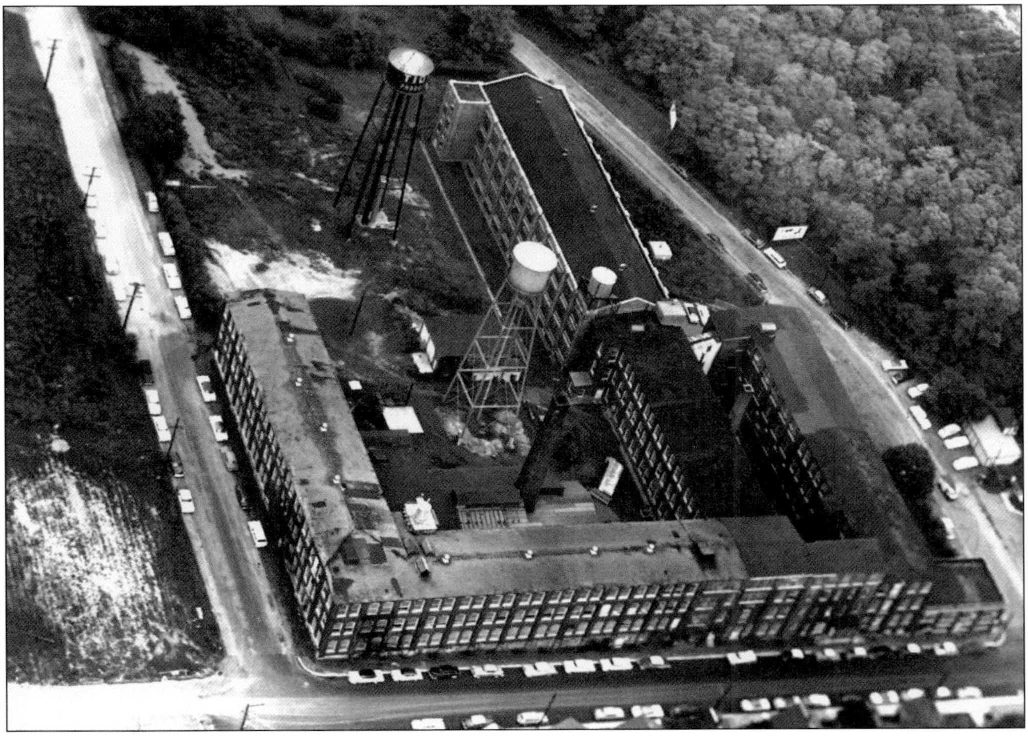

During the Depression, other companies all involved somehow with cloth began operating in the building complex, including the Patrician Piece Dye Works, Columbia Sports Wear Mills, Little Prince, and Tidy Products. The last company's name is on one of the water towers in this aerial view, which clearly shows the various building additions. (Courtesy Columbia Historic Preservation Society.)

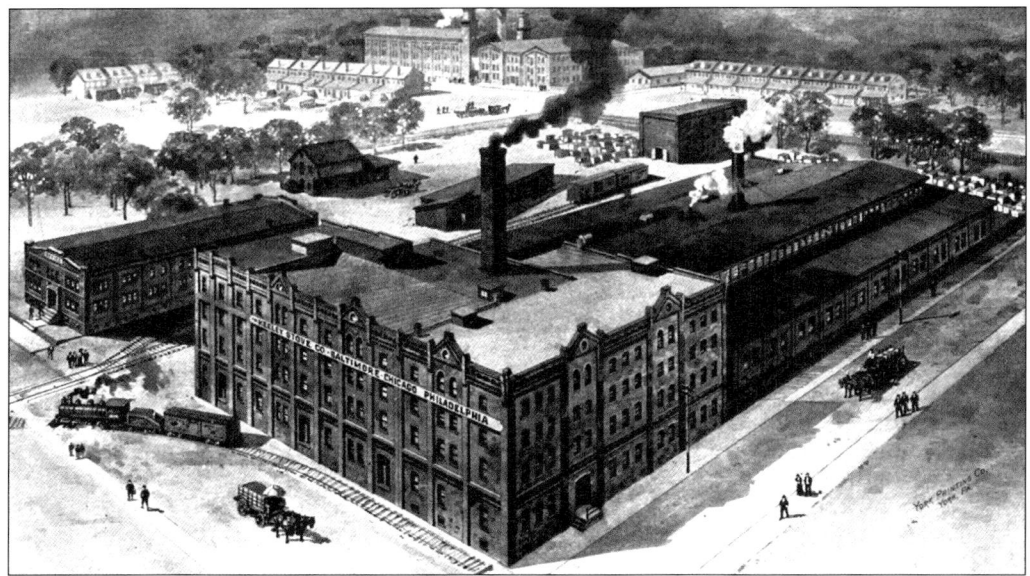

Keeley Stove Company occupied an entire square block between North Second and Third Streets and Maple and Linden Streets. The two-story building on the left along Second Street is the office, while the large building is the foundry and assembly area. In the background is the Ashley and Bailey silk mill. (Author's collection.)

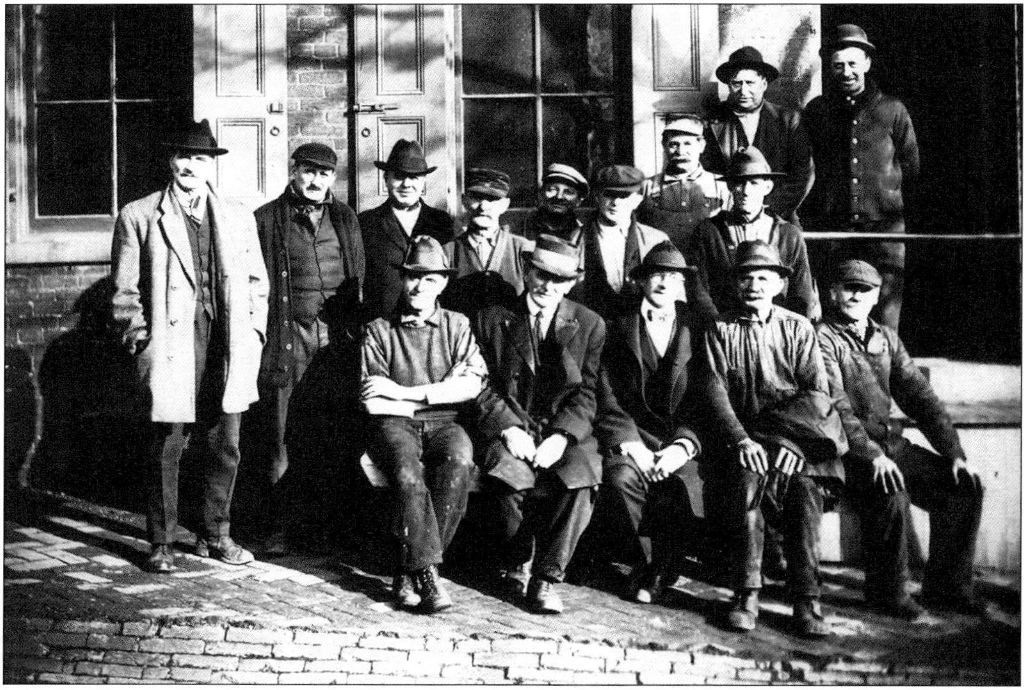

A few of the many Keeley supervisors and workers take a break to pose for their photograph. A 1926 advertisement said, "We make combination coal and wood stoves and heater, cellar furnace, combination coal and gas ranges and house heaters—in fact anything in the cooking and heating lines. Enameled stoves a specialty." (Courtesy Columbia Historic Preservation Society.)

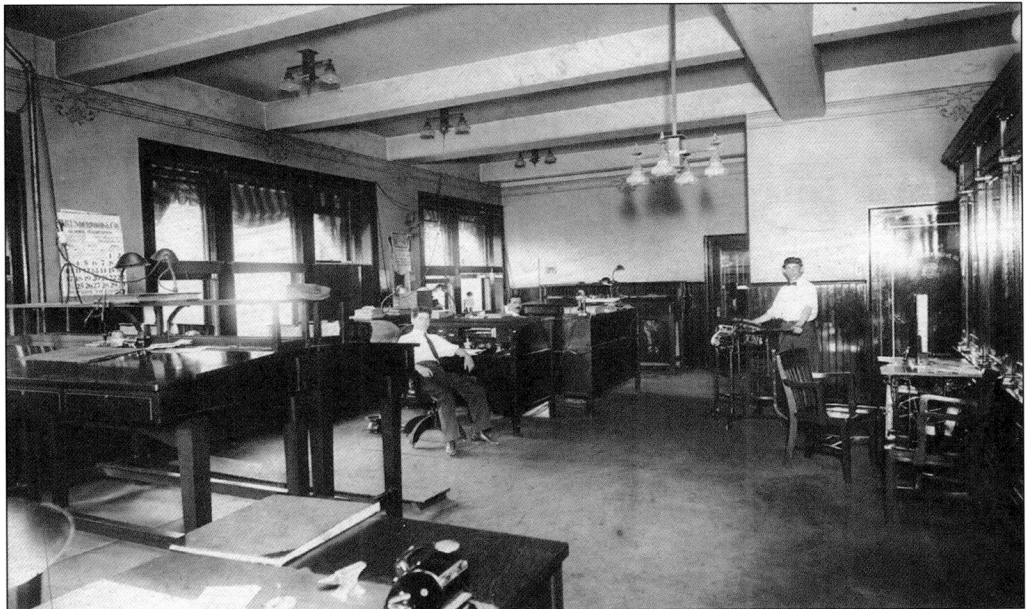

Three workers in the Keeley Stove Company pause for a bit and look toward the camera so that the photographer can capture their image. The wall calendar on the left says May 1914. Awnings outside the windows are in the retracted position, but the staff could easily unfurl them to keep out the direct sunlight. (Courtesy Columbia Historic Preservation Society.)

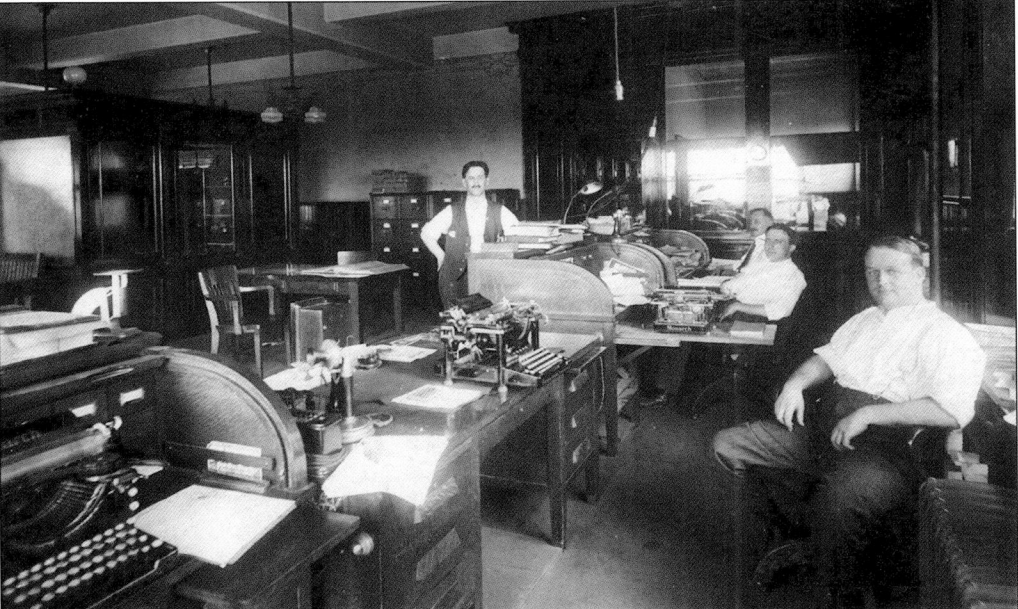

These four Keeley Stove office workers had an area filled with the most modern conveniences and equipment: electric lights, mail scale, telephones, typewriters, file cabinets, and steam heat. These workers may have dealt with sales colleagues across the United States in Baltimore, Chicago, and Philadelphia. Keeley would ship its Columbian line of stoves across the country. (Courtesy Columbia Historic Preservation Society.)

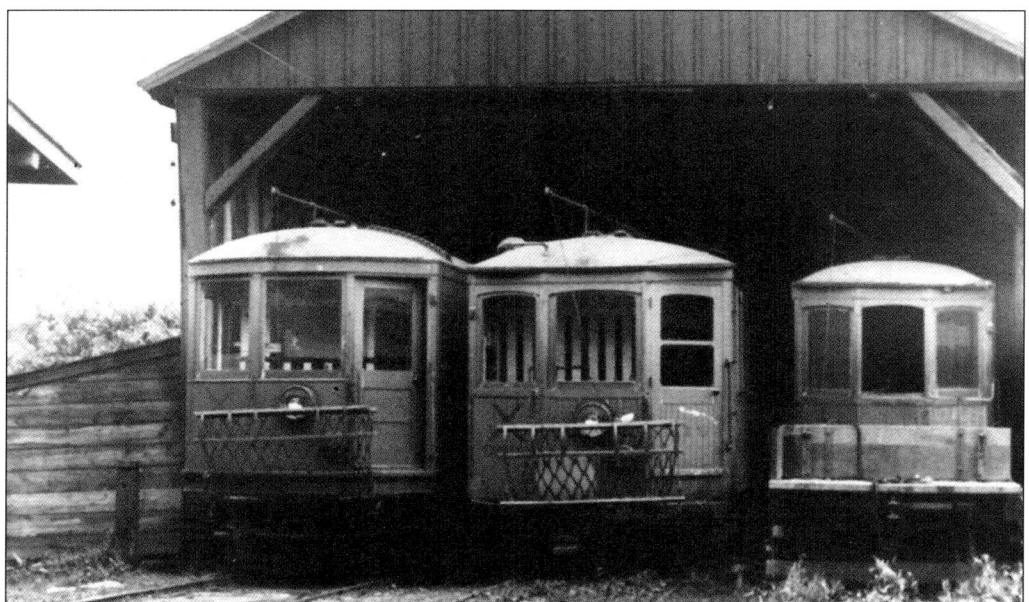

The Conestoga Traction Company had a small three-stall carbarn on Commerce Street between Walnut and Bridge Streets. Streetcars reached the carbarn by a spur off the line on Walnut Street. Inside are two passenger streetcars and, on the right, a piece of smaller work equipment. The passenger cars have their protective cow catchers fastened up. (Courtesy Columbia Historic Preservation Society.)

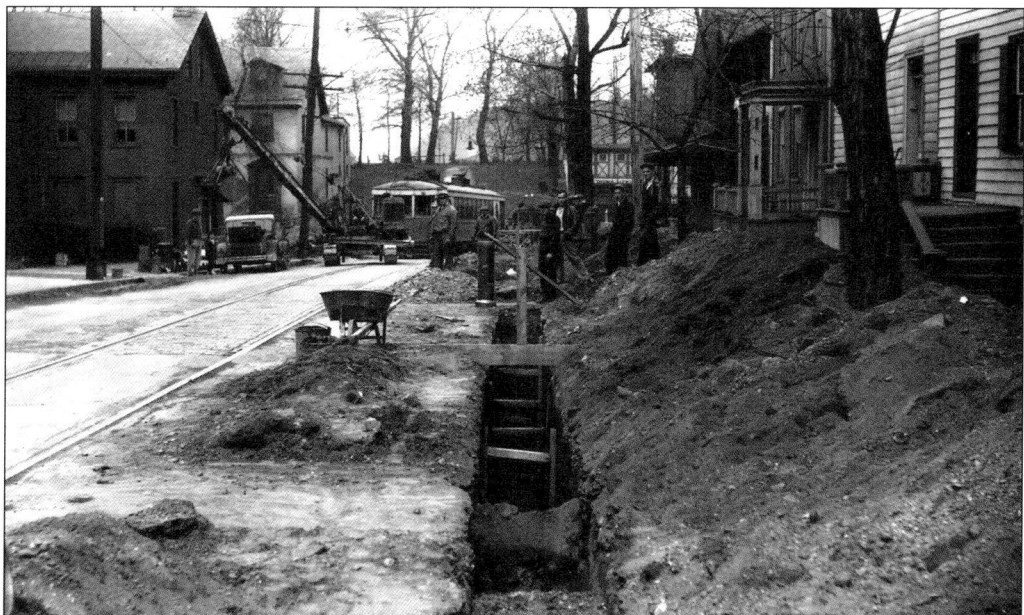

The Lancaster-bound Conestoga Traction Company trolley in 1930 swings off of Walnut Street onto North Second Street and encounters a self-propelled crane involved in installing sewer line along the east side of the street. The trolley would only run to Columbia for another eight years. (Courtesy Cleon G. Berntheizel.)

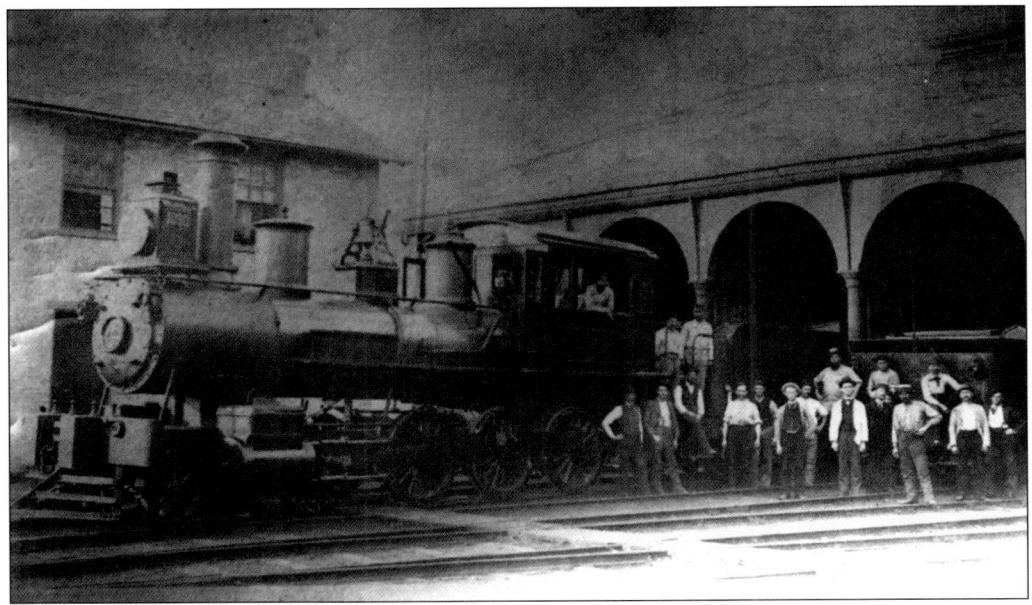

In 1863, in the midst of the Civil War, workers completed the Reading and Columbia Railroad (R&C) linking the two namesake places. The R&C built this four-stall engine house in Columbia just east of South Fourth Street between Manor Street and Shawnee Run. The tracks led to a turntable out of sight to the left. (Courtesy Lancaster County Historical Society.)

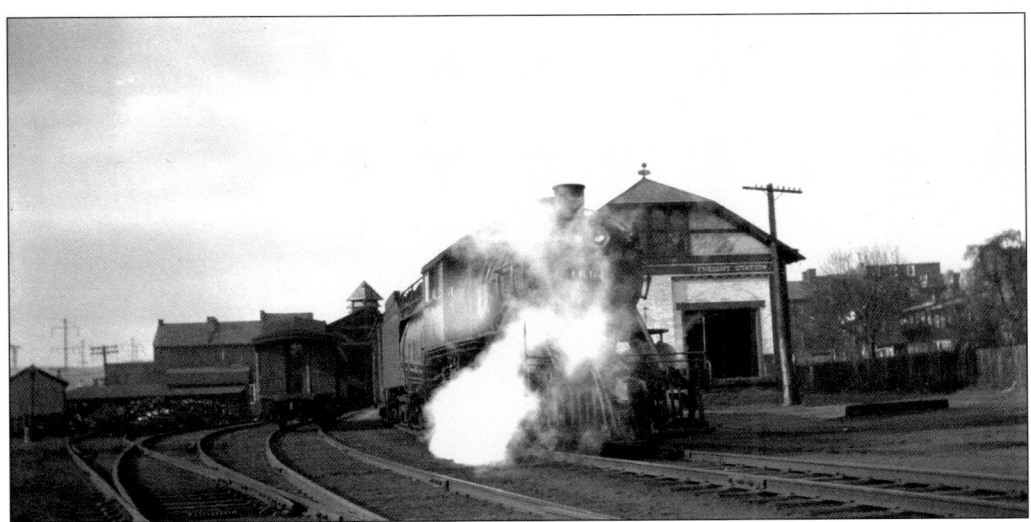

R&C No. 601, a camelback-style locomotive, is wrapped in a cloud of condensing steam. A camelback had its cab over the boiler to accommodate a Wooten firebox, which burned a mixture of bituminous and anthracite coals. The cupola to the rear belongs to the train shed of the passenger station designed by famous Philadelphia architect Frank Furness. The freight station is to the right. (Author's collection.)

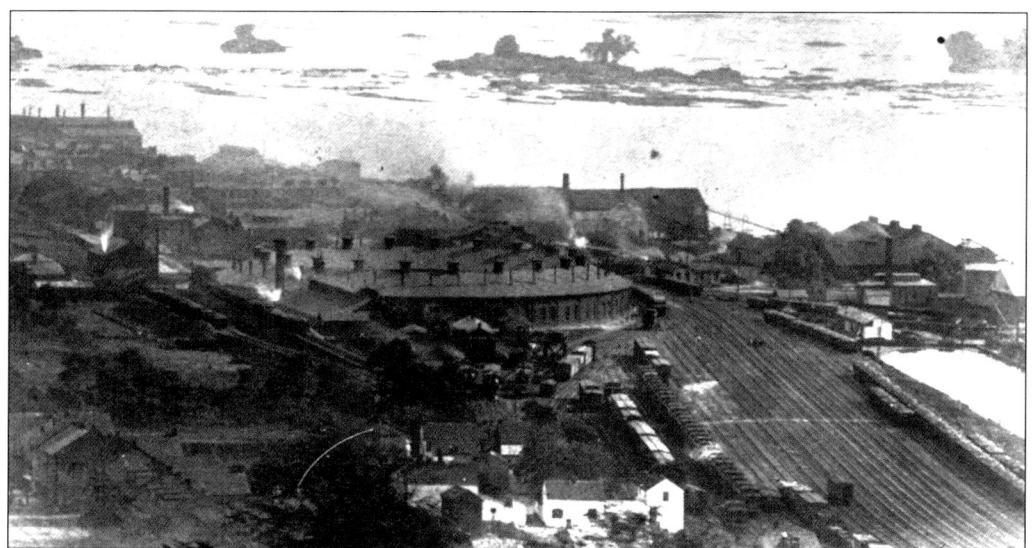

In 1874, the PRR opened a 40-stall 360-degree roundhouse at Front and Bridge Streets with a turntable in its center. The roundhouse is in the center of this view, dated 1895, with the yard in the right foreground. To the right is the canal basin and filling up the background is the Susquehanna River and its many islands. (Author's collection.)

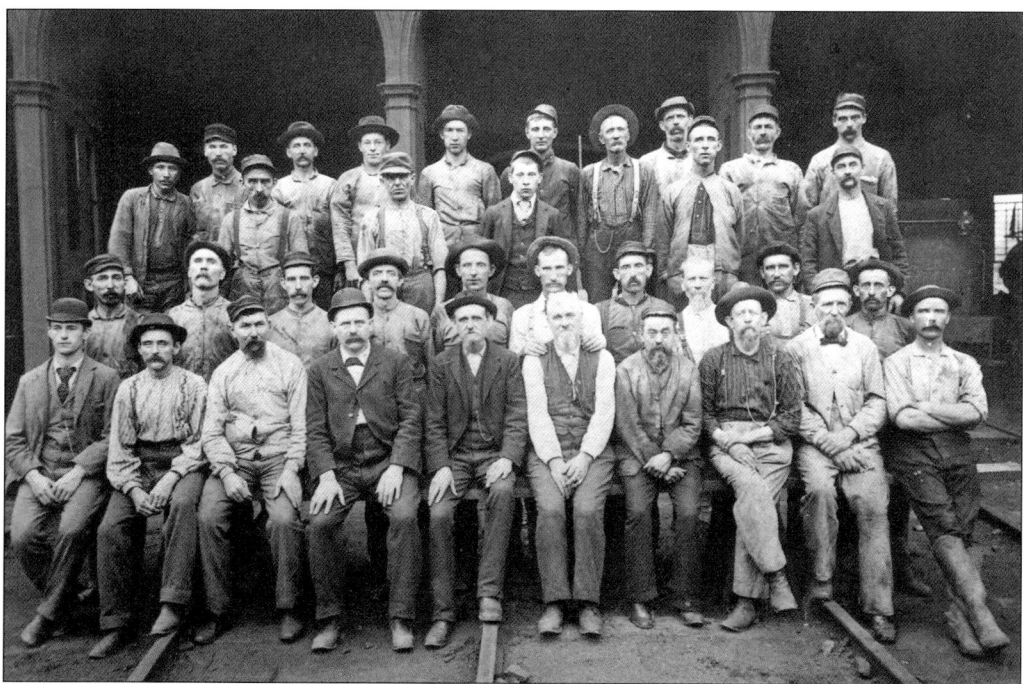

In 1874, the PRR opened a new roundhouse in Columbia at Front and Bridge Streets at the east end of the PRR's West Yard. The new structure was a complete circle totally encompassing a turntable. PRR workers and supervisors took a break to arrange themselves in front of several stalls. (Courtesy Columbia Historic Preservation Society.)

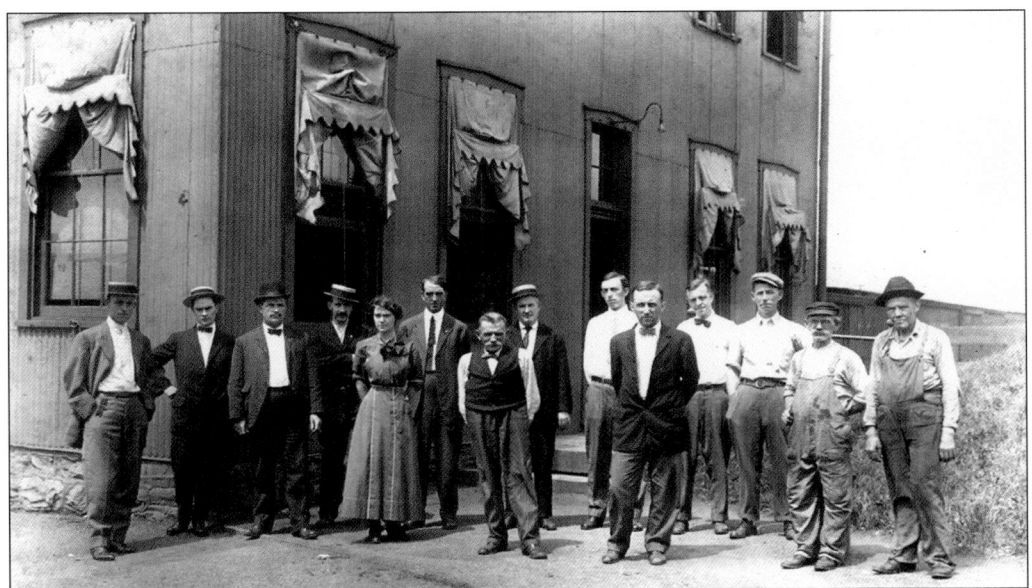

Located on North Second Street at the foot of Poplar Street was the PRR's large freight station. There workers could load and unload local freight and transfer freight between cars. Clerks could bill local customers and do all the paperwork needed to handle freight to or from any destination. In 1902, the freight station workers and clerks pose outside the freight station. (Courtesy Columbia Historic Preservation Society.)

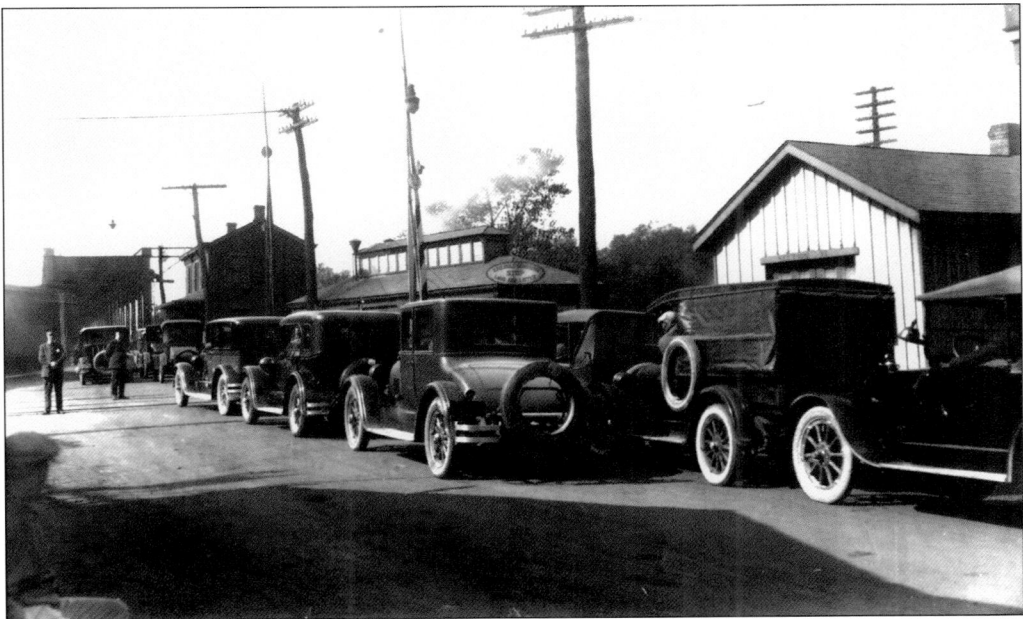

When the PRR designed its replacement bridge, it meant it to be double deck with the railroad below and a roadway on top. The PRR could never acquire land on the Wrightsville side to build an approach and so never build the roadway. By the 1920s, road traffic had grown so much that major traffic jams such as the one here at Columbia regularly occurred whenever a train crossed. (Courtesy Lancaster County Historical Society.)

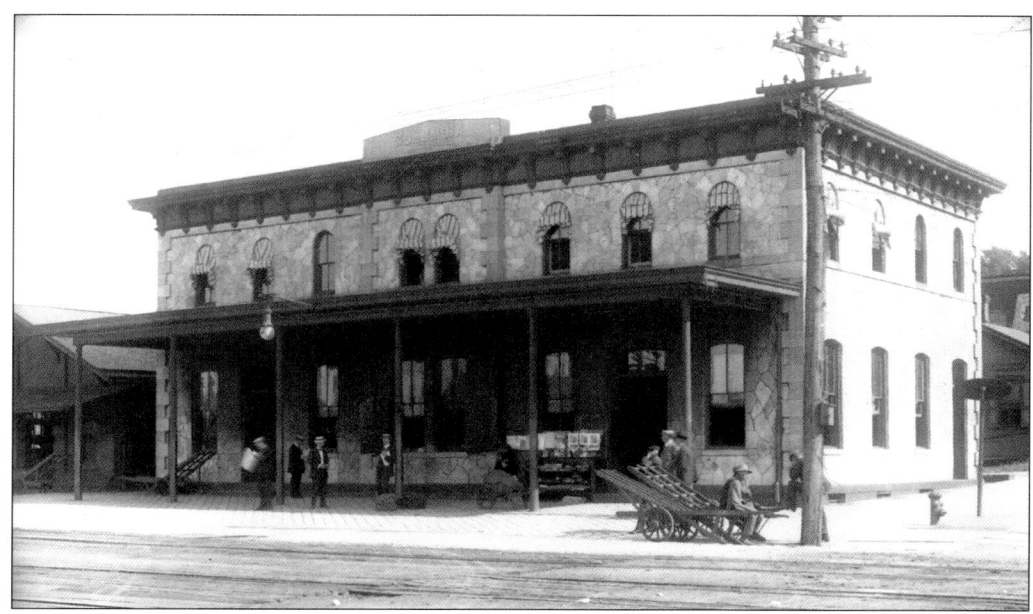

The PRR station faced North Front Street and Walnut Street was to the south. Here people await a passenger train and could buy a paper or magazine from the stand outside. Several carts, including at least two from Adams Express, are ready to handle any arriving baggage or express packages. To the left is the express building. On the second floor the railroad had offices. (Courtesy Columbia Historic Preservation Society.)

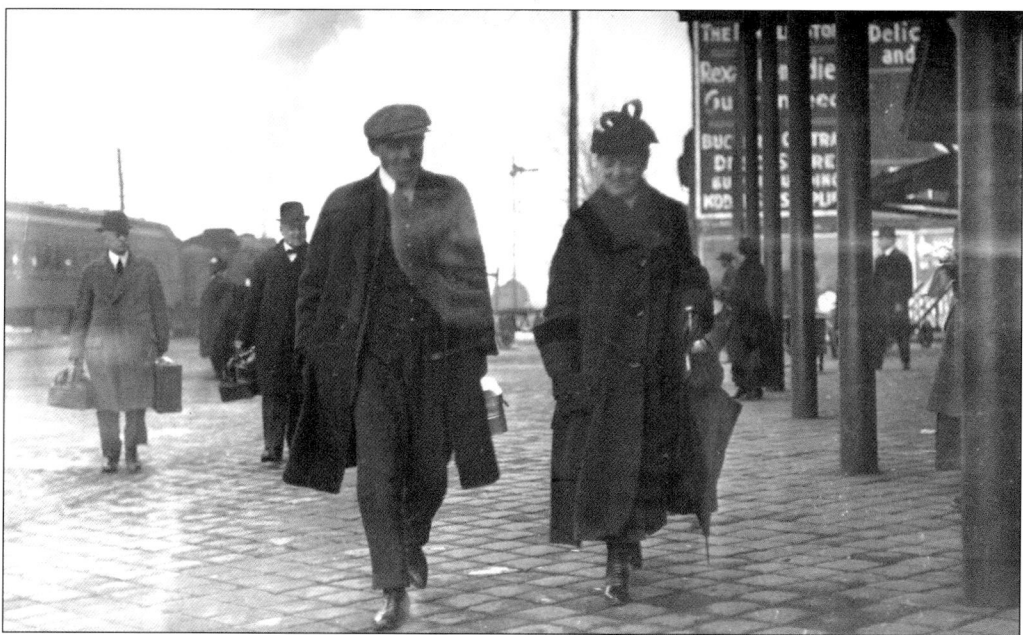

Passengers detrain from a westbound train at Columbia's PRR station on a dreary, chilly day and walk toward Walnut Street. There is a faint image of a child's face on the photograph. It is unknown if it is because of a double exposure or if it is a reflection in a waiting car's window along Walnut Street. (Courtesy Columbia Historic Preservation Society.)

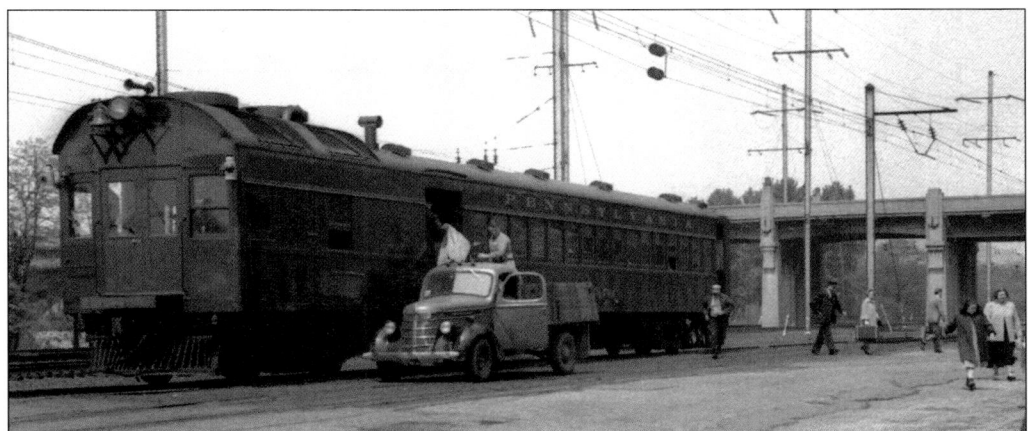

PRR No. 4662 has arrived at Columbia station. Passengers have disembarked and scatter on their various ways. The conductor heads to the station and workers transfer sacks between a truck and the train. This Lancaster–York shuttle ran until 1954, when the railroad replaced it with a bus. (Author's collection.)

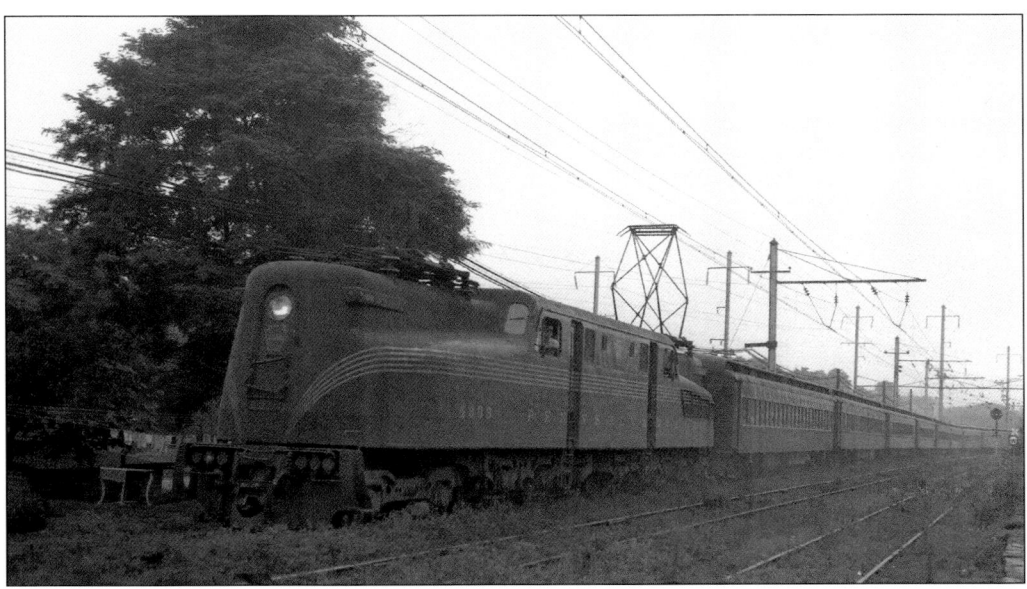

For many years, the local Independent Grocers Association ran special excursion trains to Atlantic City, New Jersey, for the day for its annual picnic. Known as the Grocers' Picnic trains, the PRR powered them either with electrics, which only ran to Philadelphia as the rest of the route was nonelectrified, or diesels. Here GG1 No. 4888 heads east on the Columbia branch with a seemingly endless string of coaches. (Author's collection.)

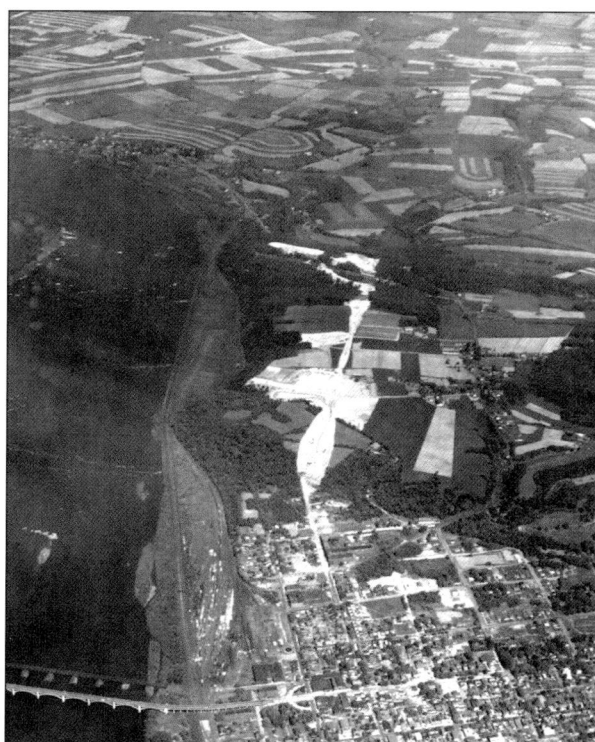

This aerial photograph gives a good view of the 1957 construction of PA 441 between Columbia and Marietta. Columbia is in the foreground with the 1930 highway and 1897 railroad bridges over the Susquehanna to the left. In the background along the river is Marietta. The new route was much more direct than the old curvy up-and-down one that is to the right of the new. (Courtesy Columbia Historic Preservation Society.)

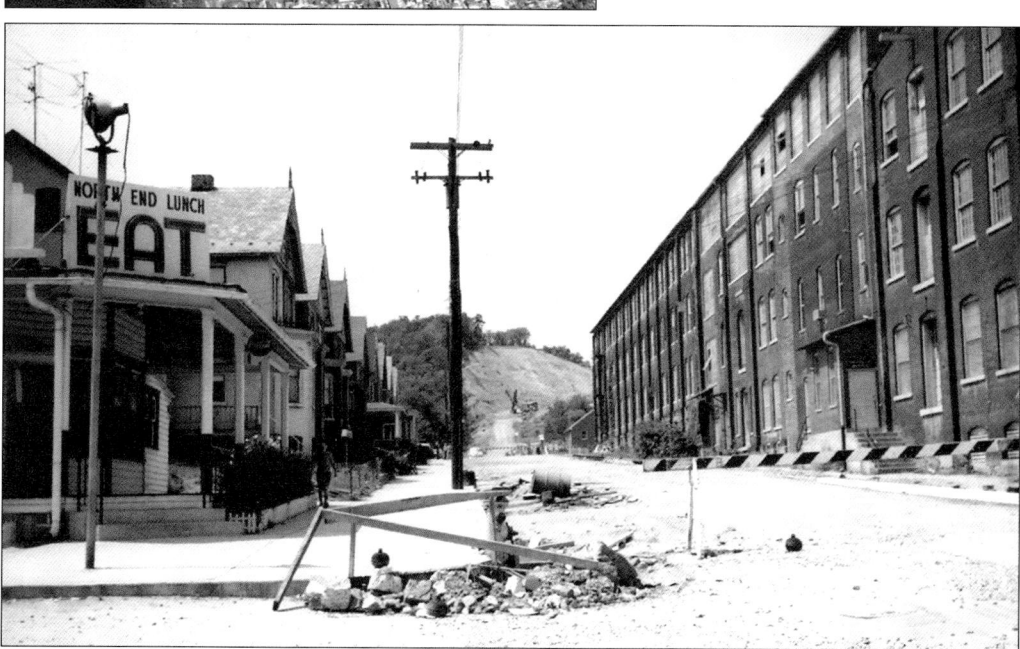

The new PA 441 started in Columbia as an extension of North Third Street. To the left is the North End Lunch and to the right is Tidy Products. Running between them is North Third Street, which will continue up into the newly dug cut in the hill in the background. (Courtesy Columbia Historic Preservation Society.)

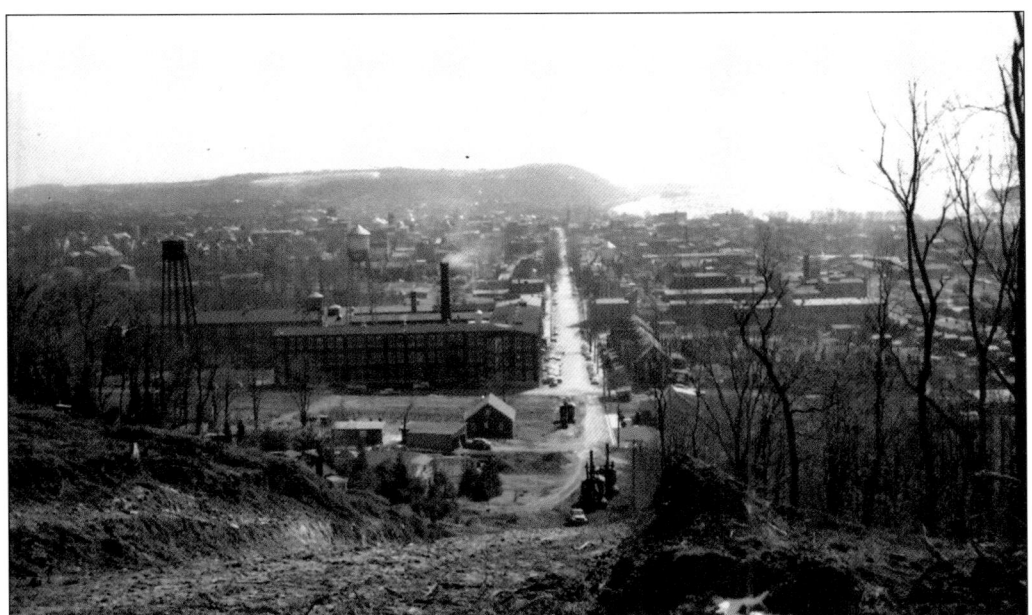

This is a 1957 view looking south from the southernmost of two cuts on the new PA 441. There is a clear view down Third Street. Tidy Products is on the left, or east side, of north Third, while the old Keeley Stove Company, now the Cared Corporation is on the right. (Courtesy Columbia Historic Preservation Society.)

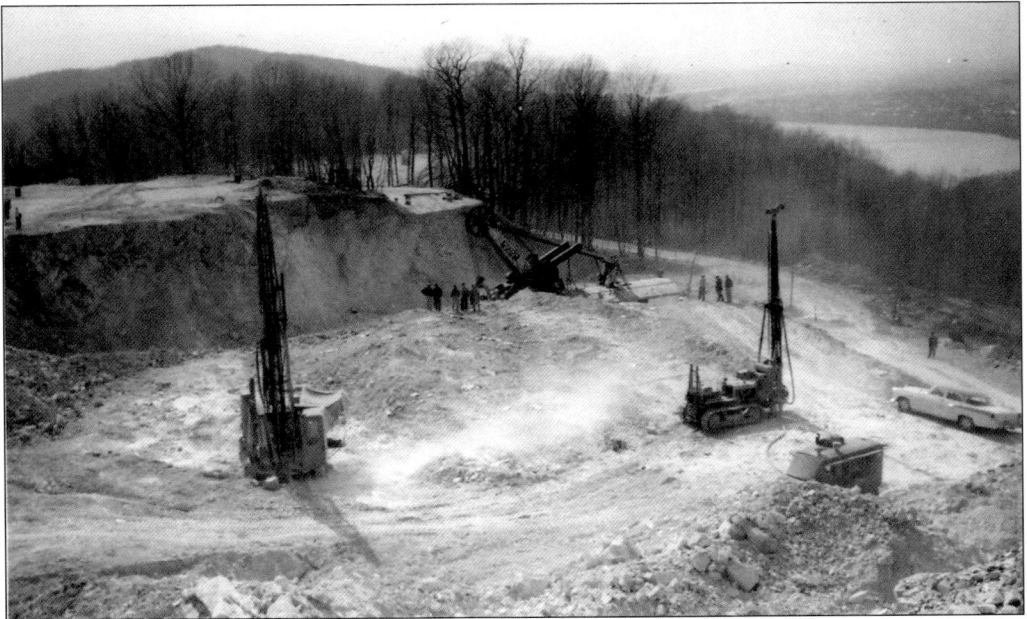

This view is from the eastern side of the southern cut looking west over the cut to the western side and the Susquehanna River beyond. Workers could use the two drills in the foreground to drill holes in the side. They could then place dynamite in the holes and set it off. The loosened rock would then slide into the cut where the shovel could load it up for removal. (Courtesy Columbia Historic Preservation Society.)

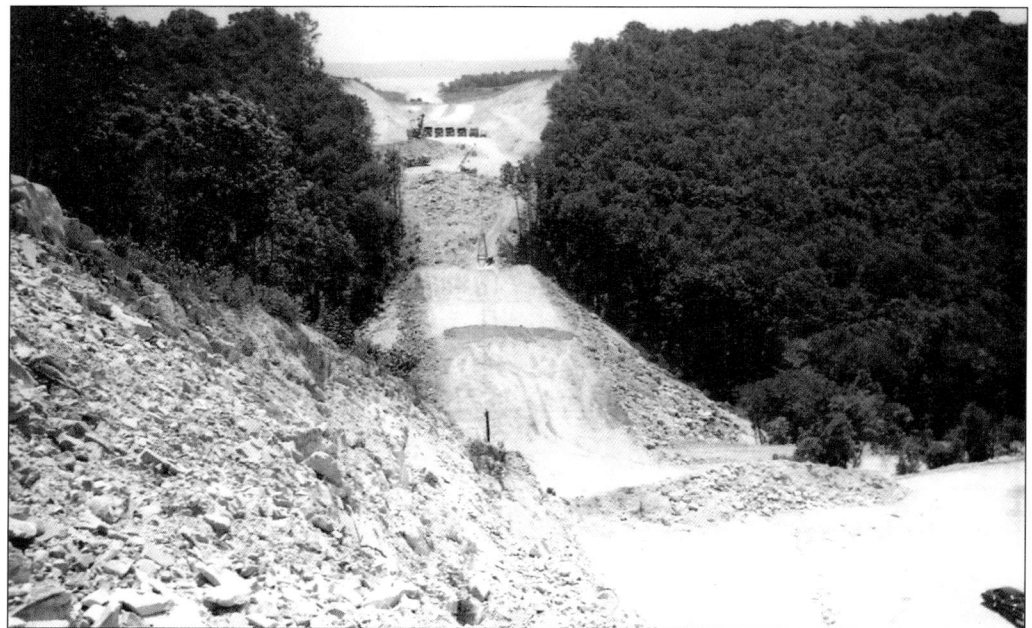

Between the southern and northern cut there was a valley with a small stream at the bottom. Workers used material from the cuts to fill the valley in. This view looks north from the southern cut, past the partially filled valley and into the northern cut, which is taking shape. (Courtesy Columbia Historic Preservation Society.)

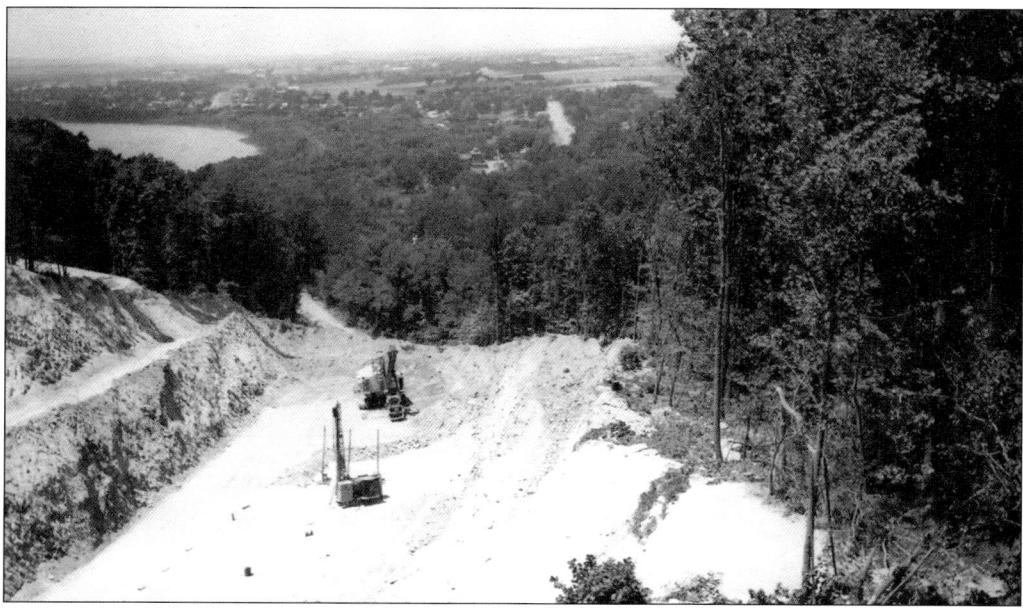

Marietta is off in the distance on the curving east bank of the Susquehanna River. A long job is ahead of the drill and shovel and their companion machines as workers use them to build the new PA 441 through the north cut through Chickies Rock. The slopes of this cut were steep and prone to frequent rock slides for years following the opening of the road. (Courtesy Columbia Historic Preservation Society.)

Two

MARIETTA

Viewing Marietta from the air or on a map gives the impression of two ice floes, each three-quarters of a mile long by one-half mile wide (at most), colliding at an angle. That is because Marietta is made from two former towns and their respective associated satellites. On the west and upstream along the Susquehanna River is Waterford bordered by Irishtown on the west and a developed farm to the north. Appearing to collide with Waterford is New Haven with Moravian Town or Bungletown to the east. The collision line is Waterford Avenue angling away from the river.

So confusing is the situation that at one time one street had the names, from west to east, United States Street, High Street, Second Street, and Third Street. Fortunately that street carries a single name—Market Street.

In Irishtown, the north–south streets are named for American War of 1812 naval heroes: Morris, Hull, Bainbridge, Decatur, Porter, Jones, and Biddle. East–west streets bore names of famous frigates of that war: Constitution, United States, Essex, and Wasp. The town or "centre" square is at the intersection of Gay (north–south) and Market Streets in the old Waterford section.

East of Grosh's addition to New Haven was Watts Station, named for an ironmaster. Between Watts and Chickes rock there were at one time six anthracite iron furnaces. The furnaces were, from west to east, Vesta, Marietta No. 2, Marietta No. 1, Donegal, Chickies No. 2, and Chickies No. 1.

About halfway downstream toward Columbia was the Henry Clay Furnace and at the north end of Columbia was the St. Charles furnace. On a hillside north of the furnaces, many ironmasters who ran the furnaces built their homes. Running all along Marietta and the furnaces was the Pennsylvania Canal and the PRR. At first they were independent, but later the railroad bought the canal from the Commonwealth of Pennsylvania.

The railroad and canal tended to act as a barrier to citizens to have easy access to the Susquehanna River. On the other hand, the railroad tended to help protect the town from floodwaters, especially after 1906, when the PRR opened the Atglen and Susquehanna (A&S) branch, which was slightly elevated.

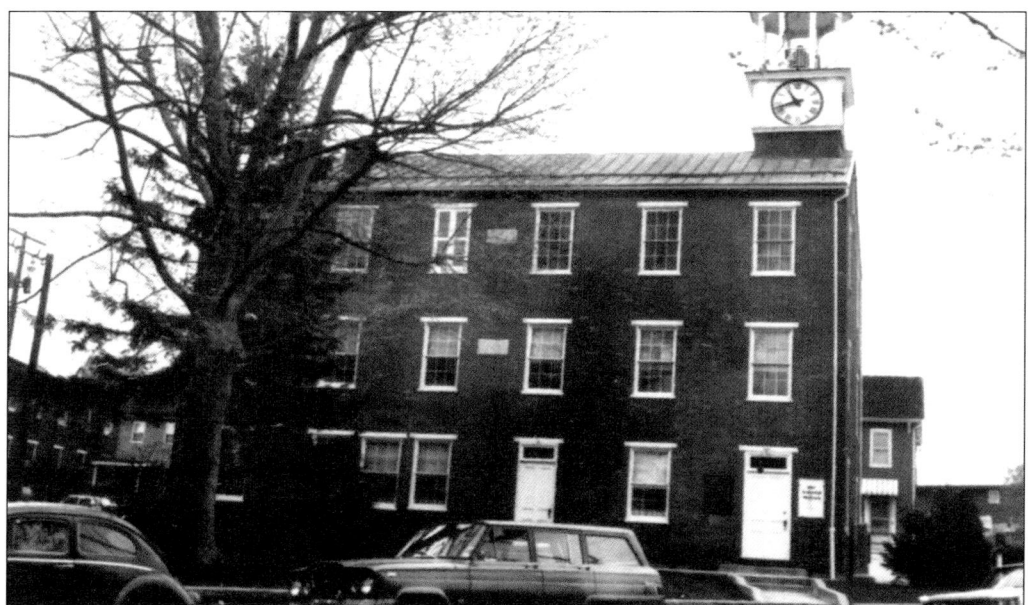

Built by Marietta Borough in 1847, this building for many years served as the town hall with the jail beneath the first floor. Marietta Restoration Associates now uses it for a museum. The building's tower with four-faced clock, bell, and weather vane has come to represent the community as a symbol widely used. (Author's collection.)

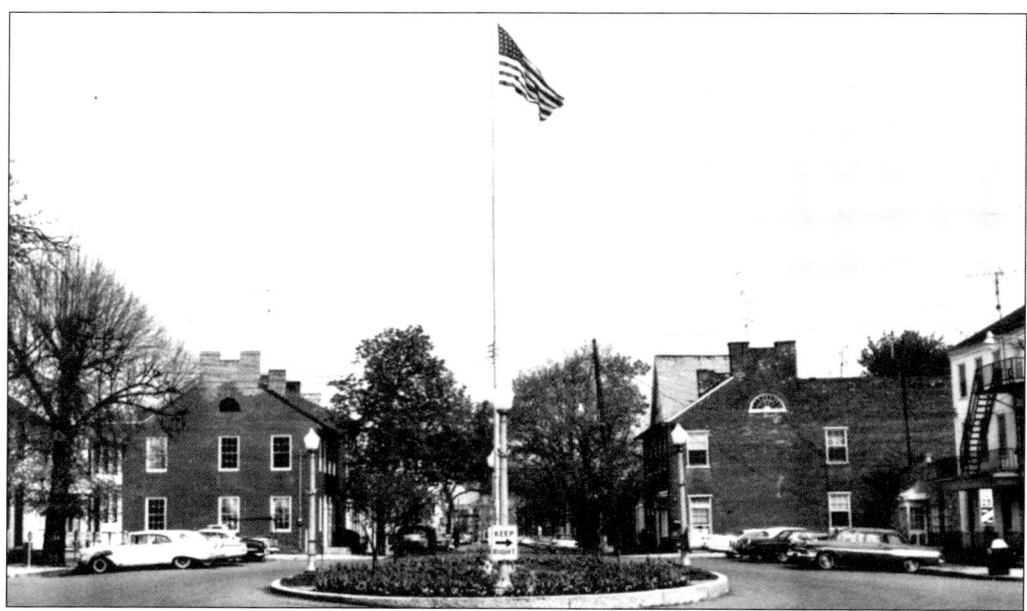

At the intersection of Gay (north–south) and High (east–west) Streets, Marietta has a small-town America town square (or centre to use the European spelling on an 1875 map) complete with flagpole in a flower-decorated island. Looking east along High Street, its intersection with Waterford Street is off in the distance. (Author's collection.)

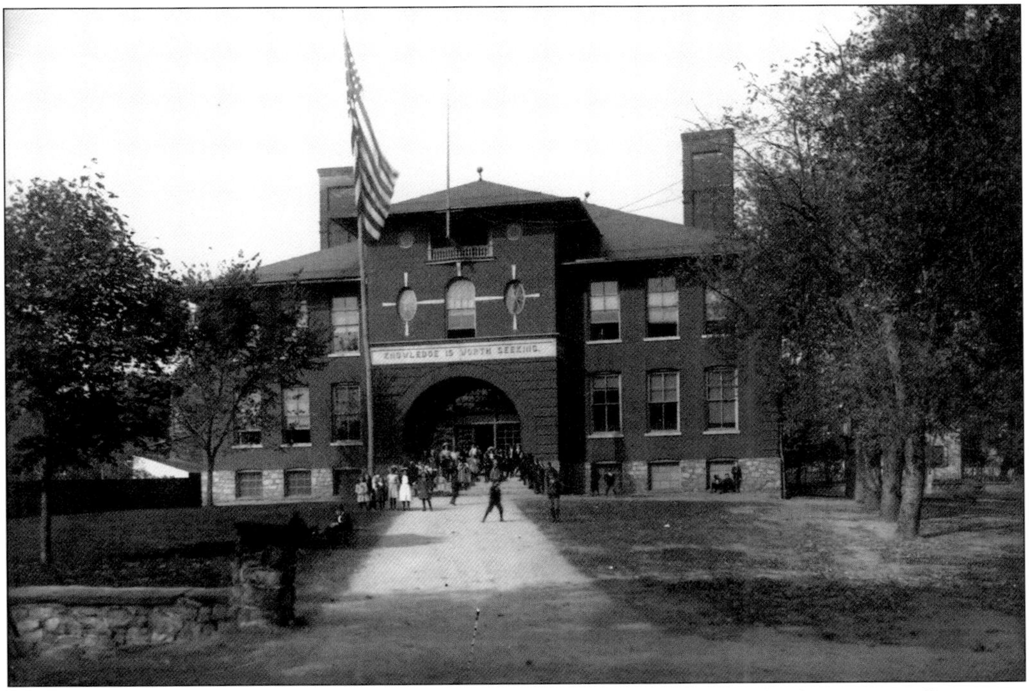

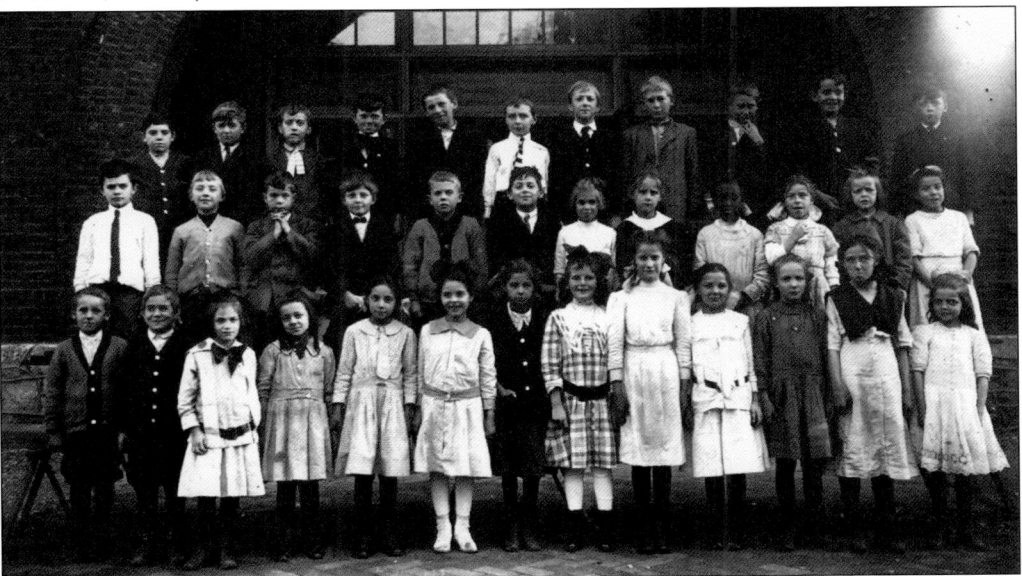

Students are spread out over the grounds and the steps leading to the arched entrance of Marietta High School. Over the arch in the horizontal white stone is the saying "Knowledge Is Worth Seeking." In 1933, an extension was placed on the building's entrance to handle an increase in students. (Courtesy Columbia Historic Preservation Society.)

In what is almost a universal tradition across the country, students line up outside on their school's steps to have their picture taken. The Marietta schools are now part of Donegal School District, which includes not only Marietta, but also Mount Joy Borough, Maytown, and the areas around these communities. (Courtesy Lancaster County Historical Society.)

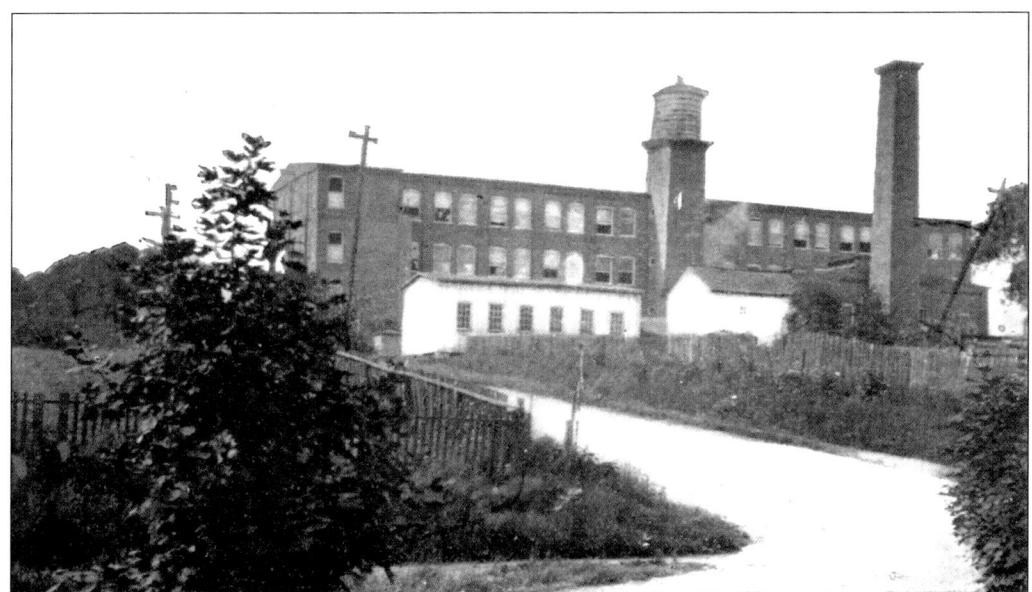

Ashley and Bailey had an operation in Marietta, as well as Columbia. Built in 1897, at the corner of East Walnut and North Pine Streets, the building is on the National Register of Historical Places and now is the home to Silk Mill Condominiums. Marietta Silk Company also started in the town. (Author's collection.)

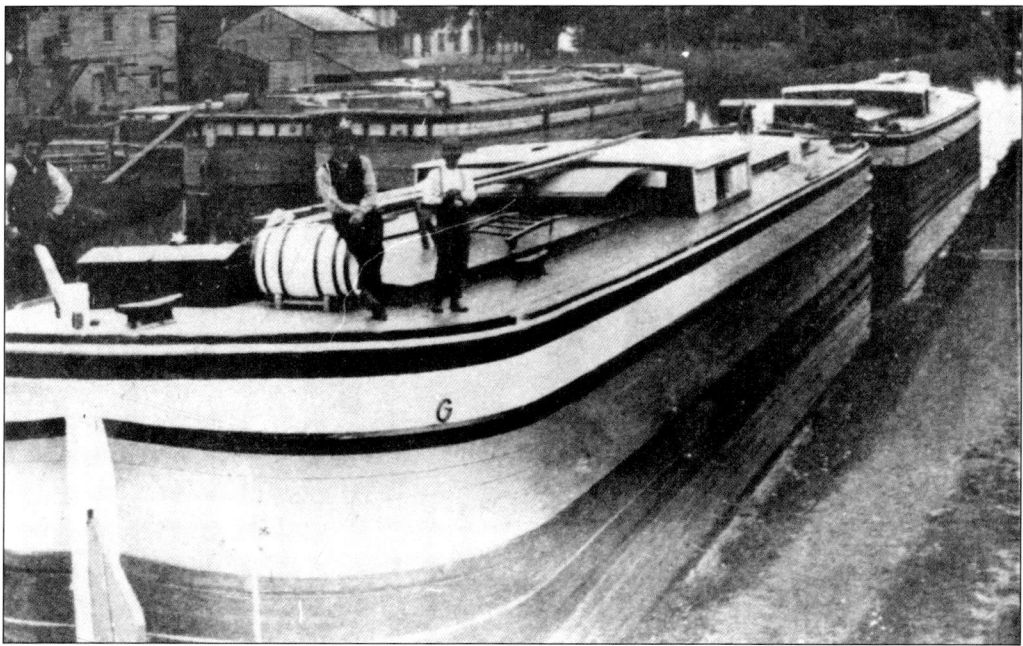

Canal boats, drawn by mules, were an economical transportation method. However, the Pennsylvania Canal passing through Marietta, like all in northern climates, was unavailable in wintertime when it was drained to minimize damage from freezing water. In spring, floods could wash out sections. Railroads proved much more reliable throughout the year. (Courtesy Lancaster County Historical Society.)

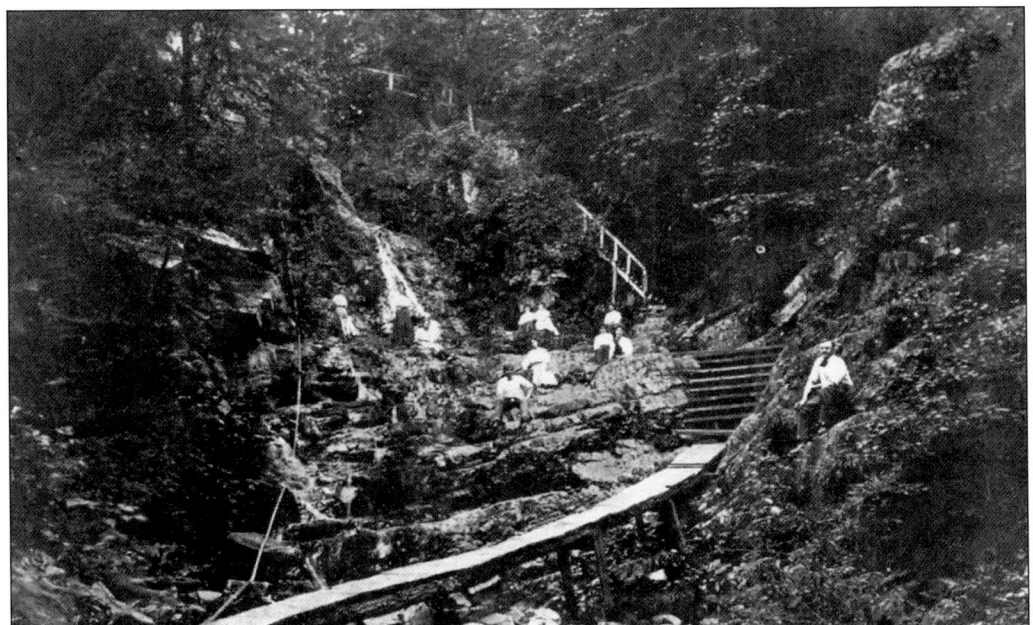

At Wildcat Falls, visitors found a path crossing over the stream on a narrow wooden bridge, stairs, and handrails leading to the falls and going up the hillside parallel to them. A popular summertime destination, both local and out-of-town tourists would take a ferry from Marietta to cross the Susquehanna River over to the York County side to reach the falls and the nearby hotel. (Author's collection.)

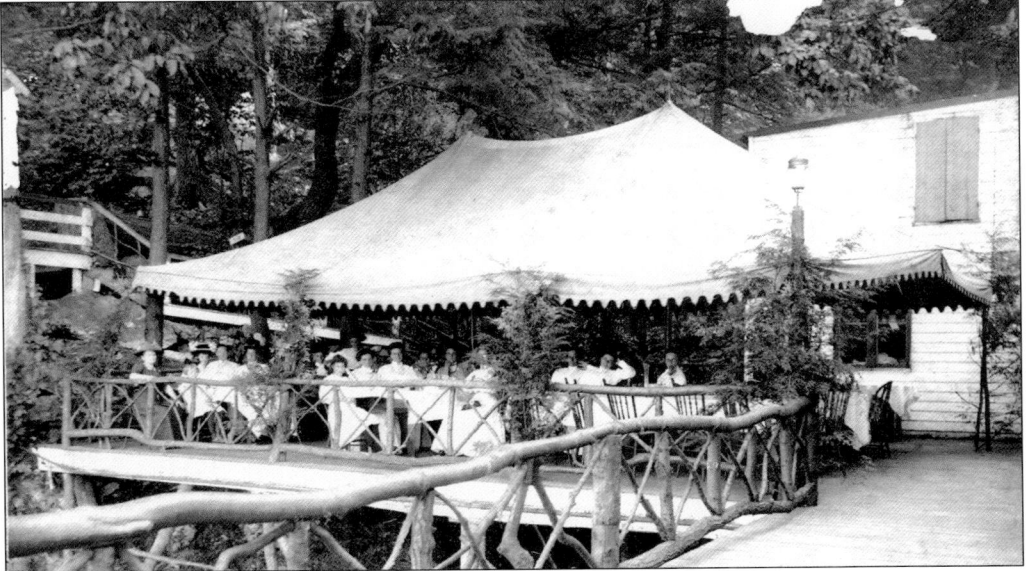

Wildcat was a summer getaway across from Marietta where people could use a ferry to cross over the river and enjoy a waterfall, dine on a wooden deck, and enjoy the cooling breezes. The York County side directly across from Marietta has always had close ties to the town with the Marietta Gravity Water Company piping water gathered from the hills under the river to supply the town. (Courtesy of Cleon G. Bernteizel.)

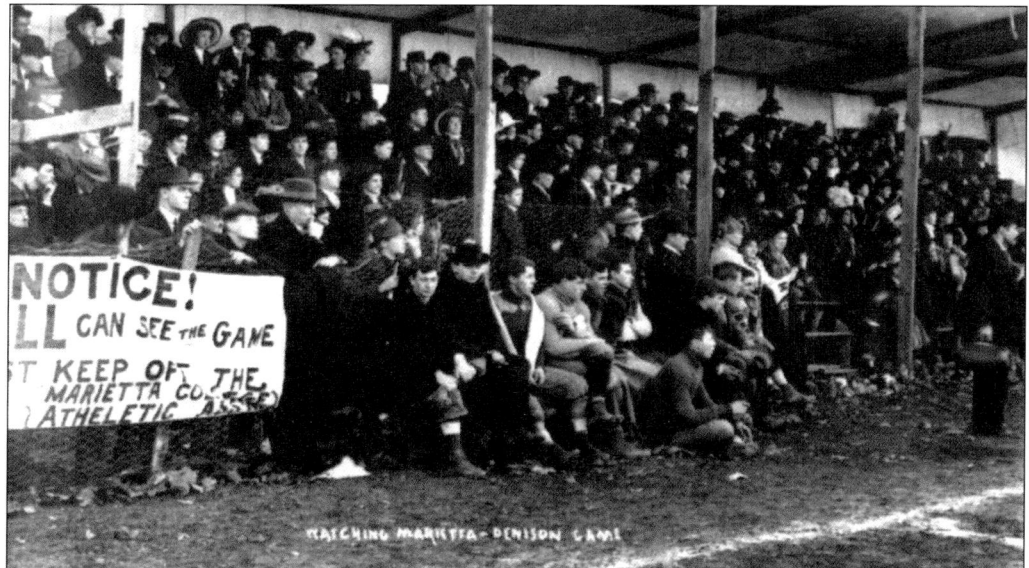

Baseball fans watch a game between a Marietta team and one from Denison farther west in Pennsylvania along the Lincoln Highway toward Pittsburgh. Apparently the sign admonishing fans to stay off the field so all could see was not enough, so another restraint was strung—chicken wire. Fans along the back appear to be Plain Sect; many of their members not only are fans, but eager game participants. (Courtesy Lancaster County Historical Society.)

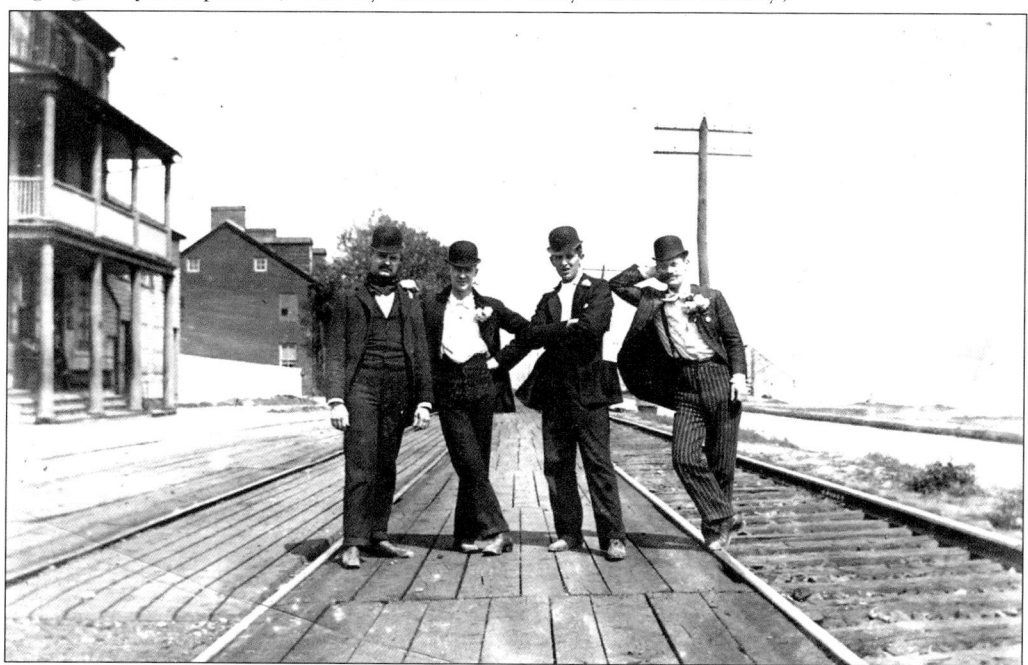

Four young men pose in a dangerous position along the busy PRR tracks at the north end of Marietta. To the right are the canal and the Susquehanna River. On the left is the Railroad House built between 1820 and 1823. The Railroad House Restaurant and Bed and Breakfast is now located here. (Courtesy Columbia Historic Preservation Society.)

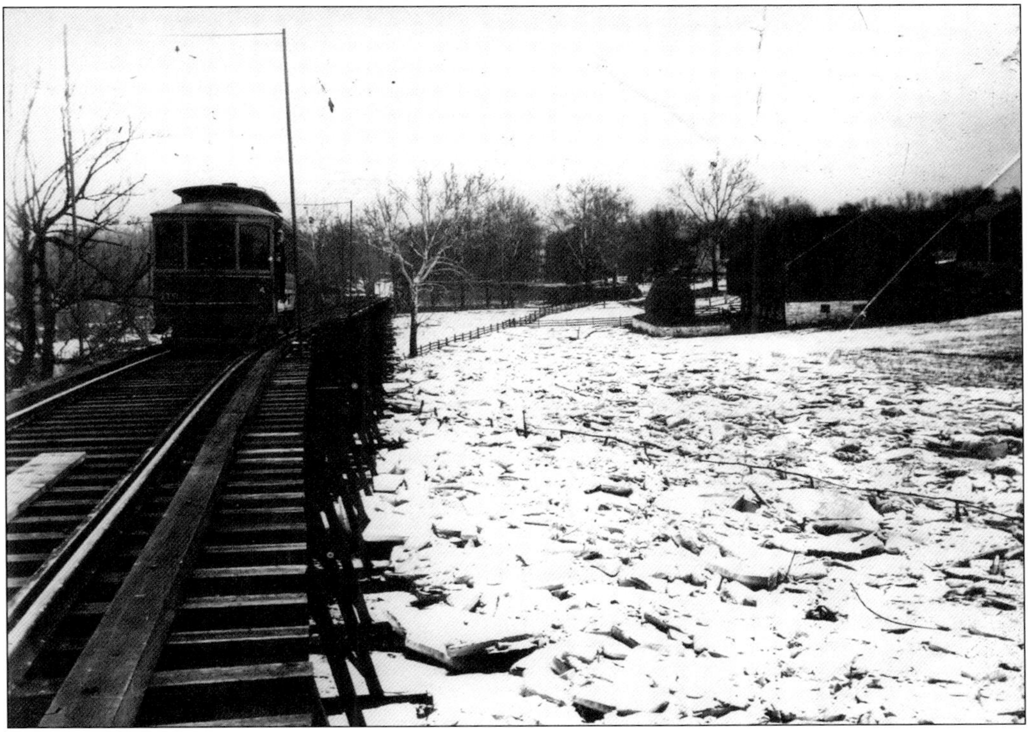

Soon after the trolley left Marietta bound for Columbia it crossed Chickies Creek on a trestle resting on concrete piers. This winter's day the ice has jammed behind the trestle and spread out over the adjacent fields. The trestle is long gone, but the piers still remain in what is now Lancaster County's Chickies Rock Park. (Author's collection.)

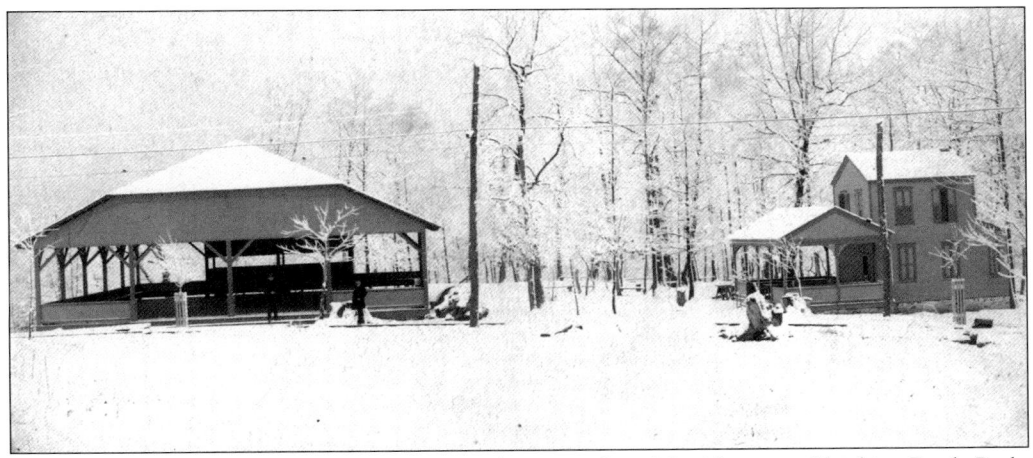

It is the last day of 1893, and snow covers the ground and buildings at Chickies Rock Park. Built by the Columbia and Donegal Electric Railway (C&D), the park started its second season come spring as a destination for trolley passengers. Conestoga Traction Company, which was the ultimate successor to C&D, continued operations between Columbia and Marietta through the park until 1932. (Author's collection.)

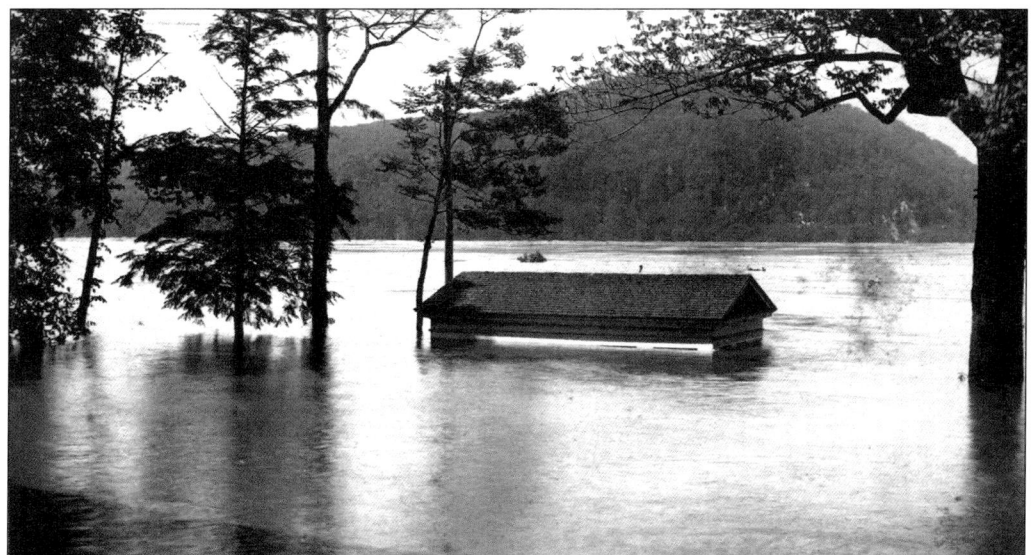

Prof. Samuel S. Haldeman, a well-known orthographer and a man with wide-ranging scientific interests, came to run his family's anthracite iron furnaces in the area and built his home at the base of Chickies Rock. On the property was a springhouse, which on June 2, 1889, was almost covered up to its roof by floodwaters. Roundtop is across the river over on the York County side. (Courtesy Columbia Historic Preservation Society.)

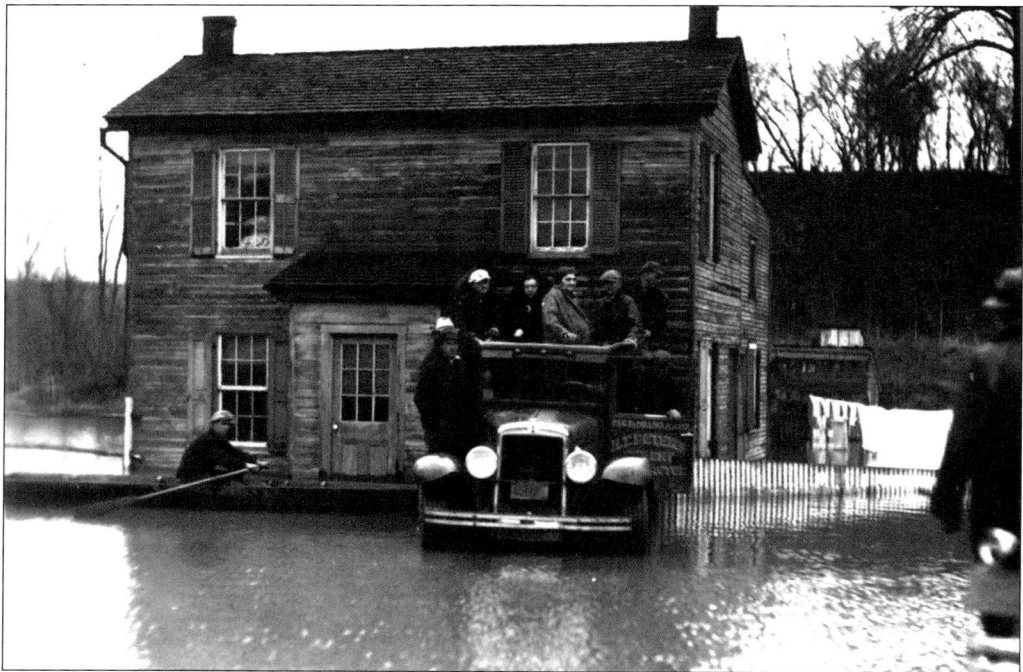

What became known as the 1936 St. Patrick's Day flood started in northern Pennsylvania when a sudden thaw caused unusually high snowfalls to melt and run off. Here a truck from H. T. Peters and a rowboat help evacuate a low-lying home. Residents moved their furniture upstairs to the second floor. (Courtesy Lancaster County Historical Society.)

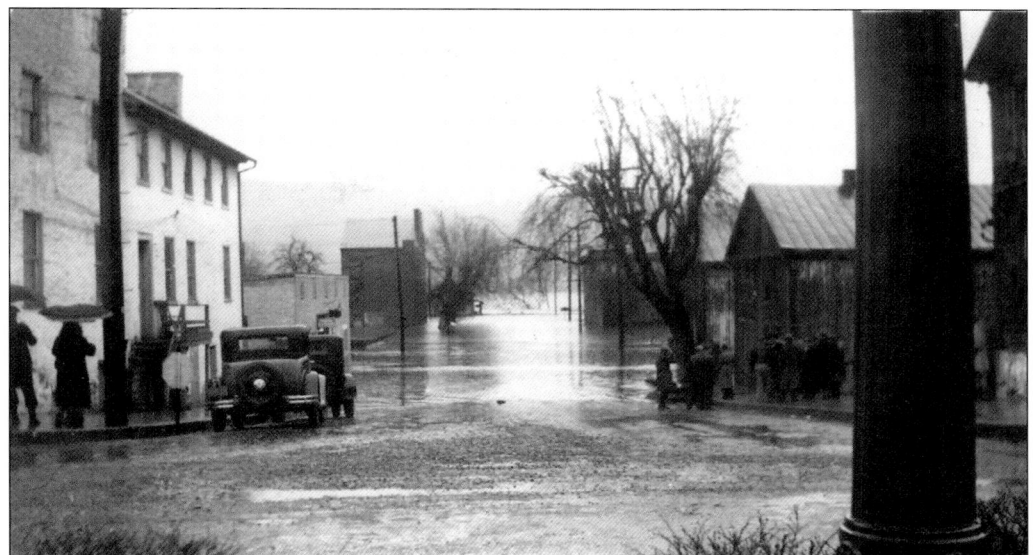

Looking west down along Gay Street in March 1936, the Susquehanna River has long since passed flood stage and has advanced several blocks inland. What happens in Marietta is the river backs up along small streams flowing into it under the raised railroad bed, which partially acts as a levee and spreads out. Typically in floods Marietta is harder hit than Columbia or Wrightsville. (Courtesy Columbia Historic Preservation Society.)

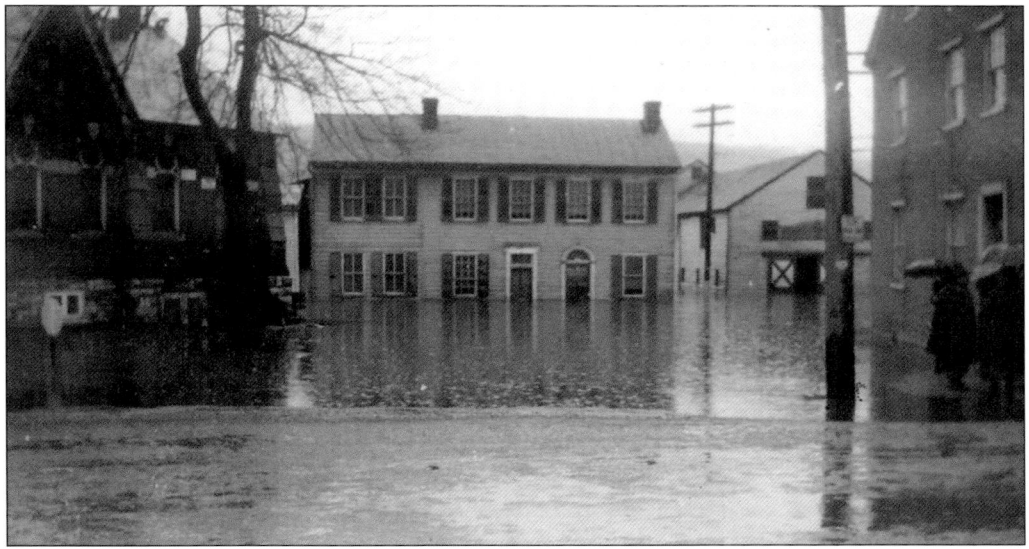

Waterford Avenue in the foreground lives up to its name on March 19, 1936, as residents would have to ford the water to get to their homes. On the left is the Zion's Reformed Church (now United Church of Christ). The water at the homes on Hazel Street is close to 400 feet away from the river's normal shore. (Courtesy Columbia Historic Preservation Society.)

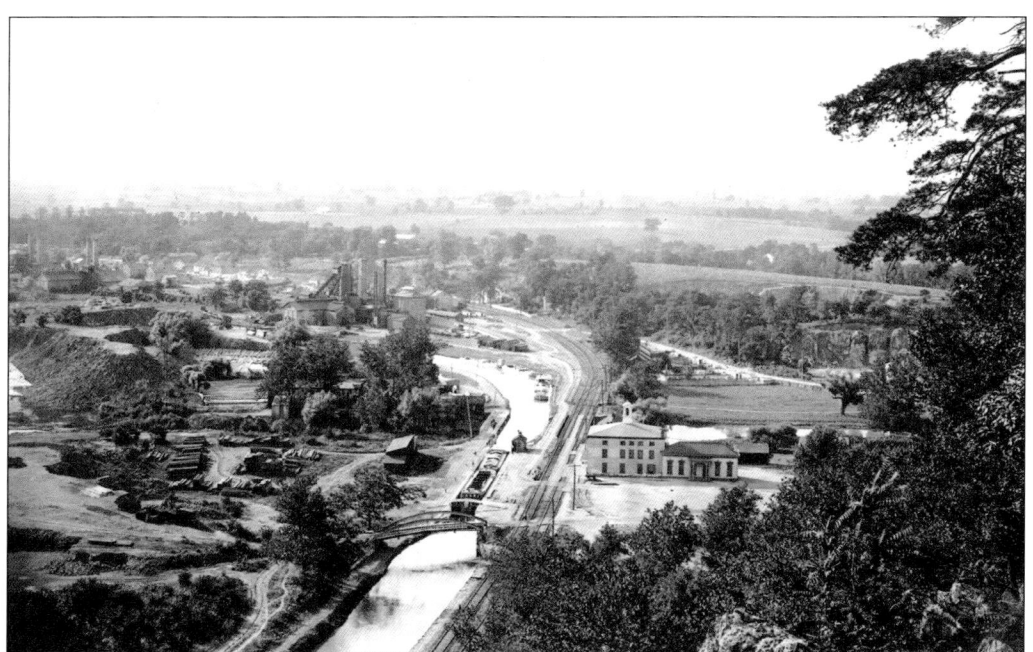

Looking north from Chickies Rock at the end of the 19th century gives a view of a sprawling industrial complex. Cutting through the industries are the canal and the PRR. In the foreground to the left is a lumberyard, and the canal lock has two boats in it. In the distance are several anthracite iron furnaces and slag piles that built up by them over the years. (Author's collection.)

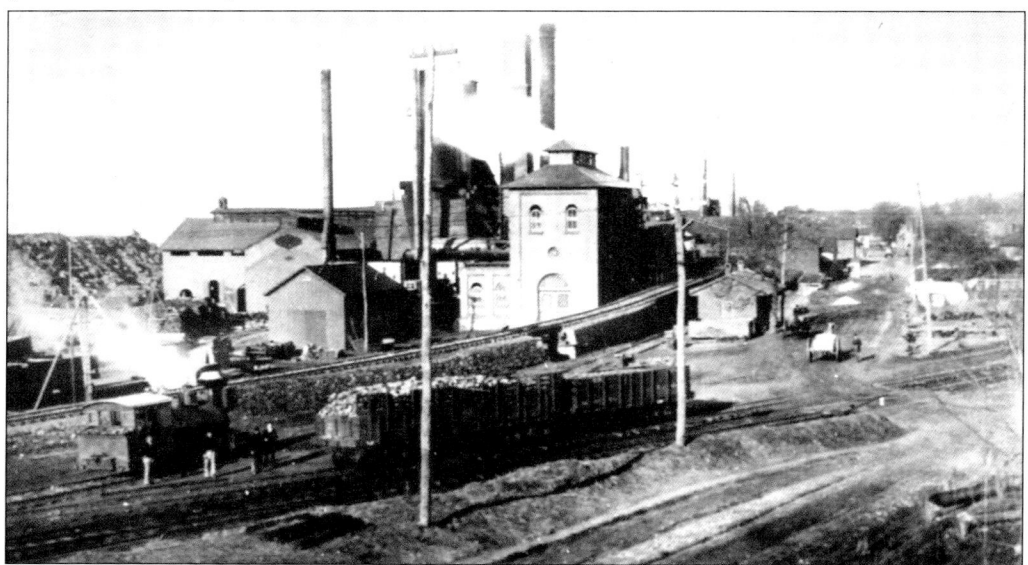

The Eagle Furnace opened for production in 1855. A decade later, the operation changed owners and got a new name, Chickies Furnace No. 2. In 1889, an extensive rebuild included construction of an engine house. Nicknamed the "happy face building" because of the appearance with windows for eyes, a round window nose, and a door mouth, the building is one of the few remaining structures from that era. (Courtesy Columbia Historic Preservation Society.)

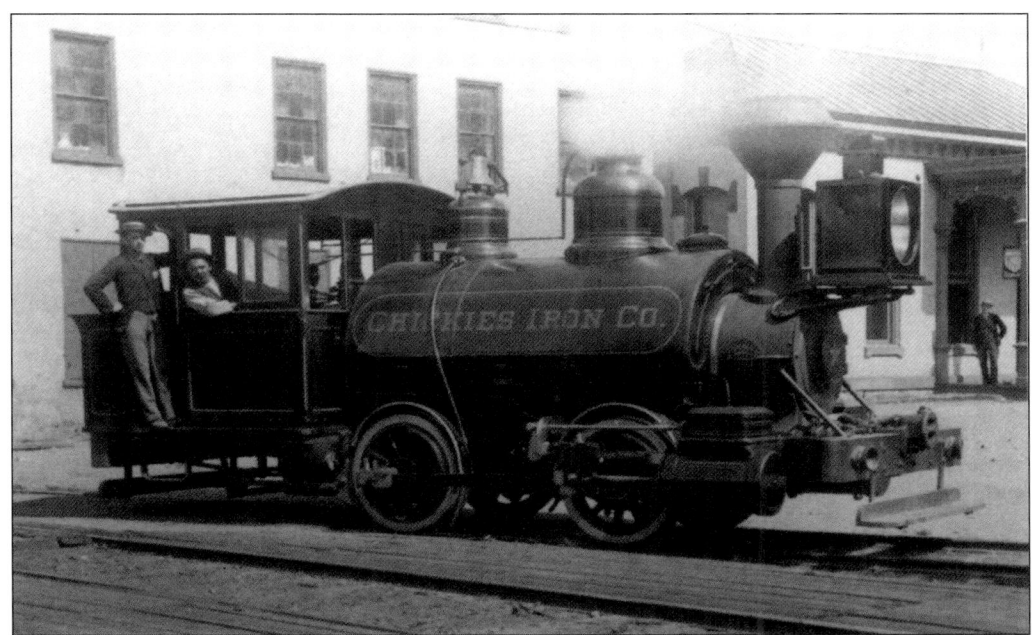

The anthracite iron furnaces dealt with many heavy loads, both incoming raw materials and outgoing iron. To shift these loads around a furnace called for railroad cars, which in turn needed motive powers. Rather than rely on the railroad to do the shifting, a furnace typically would have its own locomotive, such as Chickies Iron, so that it could work at its own pace. (Courtesy Lancaster County Historical Society.)

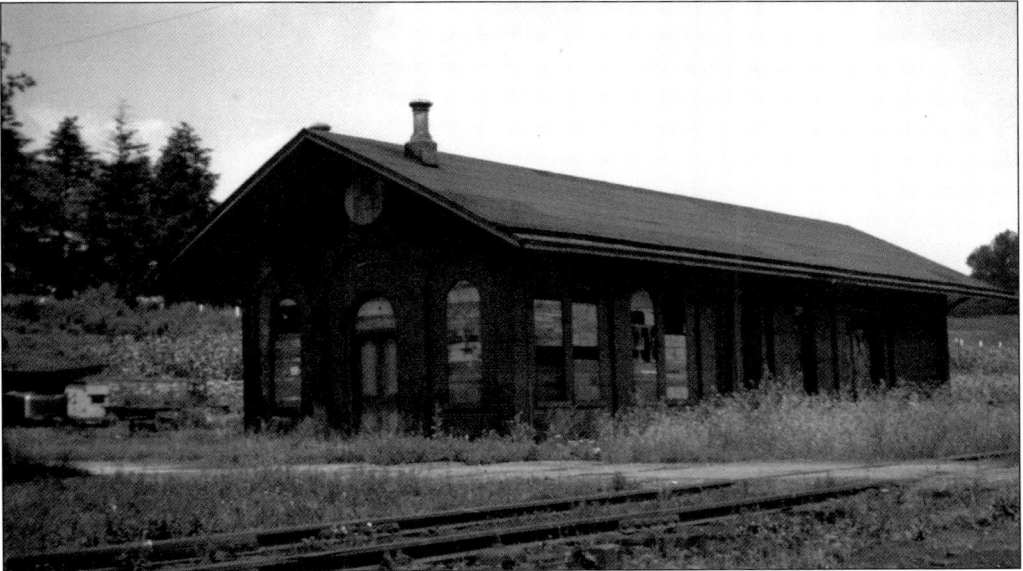

Just east of Marietta where the anthracite iron furnaces were concentrated, the PRR established a station along the Columbia branch to service the furnaces. The railroad named the station Watts after one of the furnaces. At the start of the 20th century, as the furnaces gradually closed down, the need for the station diminished and the railroad eventually abandoned it. (Author's collection.)

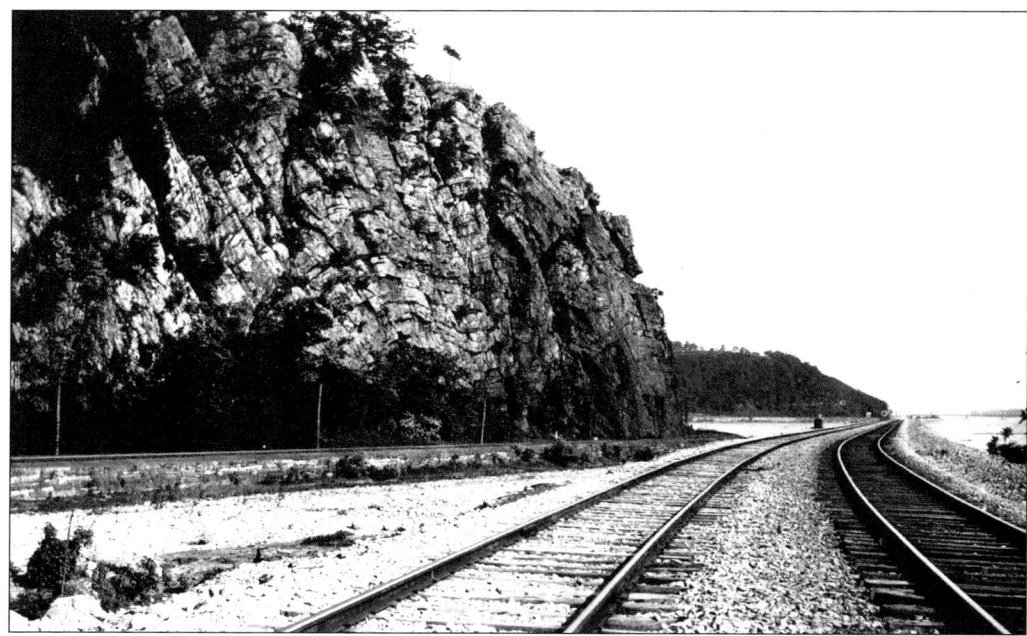

Where Chickies Rock jutted out toward the Susquehanna River, three transportation routes were crowded between the two. Nearest Chickies is the PRR's Columbia branch, which was the original line from Harrisburg. In the middle is the Pennsylvania Canal's Eastern Division. Closest to the river is the PRR's A&S branch. The PRR's assistant engineer J. P. Temple recorded scenes like this during construction of the A&S. (Courtesy Columbia Historic Preservation Society.)

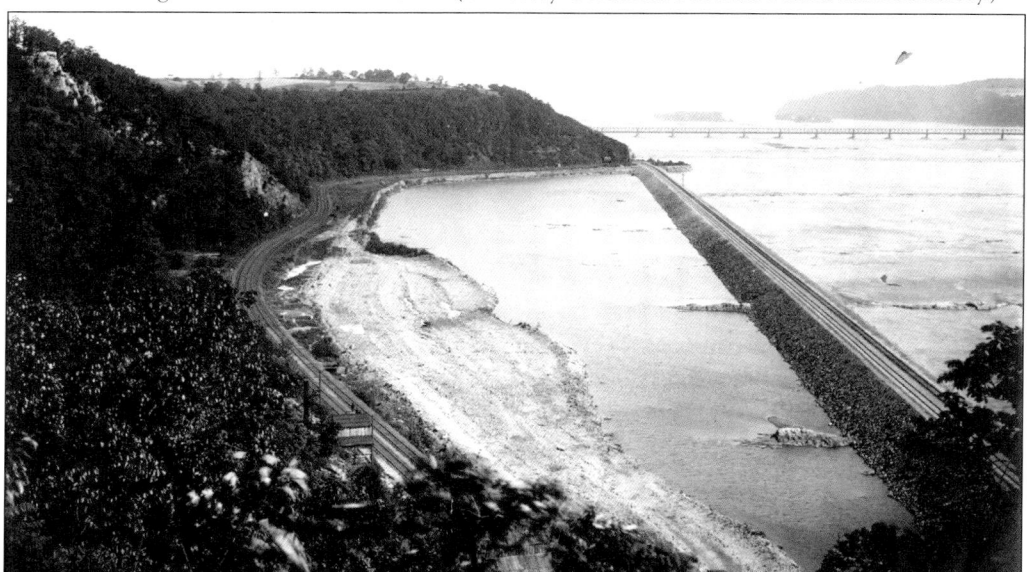

When the PRR built its A&S branch between Marietta and Columbia, it decided not to follow the original route, which curved along the base of Chickies Rock. Rather, the new line followed a straight line that cut off part of the river. The railroad named it Kerbaugh Lake after the construction company that built this portion of the route. (Courtesy Columbia Historic Preservation Society.)

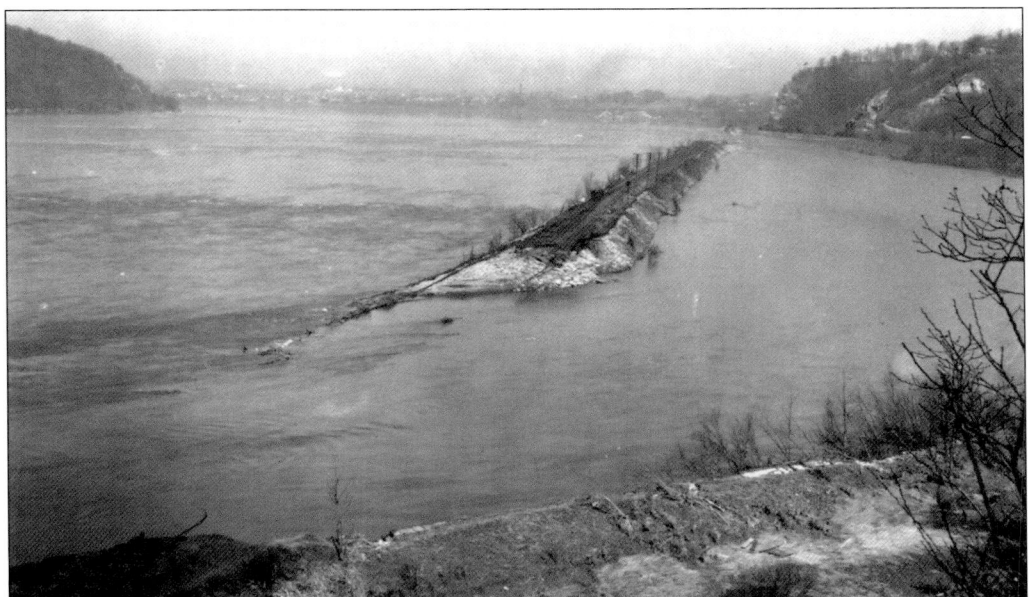

The rising waters of the Susquehanna River during the 1936 flood first broke through the PRR's A&S branch roadbed at the north end of Kerbaugh Lake near Chickies Rock. The water flowed south through the lake, through Point Rock Tunnel, and flooded the PRR's West Yard at Columbia. Then the waters broke through the roadbed at the south end forming an island of what was left. (Courtesy Columbia Historic Preservation Society.)

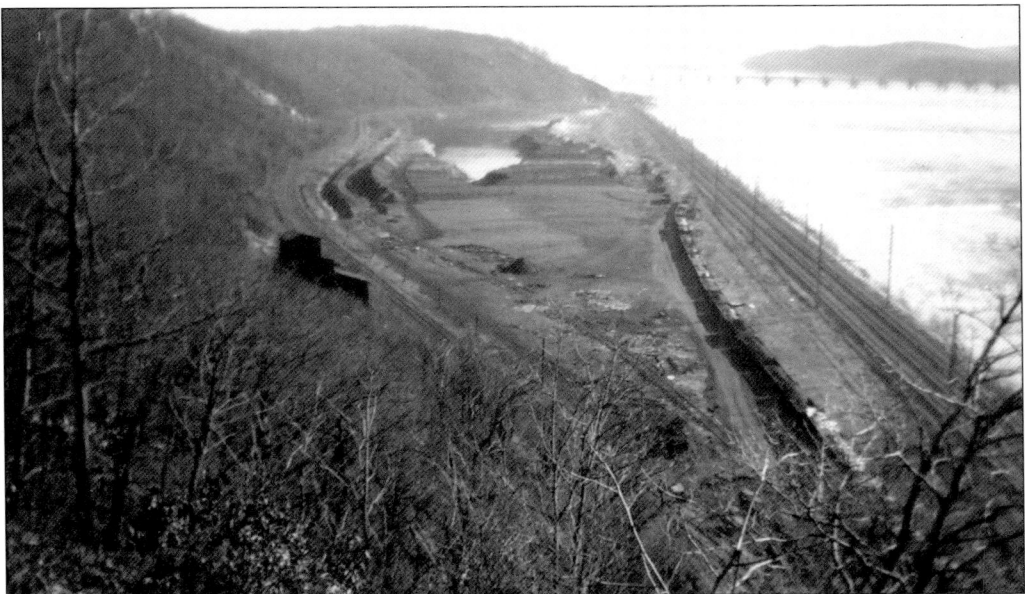

The PRR never forgot the devastation that the 1936 flood had caused and vowed to do something about it. World War II intervened and temporarily prevented the railroad from implementing a correction. However, after the war the railroad began hauling all manner of material in, some from as far way as Altoona, and started filling in the lake. The process lasted into the early 1950s. (Courtesy Columbia Historic Preservation Society.)

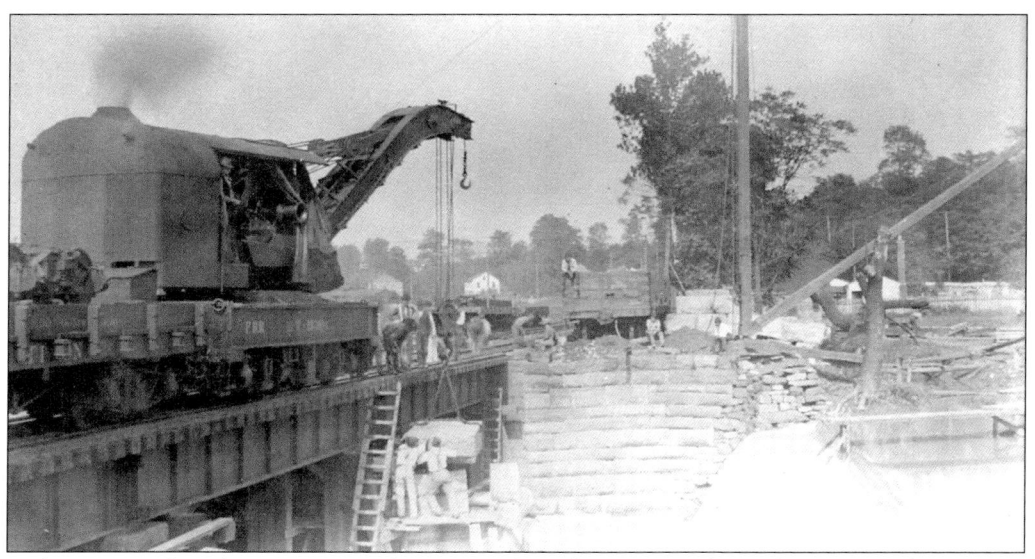

A few years after the PRR opened its A&S branch in 1906 along the eastern shore of its namesake river, the railroad improved its Columbia Branch, which now was inshore from the A&S. Here workers guide a stone into position on a pier of the bridge spanning Chickies Creek. (Author's collection.)

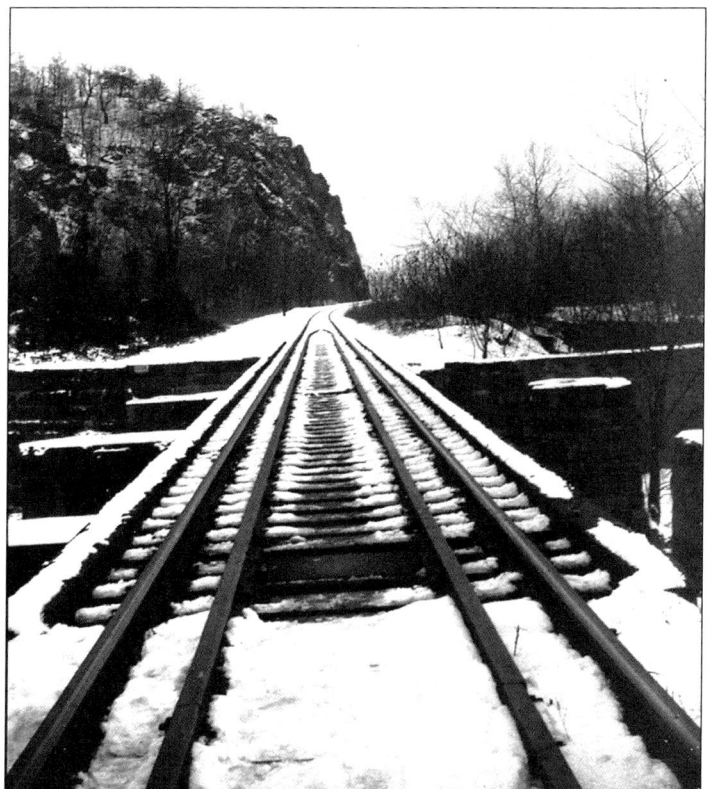

To cross over Chickies Creek going into Marietta, the bridge the PRR's Columbia branch last used was a one-track steel girder structure. Declining freight traffic along the line in the late 1950s caused the PRR to move trains over to the adjacent A&S branch and tear up the track and bridge. (Author's collection.)

Three

WRIGHTSVILLE

Wrightsville, generally speaking, slopes up more quickly and more steeply than either Columbia or Marietta. To the south there is a natural boundary, Kreutz Creek. To the north Roundtop, a hill of considerable height, lies. Once out of Wrightsville to the west, the land is rolling. The main east–west street running from the river is Hellam Street, named for the township it runs through to the west. Hellam carries the Lincoln Highway from off the 1930 bridge, the Veterans Memorial Bridge. The Lincoln Highway is now PA 462, but until 1972, when the new Wright's Ferry Bridge opened north of town, it was US 30. Hellam Street is home to most of the town's small businesses such as banks, gas stations, groceries, and restaurants.

The area's industries are along Front Street, the Susquehanna River, and the Susquehanna and Tidewater Canal.

The east–west streets, like Columbia, have tree names. Going north to south they are Cherry, Walnut, Locust, and then Hellam. South from Hellam they are Chestnut, Orange, Maple, Mulberry, Lemon, and Willow.

The north–south streets, again like Columbia, start at Front and then progress numerically toward the west.

The canal basin and outlet had a more prominent location in town than the corresponding one in Columbia. The railroad, essentially being through tracks rather than a yard like in Columbia, did not cut the canal off from the town such as what happened across the river.

The railroad had spurs along Front Street to serve its industries. To get out of town headed west, the railroad had to pass through a deep cut and then gradually work upgrade. Because the railroad was never able to acquire sufficient land to build an adequate approach road to the top of the bridge, it never installed the upper deck and roadway for which the bridge was designed.

The York Railways System's trolleys ran from the White Rose city into Wrightsville with its line stopping near the shore. Passengers could easily walk to the PRR station or to the ferry, wanting, in the summertime, to carry them to Columbia.

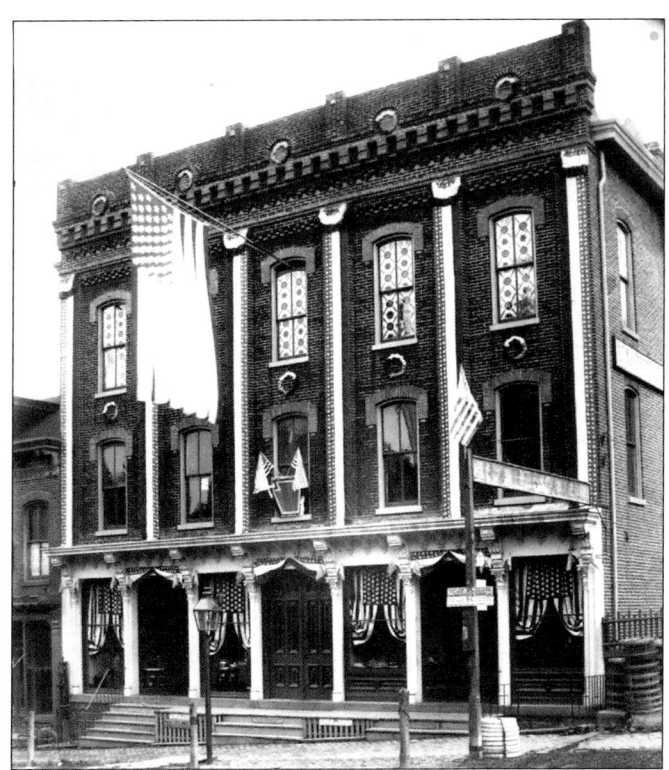

This Hellam Street building is known as the Old Town Hall building, having once served that purpose in addition to being host to a movie house and the *Wrightsville Star*, a weekly newspaper. Two identical rectangular signs on the post are for "Spence Grant prepared pure SG paints, The Wrightsville Supply Co.," a Brooklyn paint company. The 45-star flag brackets the photograph's date as being probably between 1895 and 1907. (Courtesy Historic Wrightsville, Inc.)

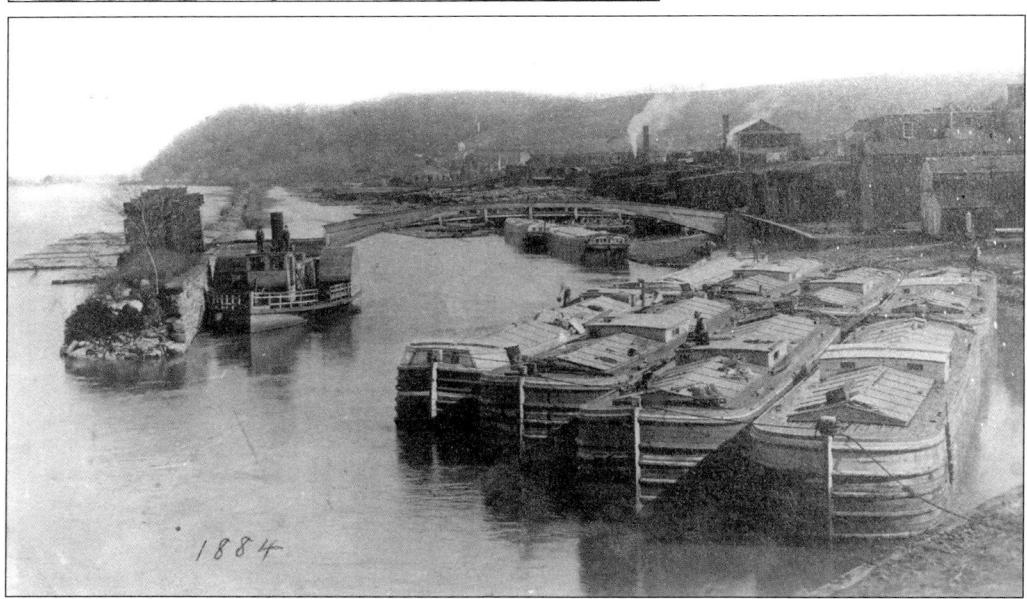

A side-wheeler tugboat and several canal boats are tied up in 1884 at the entrance to the Susquehanna and Tidewater canal. The Philadelphia and Reading Railroad owned the canal and used it to ship coal it brought down from the anthracite mines, loaded on boats, hauled across the river, and then down the west side of the river to Havre de Grace, Maryland, and the Chesapeake Bay. (Courtesy Columbia Historic Preservation Society.)

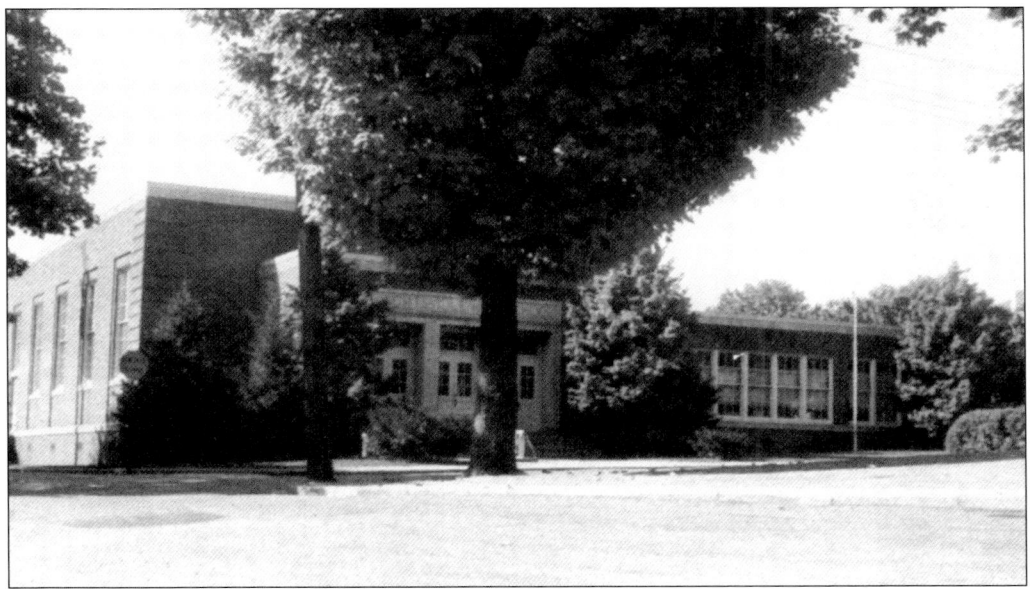

The United States Works Project Administration started the high school in 1936 as one of the many countrywide projects started to combat the Great Depression. In 1954, Wrightsville schools became part of the Eastern (York County) Joint School District. After the high school students moved to a new building well outside of town, this building became an elementary school. (Courtesy Historic Wrightsville, Inc.)

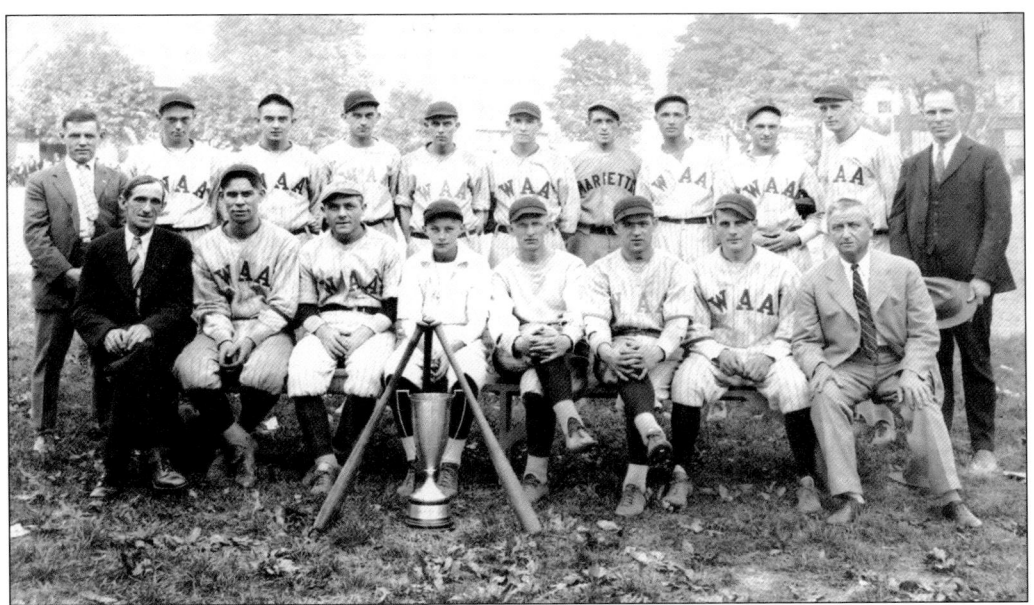

In 1929, the Wrightsville Athletic Association (WAA) baseball team won the York County championship and the trophy that went with it. The nonplaying men flanking the players all wore suits and ties back in those much more formal days. Notice the lone player from Marietta who stands out from the WAA players because of his uniform. (Courtesy Historic Wrightsville, Inc.)

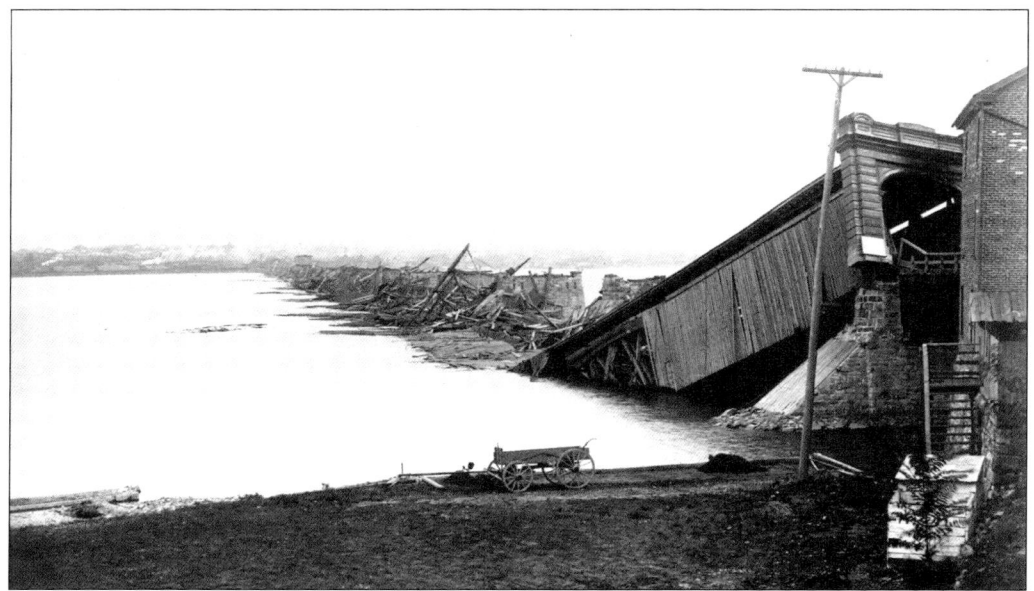
Union forces burned the bridge in 1863 to prevent Confederates that were advancing into Wrightsville from crossing. The 1867 replacement covered bridge had two iron center spans to act as a firebreak in the middle. Ironically a hurricane in 1896 left the center spans standing, but destroyed both sides of the wooden bridge. (Courtesy Columbia Historic Preservation Society.)

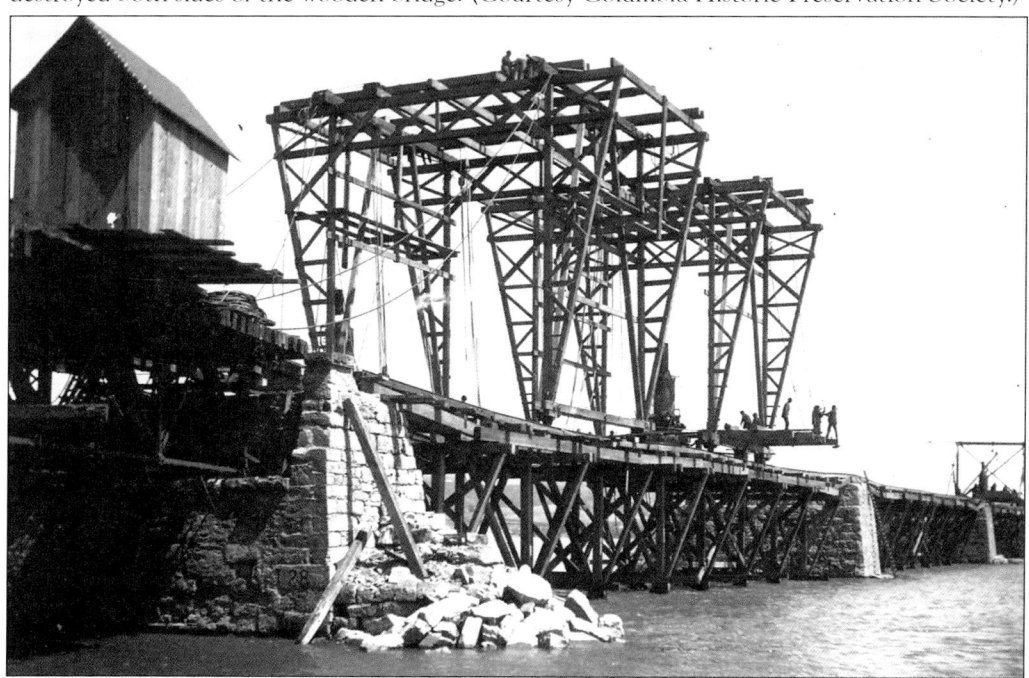
To quickly replace the destroyed 1896 bridge, the PRR hired contractors to work from both shores and repair the bridge piers where needed. Then the contractors would work out to the middle with the bridge itself. Here on the Wrightsville side, the traveling wooden frame is in place ready to position the steel pieces that would follow. (Author's collection.)

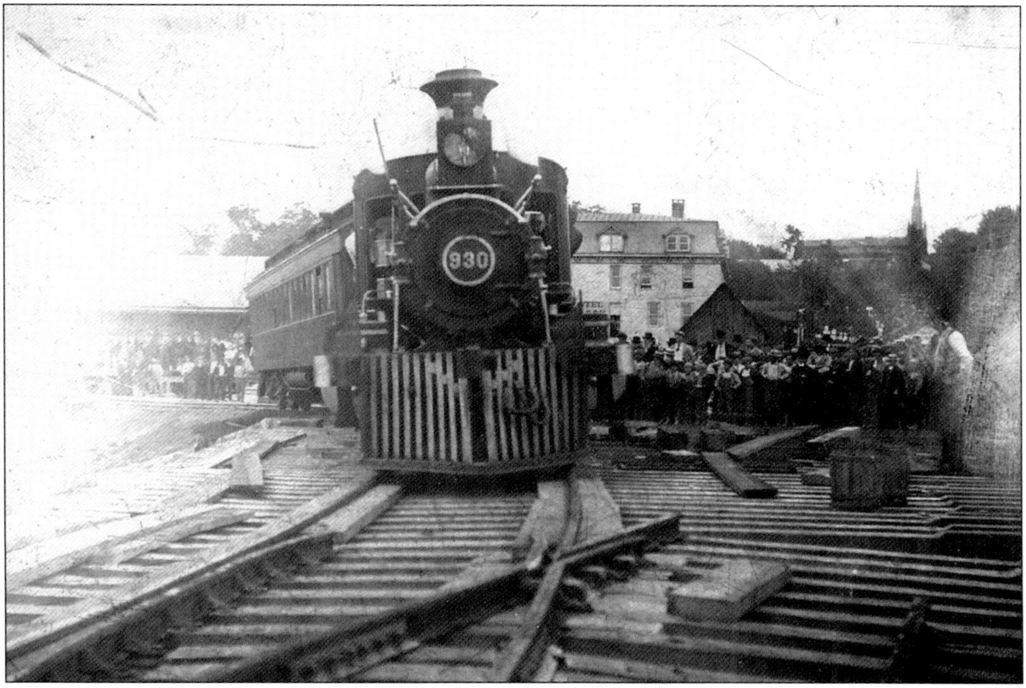

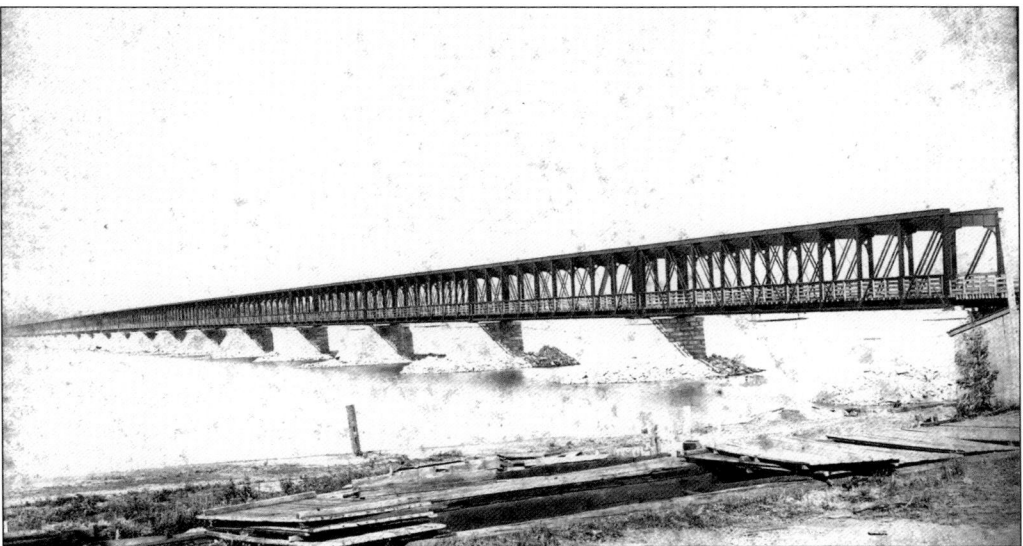

The first train over the 1897 bridge leaves Wrightsville station on June 5, 1897, and heads out onto the first span. Leading the one-car train is PRR No. 930, a G-class 4-6-0. In the background are, from left to right, the Wrightsville PRR depot, Hotel Wilson, and Trinity Lutheran Church. (Author's collection.)

In this c. 1898 photograph, the spans seemingly stretch on to infinity toward Columbia. The Susquehanna is a mile wide here so that this is a common phenomenon whenever there is haze or fog of sufficient density. Sometimes the only way to tell which shore is in the foreground is to closely examine the bridge piers, which are angled on the upstream side to break up ice. (Courtesy Columbia Historic Preservation Society.)

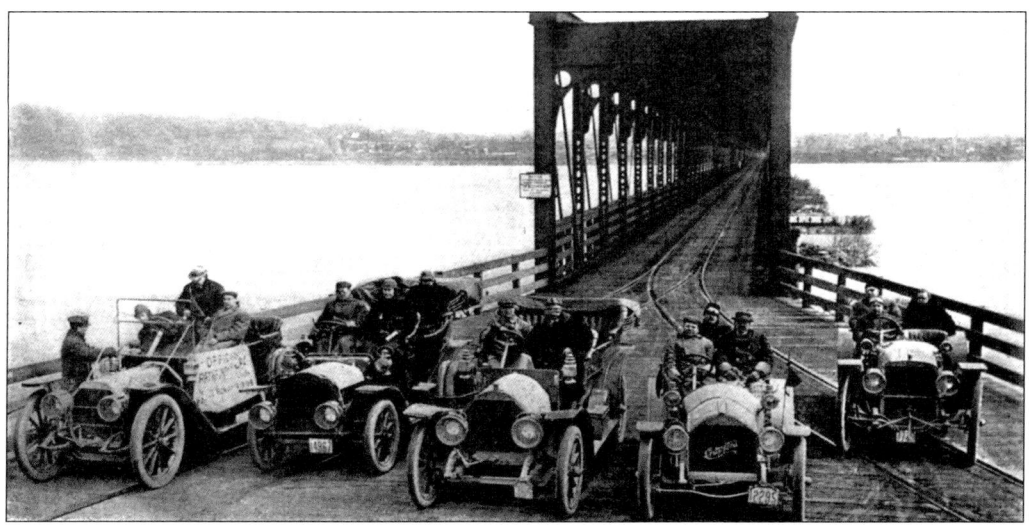

In 1909, Gov. Edwin S. Stuart established a 700-mile race that would start in Harrisburg, head to Washington, D.C., and Baltimore, and return to Harrisburg. A month before the race, pathfinders explored the route. Here five of the cars pose at the 1897 bridge, which the *Automobile* magazine called the longest railroad bridge in the country. (Author's collection.)

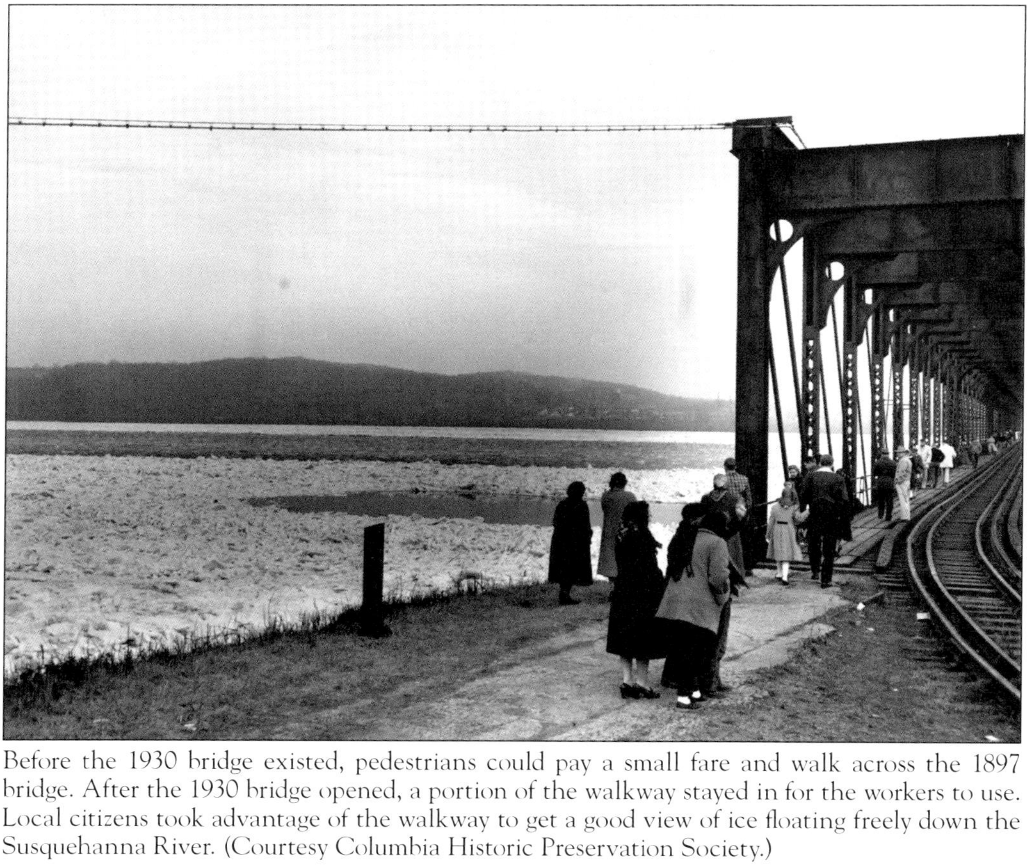

Before the 1930 bridge existed, pedestrians could pay a small fare and walk across the 1897 bridge. After the 1930 bridge opened, a portion of the walkway stayed in for the workers to use. Local citizens took advantage of the walkway to get a good view of ice floating freely down the Susquehanna River. (Courtesy Columbia Historic Preservation Society.)

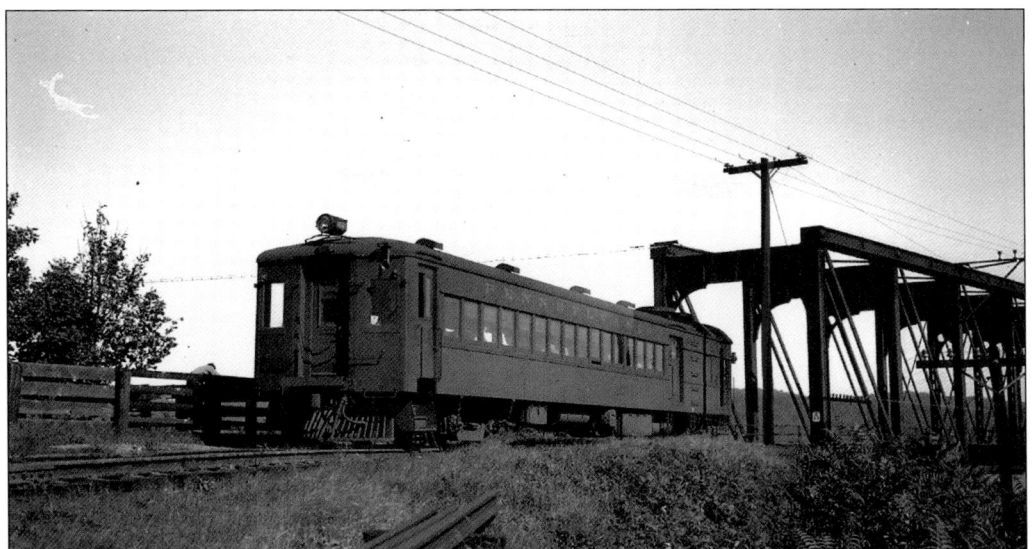

PRR No. 4662 comes off the bridge at Wrightsville on its way from Lancaster to York in July 1950. Pullman-Standard built No. 4662 in 1929. The PRR converted the self-propelled car from using gasoline to diesel in the 1940s and continued to use it until 1959. Now restored, the car runs on the Wilmington and Western Railroad in Delaware in tourist service. (Author's collection.)

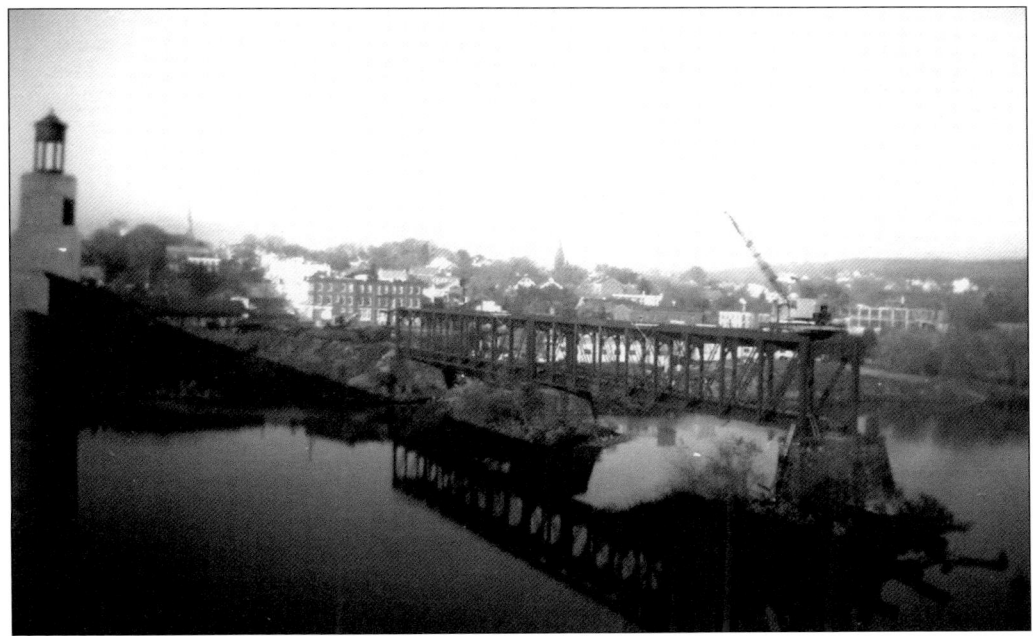

Ultimately the 1897 bridge outlived its usefulness to the PRR. The last train crossed the span in 1958, and in 1963, the railroad hired a contractor to demolish it and sell the steel for scrap. Demolition started at the Columbia side and gradually worked west to here, the Wrightsville side. (Courtesy Columbia Historic Preservation Society.)

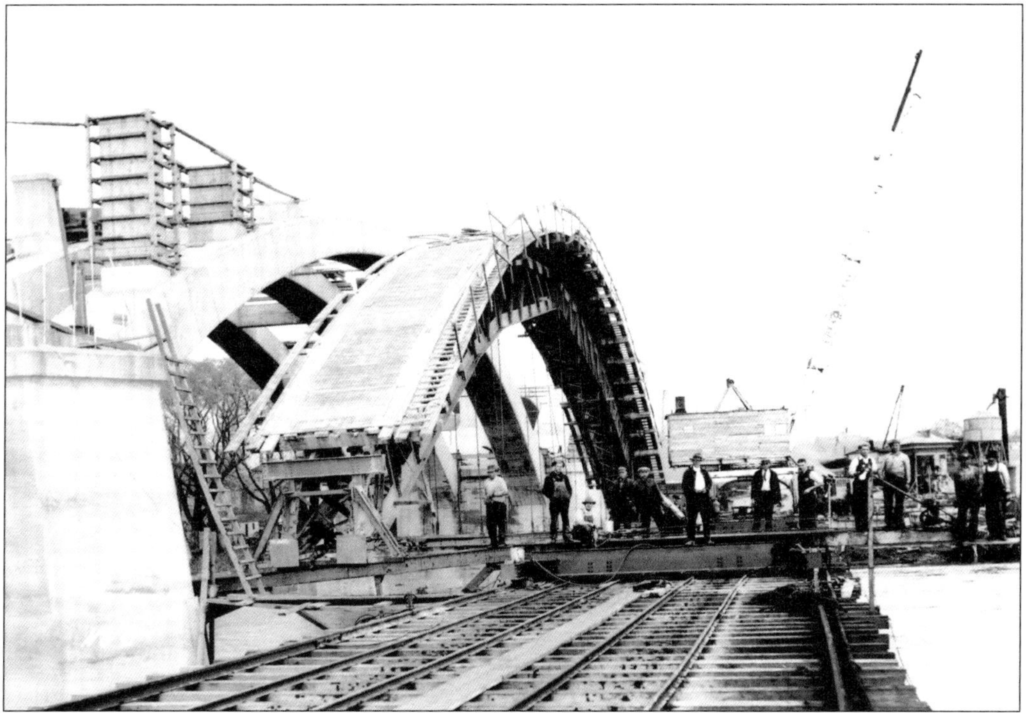

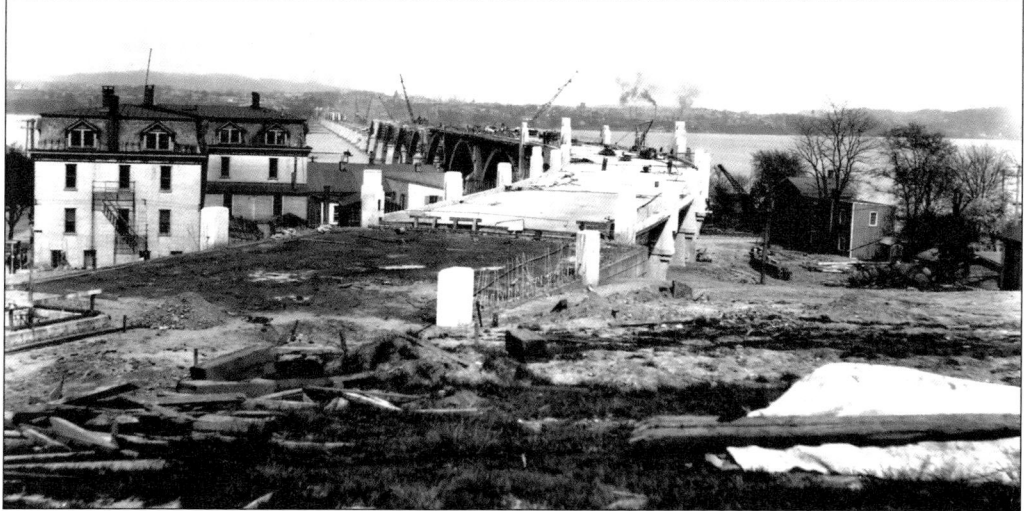

Clearly seen to the left is the rapid progress workers would make on the three arches of each span. The upstream one is finished with the vertical supports for the deck visible. The center arch has the forms in place for the vertical supports. Workers still have to complete the downstream arch and position the forms for the vertical supports. (Courtesy Columbia Historic Preservation Society.)

The curved approach from Hellam Street to the 1930 bridge at Wrightsville is almost complete with only the concrete sidewalls needing to be poured. Workers are busy placing forms, laying reinforcing bars, pouring concrete arches, and pouring the deck out over the river. The approach curves around the Hotel Wilson. (Courtesy Columbia Historic Preservation Society.)

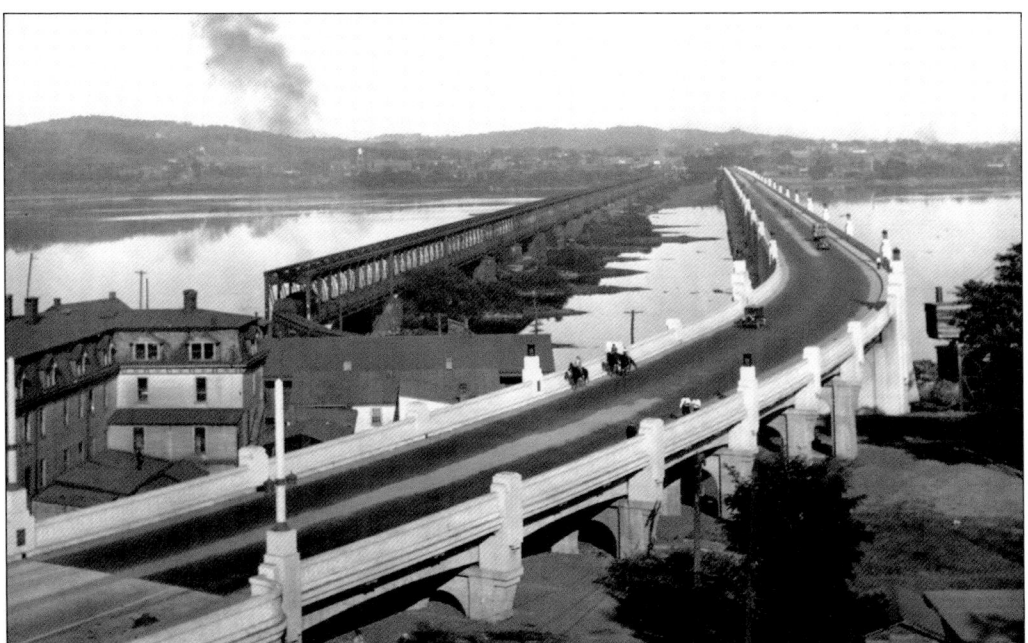

People are using four transportation modes here. Under the smoke, a PRR passenger car eastbound from York to Lancaster goes unto the railroad bridge. Three equestrians are westbound on the newly completed 1930 bridge. Automobiles travel both directions while several pedestrians use the sidewalk on the south or downstream side of the bridge. (Courtesy Columbia Historic Preservation Society.)

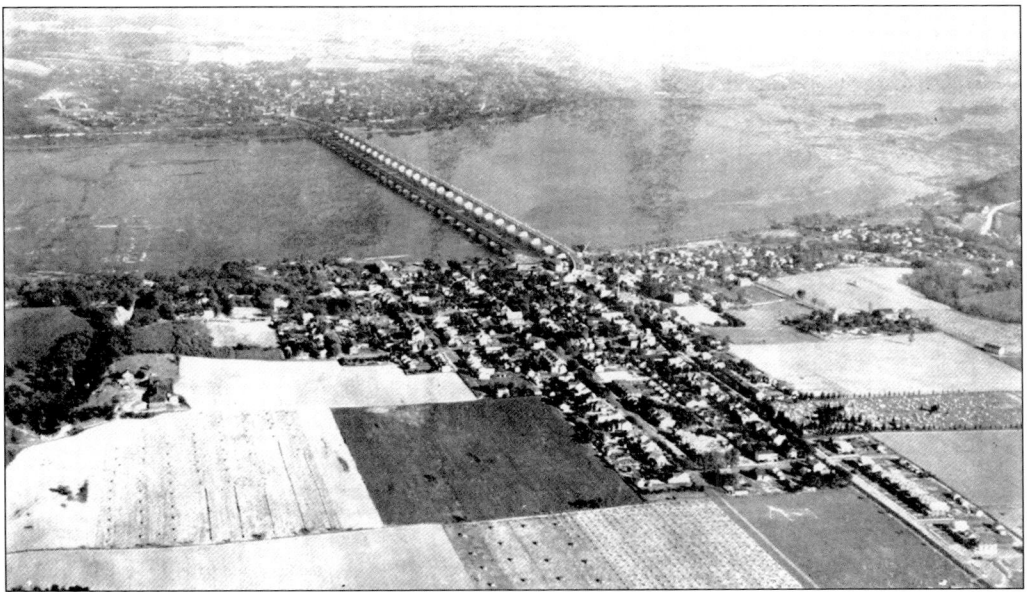

The pilot looking southeast in 1930 has a grand view of Wrightsville, the mile-wide Susquehanna River, the two bridges that cross it, and Columbia on the far side. Notice the distinct boundary between town and farms; much of the farmland has filled in with development. The Lincoln Highway extends off to York at the right bottom corner. (Author's collection.)

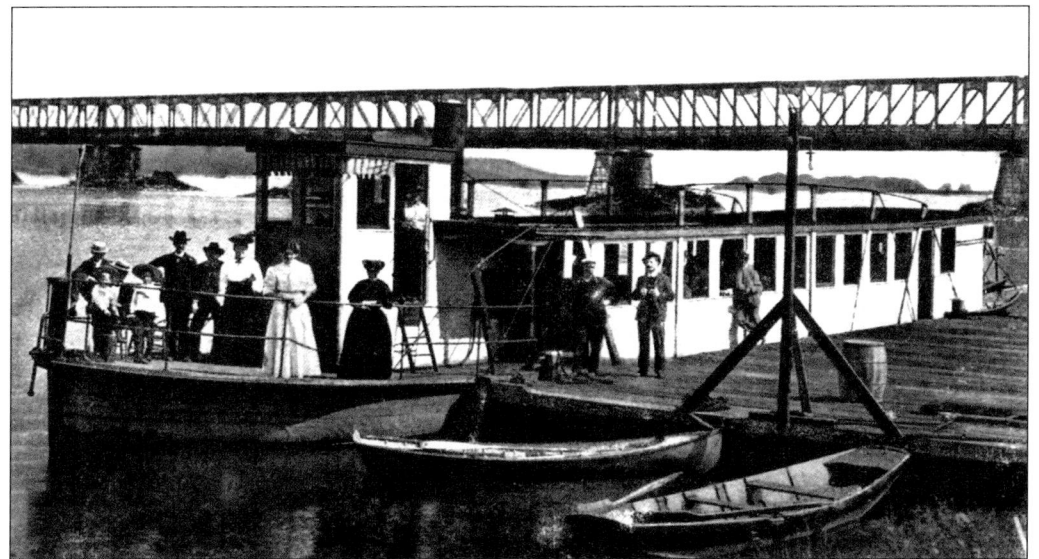

The Columbia Steam Ferry and Towboat Company ran three passenger boats from Columbia to Wrightsville from the 1890s to 1924. The steamboat names were *Henry*, *Helen*, and *Mary*, seen here docked at Wrightsville. Five cents bought not only a good cigar, but also a one-way ticket across the Susquehanna River. (Courtesy Historic Wrightsville, Inc.)

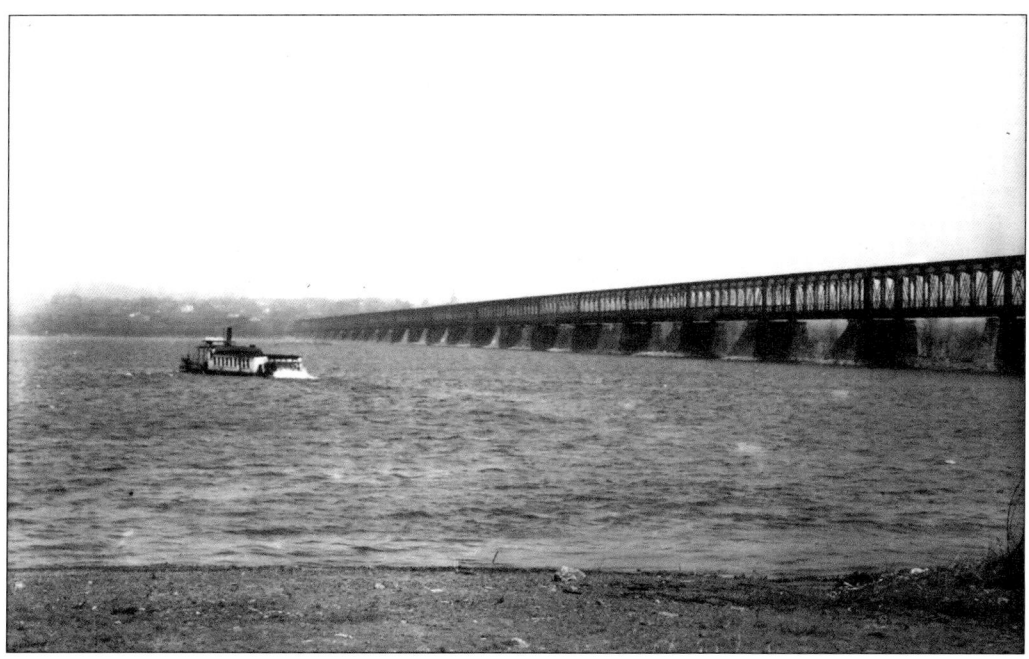

One of the steam-powered, paddle wheel ferries heads across the Susquehanna from Wrightsville. As the Columbia landing is downstream of the railroad bridge, the ferry will pass under it on its crossing. The Depression and the opening of the 1930 bridge brought about the end of this company that provided an alternative way of crossing the river. (Courtesy Columbia Historic Preservation Society.)

When Confederate general John B. Gordon's brigade occupied Wrightsville, citizens were fearful that the rebels might destroy the town. They did not, and Wrightsville's chief burgess, James F. Magee, sent his daughter to invite Gordon to his home, appearing here in 1976 much as it did back in June 1863. (Courtesy Historic Wrightsville, Inc.)

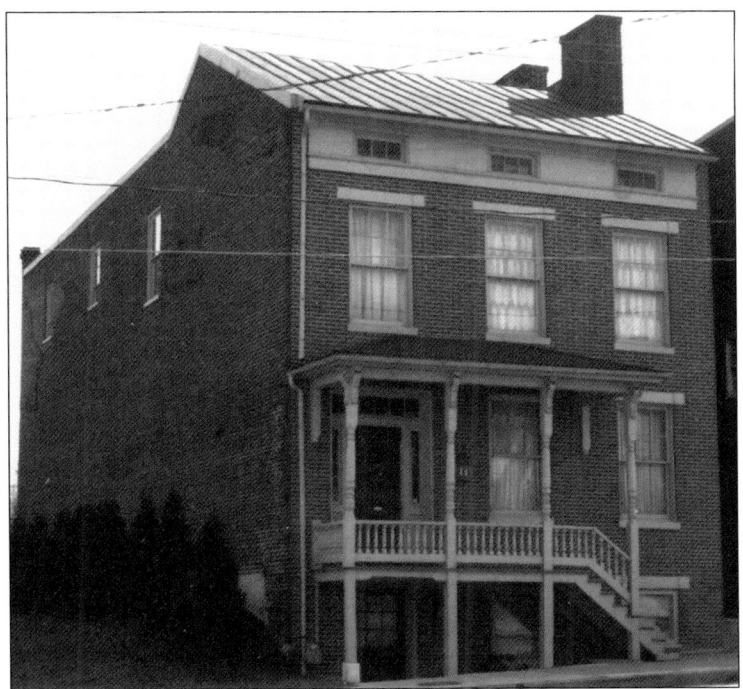

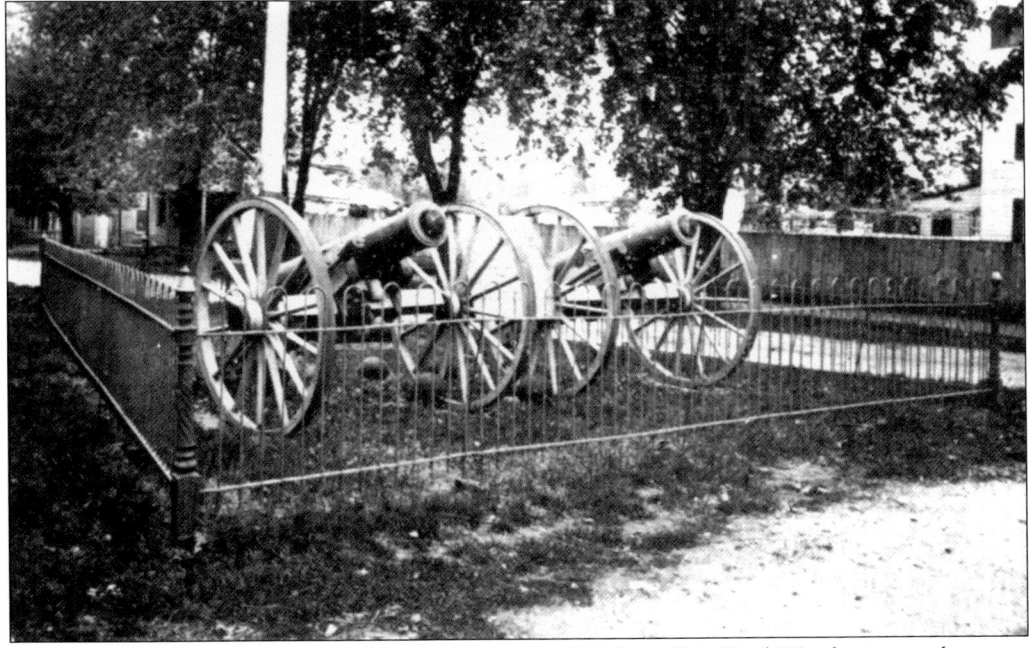

To have a permanent, always-visible connection to Wrightsville's Civil War heritage, the town has long displayed cannons along the north side of the Lincoln Highway along with cannon balls. Originally, the cannons' supports were wheel sets as shown here about 1900. When the wheels deteriorated, individual concrete mounts took their place. Still later came the present single-concrete mount holding both cannons. (Courtesy Historic Wrightsville, Inc.)

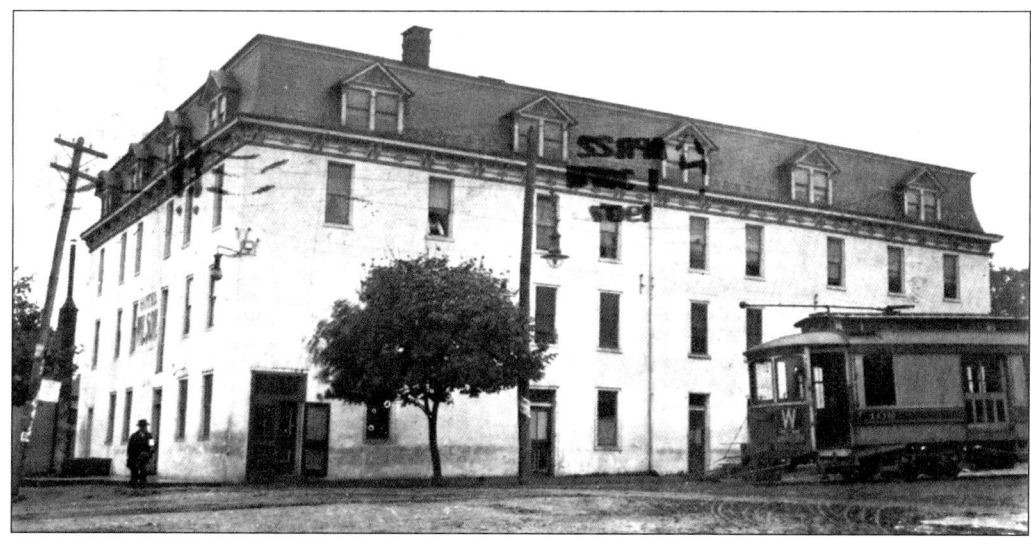

In 1907, the trolley is at the end of the line from York to the west at the Hotel Wilson. From this stop it was a short walk to catch a ferry or a PRR passenger train. Shortly after the 1930 bridge opened, the hotel ceased operation and was torn down. (Author's collection.)

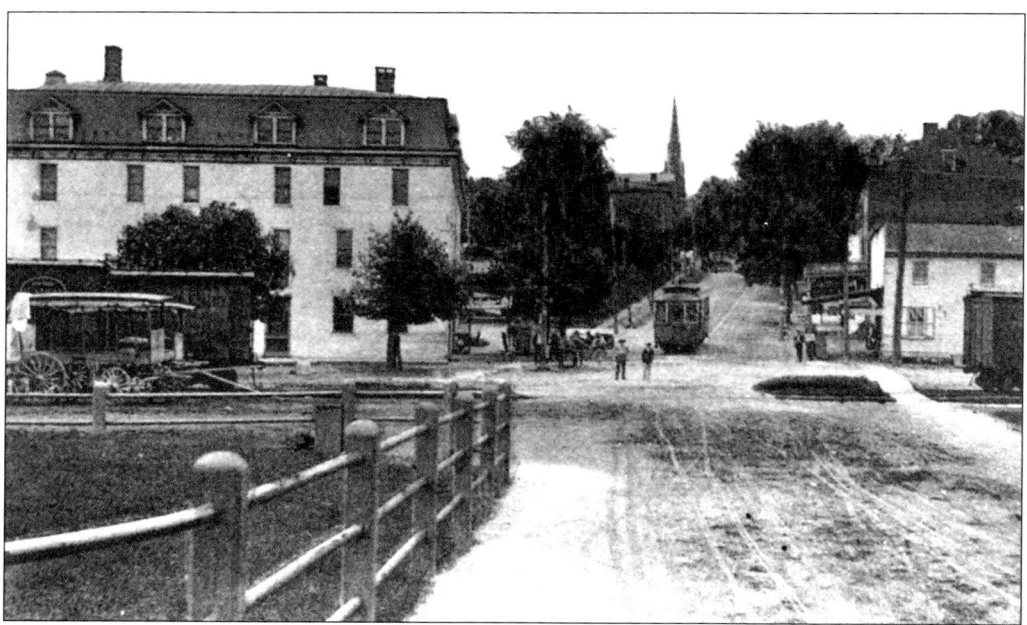

This picture was taken before 1909 (the Hoober building is not in the picture) and after 1905 (the trolley is at Front Street). The trolley is at the foot of Hellam Street at Front Street. Hotel Wilson is to the left. The view is from close to the Susquehanna River and a block downstream from the ferryboat landing. The spire is on Trinity Lutheran Church farther west on Hellam Street. (Courtesy Historic Wrightsville, Inc.)

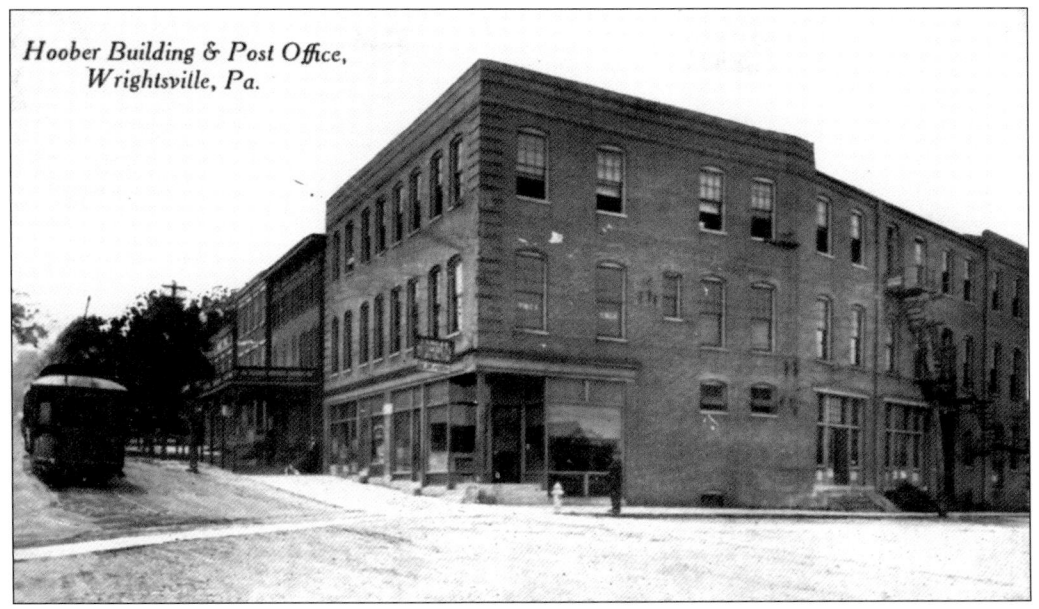

Hoober Building & Post Office, Wrightsville, Pa.

At the foot of Hellam Street at Front Street on the northwest corner stands the Hoober Building. Built in 1909 by R. S. Magee, over the years the building has been home to the post office, trolley waiting room, local newspaper business office, YMCA, cigar and newsstand, cigar manufacturing company, plumbing store, machine shop, hosiery mill, restaurant, and apartments. (Courtesy Historic Wrightsville, Inc.)

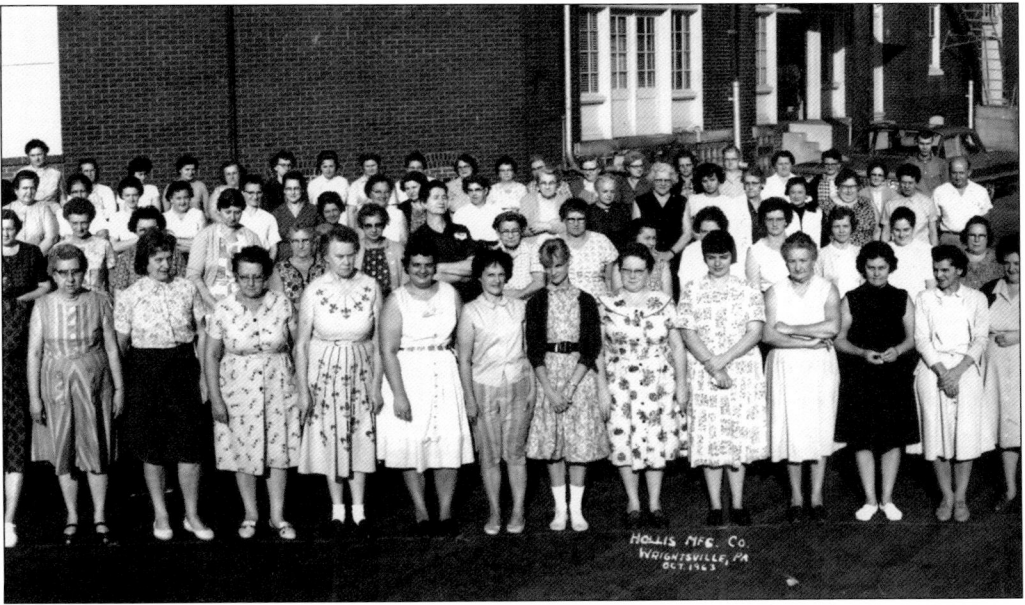

In June 1939, R. W. Hollis Jr. and his wife established a partnership, named it Hollis Manufacturing Company, and began making women's and children's clothing. The company bought the Hoober Building in 1947 and ultimately occupied it all except for the Villa-Mar Restaurant. In October 1963, employees gather for a photograph outside the building. (Courtesy Historic Wrightsville, Inc.)

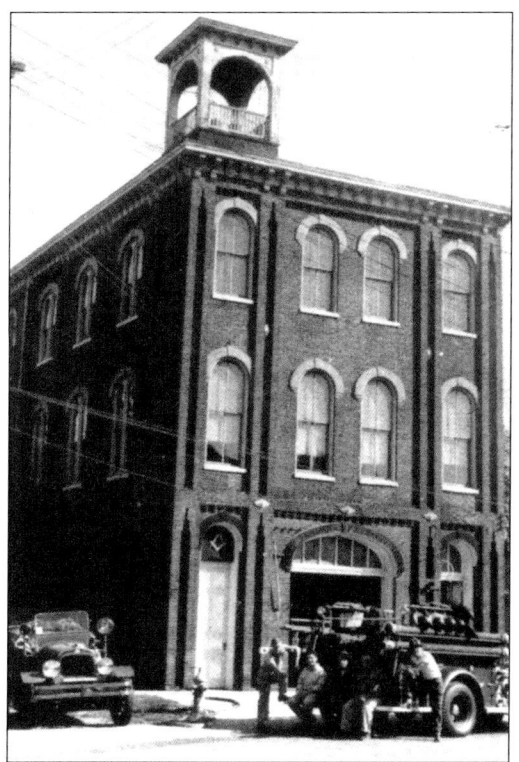

The Pennsylvania Railroad Company donated the land for a firehouse at Second Street and Garden Alley. Completion of the $5,726 (about $130,000 in today's dollars) building was in about 1890. The council ordered a bell in 1892. Official incorporation of the Wrightsville Steam Fire Engine and Hose Company No. 1 was in 1893 with 60 members. (Courtesy Historic Wrightsville, Inc.)

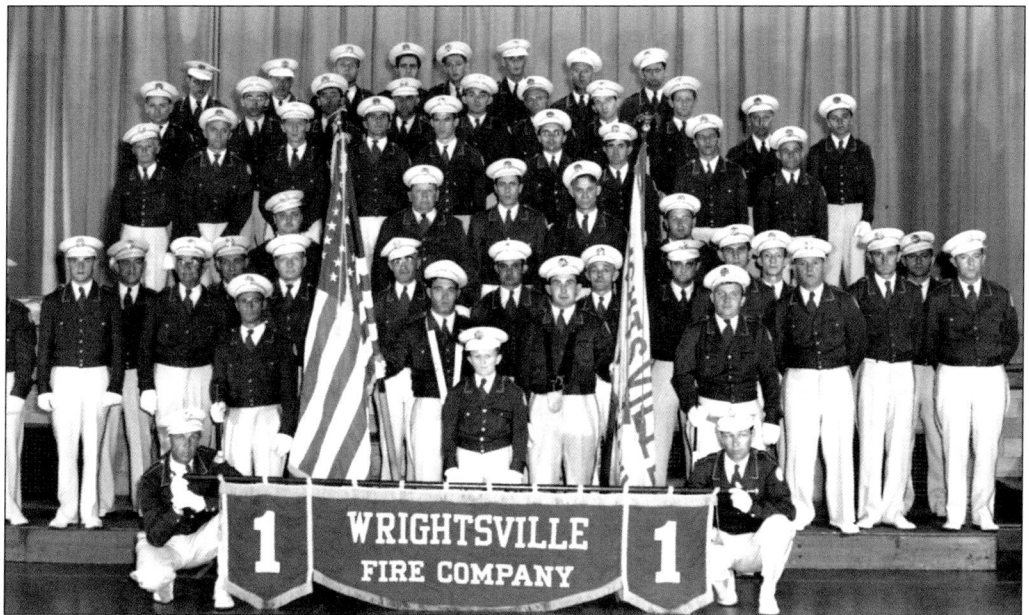

The Wrightsville Fire Company No. 1 set up its Marching Club on October 14, 1946. For parades, members wore white caps, trousers, and shoes with jackets of royal blue and gold. Marching in parades provided members with camaraderie and publicity for the fire company. The club disbanded in December 1955. (Courtesy Historic Wrightsville, Inc.)

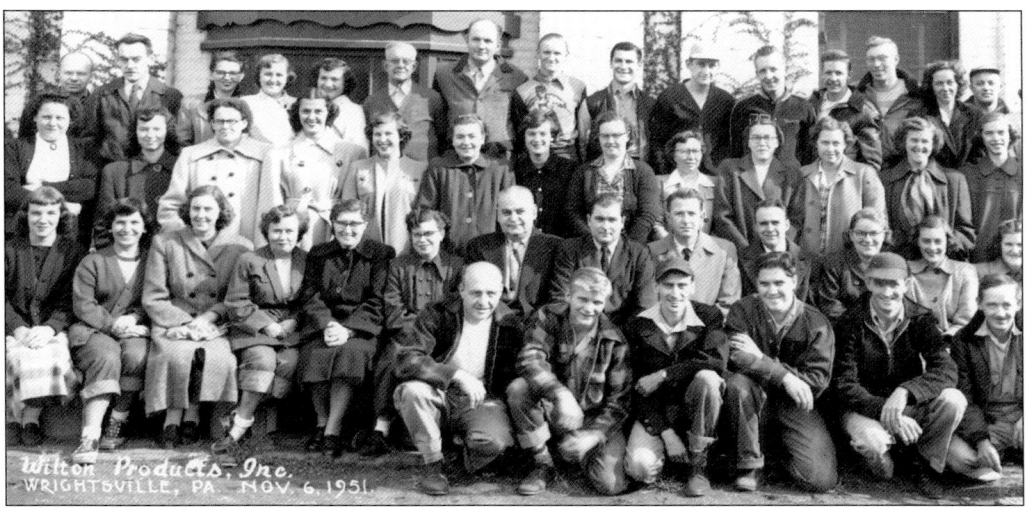

Wilton Products was one of several operations the Wilton family set up in Wrightsville. The company was the source of brass, iron, and aluminum decorative castings and hand painted many of them. The operation centered on a large four-and-half-story brick building erected in 1862. Some employees pose for a photographer who came down from Harrisburg to capture them on film. (Courtesy Historic Wrightsville, Inc.)

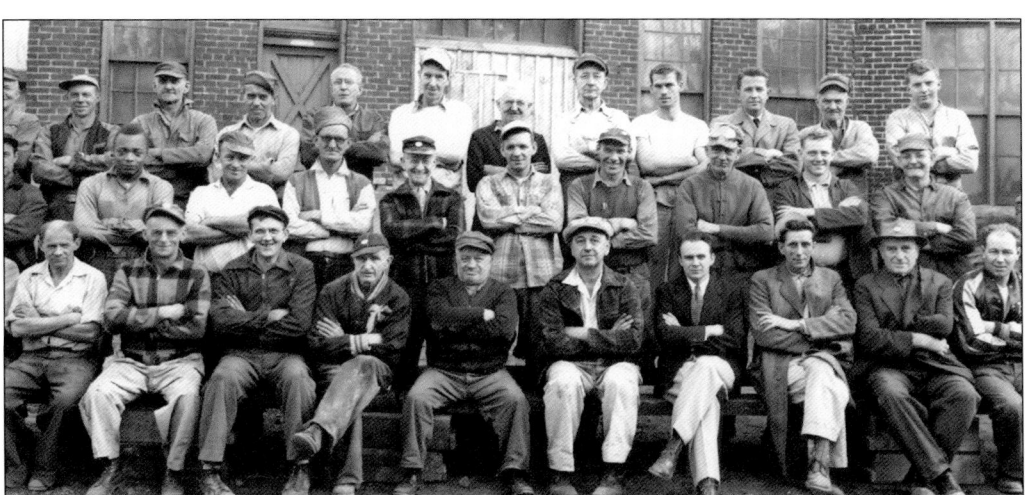

Another Wilton operation, Susquehanna Casting Company, which made iron castings, was located along North Front Street. The company gradually evolved into Wilton Brass Company and that, in turn, became Wilton Armetale, maker of the well aluminum-based alloy used in metal food dishes. The Harrisburg photographer lined up Susquehanna employees for a group picture the same day he visited Wilton Products. (Courtesy Historic Wrightsville, Inc.)

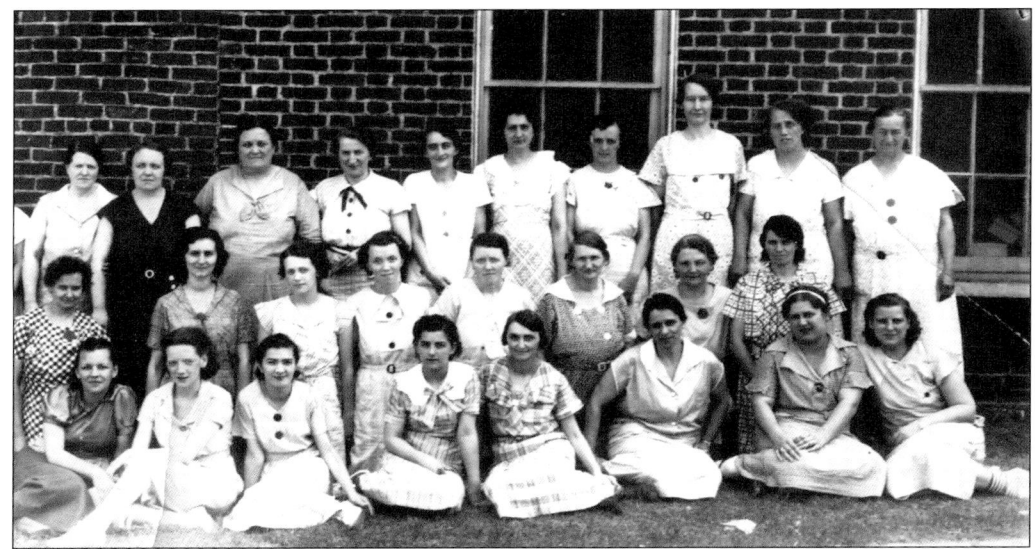

Standard Garment Company's manufacturing plant was located on the south side of Hellam Street in Wrightsville. The company also had a plant in Columbia on Locust Street above Sixth Street making ladies garments. In May 1936, in the midst of the Great Depression, the women workers formed three rows for their picture. (Courtesy Historic Wrightsville, Inc.)

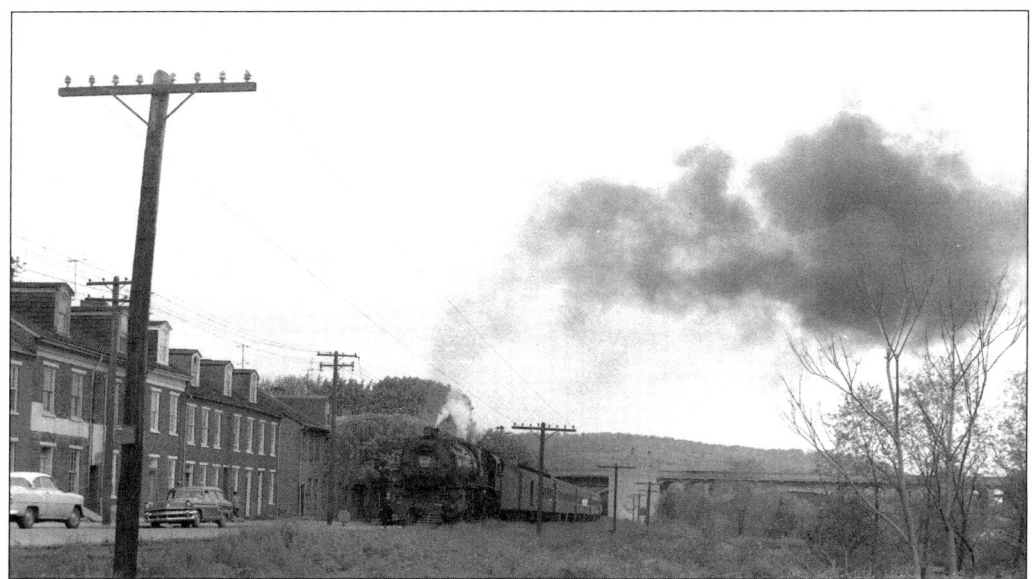

In May 1955, a rail fan excursion ran over the PRR Frederick Branch and passed through Wrightsville on its way to Gettysburg. Leading the special train was K4s Pacific steam locomotive No. 7133. The PRR built No. 7133 in its Juniata Shops in Altoona in July 1918 and retired the locomotive in September 1956. (Author's collection.)

Bibliography

Abendschein, Frederic H. "The Aglen & Susquehanna: Lancaster County's Low Grade." Pennsylvania Railroad Technical and Historical Society *Keystone* (Winter 1994): 10–25.

———. "A Bridge Too Many." Pennsylvania Railroad Technical and Historical Society *Keystone* (Winter 2002): 15–22.

Clark, Edna, et al. *Columbia Bicentennial History 1788–1988*. Columbia, PA: Mifflin Press, 1988.

Denney, M. D., John D. Denney, et al. *Columbia Civil War Centennial, 1863–1963*. Columbia, PA: 1963.

Denney, John D., Jr. "A Sentimental Journey . . . The Story of the Reading & Columbia." Pts. 1, 2, and 3. Reading Company Technical and Historical Society *Bee Line* 1 (1992): 5–9; 2 (1992): 4–12; 3/4 (1992): 29–36.

———. "Columbia on the Pennsy." Pennsylvania Railroad Technical and Historical Society *Keystone* (Autumn 1994): 21–52.

———. *Trains of the Pennsylvania Dutch Country*. Columbia, PA: Mifflin Press, 1966.

———. *Trolleys of the Pennsylvania Dutch Country*. Columbia, PA: Mifflin Press, 1973.

Gable, Charles Hull, et al. *The Sesquicentennial of the Founding of Columbia, Lancaster County. Pennsylvania*. Columbia, PA: Press of Columbia News, 1938.

Kloidt, Bill, Sr. *Columbia . . . The Gem*. Columbia, PA: Mifflin Press, 1994.

Lehman, Donald I., Sr., et al. *Wrightsville, 1736–1976*. Wrightsville, PA: 1976.

Morse, Jean Gaus Motter. *The Sixth Street Indians*. Columbia, PA: self-published, 1993.

Myers, Naomi, et al. *Marietta Sesquicentennial 1812–1962*. Marietta, PA: 1962.

Nye, W. S., and John G. Redman. *Farthest East: Wrightsville, Pennsylvania*. 1963.

Swiger, Anna M., et al. *Columbia, Pennsylvania, From Shawanah Indian Town, 1726, To Columbia, Pennsylvania*. Columbia, PA: 1977.

Discover Thousands of Local History Books
Featuring Millions of Vintage Images

Arcadia Publishing, the leading local history publisher in the United States, is committed to making history accessible and meaningful through publishing books that celebrate and preserve the heritage of America's people and places.

Find more books like this at
www.arcadiapublishing.com

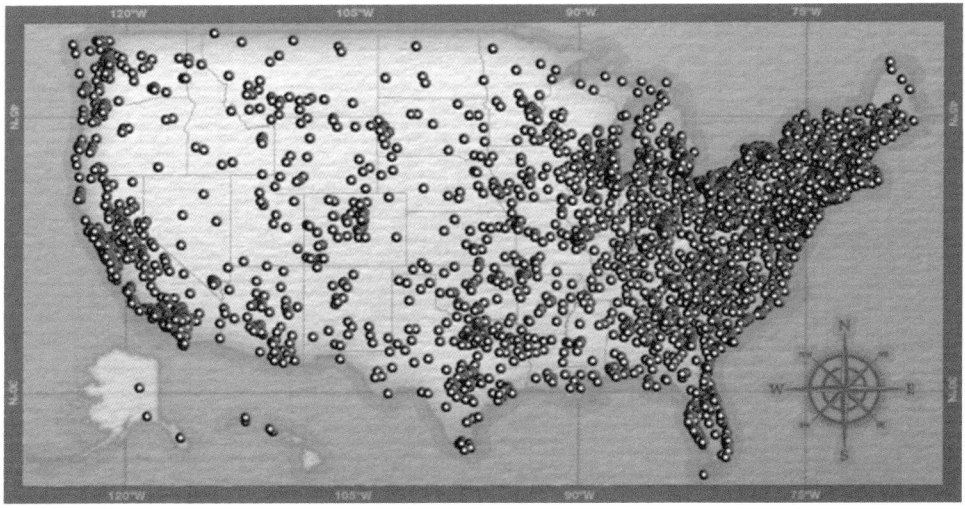

Search for your hometown history, your old stomping grounds, and even your favorite sports team.

Consistent with our mission to preserve history on a local level, this book was printed in South Carolina on American-made paper and manufactured entirely in the United States. Products carrying the accredited Forest Stewardship Council (FSC) label are printed on 100 percent FSC-certified paper.

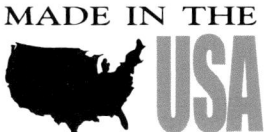